REACHING FOR THE MOON

the (questionable) treatment; there were no antibiotics at the time[2]. Doris suffered for months, describing the pain in her side in many, many diary entries.

Two major experiences change Doris during her stays in the hospital. While she remains an incorrigible flirt, Doris also discovers a real gratitude for her blessings. She looks at life and regrets ever worrying her parents. She repeats the phrase, "I'm glad I'm alive," like a prayer dozens of times through the pages of her diaries, and her attitude develops into a deeper passion for living. Her delight in the natural world, the pleasures of the table, her deep love for her horse Mac and best friend Marjie Dana, and her attraction to almost any man, gentle or otherwise, stem in part from her relief at having survived such pain and suffering.

Doris's other life event is falling headlong into a hero-worshiping romance with her intern, Dr. Abel D. Scott[3]. Any psychologist can explain the common story of a patient falling for her doctor or an accident victim loving her rescuer—a classic case of transference. Doris imbues masterful, heroic qualities to her doctor, imagining him in love with her. They begin a correspondence and her evocative fantasy life revolves around him. Her discovery that he is married with children does not sway her. In Portland, she essentially stalks him to his home where she peers into his windows and at his clothes drying on the clothesline. She visits him at his office, inventing reasons to unburden her heart to him. In what is to the 21st century reader a shocking lack of boundaries as well as frankly unethical medical behavior, Dr. Scott encourages her, and in fact, seems to return her affection[4]. The denouement of their "rescue romance" comes in June 1929, when a line is crossed and the scales fall from both their eyes.

Doris's removal to California and Arizona does nothing to alleviate

---

2 Penicillin was not discovered until 1928, and it wasn't generally available until World War II.

3 Because the doctor practiced in Portland for many years, his name has been changed in this book.

4 Dr. Scott is practicing before the legal guidelines that came in the 1960s and 1970s, putting a stop to romantic doctor-patient relationships, excessive paternalism, and highly inappropriate over-familiarity.

her desire; absence, after all, makes the heart weave elaborate fantasies. As Doris explains in her diary in January 1928, her illness was so bad that her father sold his business and the family home on Culpepper Terrace. He moved them all to Los Angeles where Doris could enjoy the benevolent weather of California for her health. Family lore tells this differently, and the newspaper and stock market of the time support the alternate story: Doris's father, architect and builder Luther R. Bailey, had gone bankrupt. He could no longer sustain the elegant lifestyle the family had enjoyed in Portland, and he joined some relatives in Southern California, where he hoped to capitalize on the growth of the suburbs in the Los Angeles area. Doris briefly enrolled at Hollywood High School at the acme of the silent-film era. Just driving around town was a glamorous adventure. The Baileys did not stay in Los Angeles long, however. The glittering opportunities in Arizona real estate called to Luther, and in the spring of 1928, the Baileys took up residence in Phoenix.

The family remained in Phoenix for four years, as Luther desperately tried to make a go of real estate in the waning years of the once-Roaring Twenties. Doris says succinctly in December 1929, "Daddy says there's no money," and for once, he wasn't sugar-coating it for Doris's sake. A few years later, the Baileys' real estate holdings will be sold at a bankruptcy auction for just $400, including parcels belonging to several other would-be investors. The Great Depression is most definitely on its way. Doris returns to Portland to school in the fall of 1928. She lives with the Marshall Danas[5]—Marjie's family, in Marjie's bedroom—while Marjie attends college. Later, in September 1929, Doris becomes a boarder at St. Helen's Hall, and enjoys a last refreshing burst of girlhood in the dorm and classrooms of her beloved school.

Doris finds herself left behind again and again as her friends finish school and she struggles to keep pace. The two years of missed classes mean that Doris is almost 20 and still trying to finish at St. Helen's Hall. Her friends are already off to college or getting married. She doesn't mention it in the diaries, but that was when Doris began lying about her age to fit

---

[5] Marshall Dana was a prominent Oregon man, editor of *The Oregonian* newspaper and active on dozens of committees, clubs, and organizations.

in, and this white lie lingered until Doris was a robust 92 and her collected friends in Occidental, California, were planning her 90th birthday party. She had to break her silence then—and at last rid her friends of the mistaken belief that she was born the same year the *HMS Titanic* went down. ("Oh, how I hate the *Titanic*," she told me some years ago, still swearing me to secrecy. A plethora of unwanted *Titanic* memorabilia she had received as gifts over the years was left behind after her passing.)

In Arizona, Doris formed another deep bond—between girl and horse. Her red roan, Mackay, whom she called Mac, is well remembered in the chapter of Doris's autobiography, *Love and Labor*, called "My Strawberry Roan."[6] In that memoir, Doris describes her father catching her in the shocking act of gambling over racehorses with Mexicans and rodeo dudes. Her diaries from the time tell a different story—no remembered dialogue, and less of a blow-up with Daddy. Doris loves her horse, and she loves to race—and win. She talks horses with the cowboys in Phoenix and up in Prescott at the rodeo. She swaps horse stories with the interns in Oregon in the hospital, and with any young man who happens to speak well of the country and fresh air. In Portland, she escapes to the countryside whenever possible to ride a rented horse. She misses Mac terribly. In Oregon, she longs for the dry desert air and the velvety nights (although in Arizona she pines for the cooling rains and evergreen mountains of the Beaver State). Alas, by the end of 1929, when there is "no money," there will be no horse in Arizona, either—a heartbreaking, bitter reality for the spoiled only surviving daughter[7] and sister of the Bailey family.

The diaries give us an unexpected peek into how times were changing in the United States culturally, socially, and technologically, for women in particular. Although Doris is writing during Prohibition, she seems to have no trouble finding an intoxicating beverage. In her 1925 diary entries, she had sneered at a neighbor woman "placidly smoking" on her back

---

6 See "My Strawberry Roan," in *Love and Labor*, Doris B. Murphy, IUniverse, 2006

7 The Baileys' first daughter, Elizabeth Lee, died in infancy. Willie Doris (Mother) mourned Elizabeth the rest of her life, and Doris felt the sting of never measuring up to a dead baby sister. She recounts this in *Love and Labor*.

porch[8], but just four years later Doris is attempting to smoke Luckies in public and giving herself a headache in the pursuit of cigarette-chic. She receives a crystal radio set her second time in the hospital in 1928, and by 1929 is listening to a proper radio in the Danas' home and hearing the local bandleader on the airwaves. She knows some popular tunes in earlier diaries, but by the end of this volume, she is buying and listening to records in the booths at the Marty Music Store in Portland. She repeatedly references popular music and even makes "My Sin" her theme song with George Tift, her first "true love."

Although Doris tussles with boys in the back seat, in the moonlight, or in the darkened parlor, she remains a virgin. She likes to have fun, but she hasn't forgotten her class or station in life. She has some close calls and writes that she feels "ashamed" after. In diary entries, which seem alarming to readers in the 21st century, Doris writes of boys (and doctors) who will not take no for an answer. Some entries in particular are startling to our rape-culture awareness, such as when a boy is going to kiss her whether she wants to or not, and how he has to "fight" for a kiss. In other entries, she kisses a little too much and is "slut-shamed,"[9] by the very boy she has kissed. Date rape existed, but naming it and publicizing it as wrong is nowhere on the horizon; for Doris, this battle to protect her virginity is part of life. Women did not yet understand that they could say no to so-called "petting parties"[10]—or a joyful yes, rather than play coy games, as Doris does so frequently.

In the mid-1920s, an important cultural and social study called *Middletown: A Study in Modern American Culture*, by husband-and-wife team Robert and Helen Lynd, was conducted on typical American attitudes and behaviors. The Lynds approached the study of Americans

---

[8] *I've Got Some Lovin' to Do: The Diaries of a Roaring Twenties Teen (1925-1926)*, Indie-Visible Ink, 2012. p. 82

[9] A 2012 election-year term invented when an outspoken young woman, Sandra Fluke, spoke at a Congressional hearing about the need for birth control services and was excoriated on conservative television and radio talk shows.

[10] See Glossary, Appendix I

"as anthropologists would a primitive society."[11] Doris is not as unique as we might think, and could very well be a typical study participant. Her frank portrayal of petting parties is exactly as described by teens in the Middletown study. Teens cited in the study agreed that "nine out of ten boys and girls of high school age have petting parties." And in particular, the distress of Victorian-era parents faced with Jazz Age children is played out between Doris and her parents. How did Doris get away with all this running around and borderline behavior? The Middletown study quotes one 1928 father saying, "These kids aren't pulling the wool over their parents' eyes as much as you may think. The parents are wise to a lot that goes on, but they just don't know what to do, and try to turn their backs on it."[12] That explains a lot. Not surprisingly, movies and popular music, asking couples to "dance cheek to cheek," get a lot of blame from adults in 1928. "Some high school teachers are convinced that the movies are a powerful factor in bringing about the 'early sophistication' of the young and the relaxing of social taboos.... The judge of the juvenile court lists the movies as one of the 'big four' causes of local juvenile delinquency."[13]

The three years depicted in volume two of The Doris Diaries swing between the highs of delirious love and nature-worship and the lows of near-death, illness, and melancholia. Doris matures a good deal in these three years, from her essentially shallow observations before her illness to her running leaps at real love at the end. Despite being thwarted at many turns, Doris is mostly irrepressible. She again displays her developing voice in her prose, and states her desire to write, to be an author, and to write a book on several occasions. She wants to be swept away with love and find her ideal man, but she is not much drawn to domesticity. She feels envious of a friend's wedding gifts, but in her view, those who have married don't seem very happy, and she has zero interest in producing children.

On December 31, 1929, with her high school years at last behind her, Doris stands on the cusp of a new decade. A blossoming proto-feminist,

11 Obituary of R.S. Lynd, *The Washington Post*, Nov. 3, 1970
12 *Middletown: A Study in Contemporary American Culture*, Robert S. and Helen Merrell Lynd; Harcourt, Brace and Company, 1928; New York. p152
13 Ibid., pp267-268

she wants the freedom of the open desert air, but is held back by her father's dictum to stay inside—a literalization of her metaphoric life quest. With crushing economic woe before them, and her future just narrowly open, Doris must learn to behave and be good, earn her parents' and society's approbation, or break free and chase whatever dreams lie ahead. From the perspective of the year 2013, I can tell you that she did chase her dreams, and catch most of them. The coming volumes of the Doris Diaries will show just how she did it.

The Baileys in Portland

Doris's father, Luther Raeford Bailey, was a respected architect in Portland. Born in Alabama in 1872, Bailey was raised in Hackneyville, and attended Southern University in Alabama; he gave the valedictory address at graduation. He met Willie Doris Upshaw in Atlanta and they married in 1901; Bailey took his wife to Boston and was graduated from Boston College with his master's degree in architecture. They had two of their five children there. These were William Raeford Bailey (Rae), born in 1902 (who became my grandfather), and Elizabeth Lee Bailey, born in 1906 and died in 1907[14]. Brother Joseph Albert Bailey was born in 1908 in Portland, and he and Doris were quite close; Joe is one of Doris's companions in many outings in this book. Doris was next, born in 1910 in Portland. Youngest brother, Jack, baptized John Upshaw Bailey, was born in 1918 and was the baby of the family.

Luther Bailey arrived in Portland in 1908. In 1910, he was the president of the Portland Realty and Construction Company. In 1911 he established a building contractor business under the name L.R. Bailey & Company; he served as president and manager. His World War I draft registration card lists his occupation as "architect" and his employer as "self." He worked from offices in the North Western Bank Building, and was generally listed as an architect in the Portland city directories between 1912 and 1940, except for the short period when they lived in Phoenix.[15]

Bailey's designs and buildings included Colonial Revival, Prairie

---

14 See Doris Bailey Murphy's autobiography, *Love and Labor*, p20, for Doris's feelings.
15 Kim Fitzgerald; see also Roy Roos' excellent book, *The History and Development of Portland's Irvington Neighborhood*, 1997

School and Craftsman style homes. In addition to building his own houses on speculation, Bailey contracted with other real estate speculators, such as Edgar W. Smith for whom he built most of the houses on an entire block between NE 19th and 20th avenues and Siskiyou and Klickitat streets[16]. Bailey designed and built the McAvinney Fourplex at 2004 NE 17th Avenue in Portland, which is on the National Register of Historic Places.[17] Other houses that Bailey designed and built include the 1911 Eugene Langdon House (2722 NE 22nd), the 1912 H.P. Palmer House (2410 NE 22nd), the 1912 George W. Hazen House (2106 NE 26th), the 1916 P. Schoniger House (3446 NE 19th), and the 1917 Edgar W. Smith House (2338 NE 20th).

By the 1920s, Bailey constructed houses in the Alameda and Rose City areas "numbering in the hundreds."[18] He designed the Highway Theatre at 5233 SE Sandy Blvd. and a block of commercial buildings in the same area. Family letters mention a school and church that he designed and built; letters and news clippings also indicate that Bailey was involved in the building of Vista House at Crown Point, designed the Rose City Park Clubhouse, and built a lodge on the slopes of Mt. Hood.

Willie Doris, born in 1878, was an Atlanta (Georgia) belle and daughter of a circuit-riding Baptist minister. Because of her slightly lower social status as a preacher's daughter, she was one of few young ladies at her college who did not have a "Negro" maid to assist her, according to family lore. She attended Judson College in Marion, Alabama, where she studied literature and history. Willie Doris was active in her church and community; she was the Church Hostess in charge of luncheons and dinners (Doris often notes her parents going out or serving at her mother's luncheons). In newspaper accounts of the weddings of Doris's friends, Mrs. L.R. Bailey reigned over the tea and coffee service.

Willie Doris was a great reader, and felt the lack of a branch library on

---

[16] Note that in 1933 all the streets in Portland were given the N, NW, SW, SE and SW declaration, and numeration on many of those streets also changed.

[17] Number 05001147 in the National Register database; the building was built in 1913 and listed in August 2005.

[18] Fitzgerald; Roos.

the east side of the river. She was the motivating force in the establishment of the Rose City Park Library near 44th Avenue and Sandy Boulevard, according to family papers.[19] Willie Doris believed she was related to Robert E. Lee though her grandmother and was very proud of her Southern heritage. She was a charter member of the Robert E. Lee chapter of the United Daughters of the Confederacy and was active in that organization for many years. Her first daughter, Elizabeth Lee Bailey, was likely named for her esteemed distant cousin. Willie Doris kept her southern accent all her life, while Luther lost his early on, according to Doris. "Social position, proper behavior, and good manners were of the utmost importance to her," Doris writes.[20]

Luther Bailey and his family left Oregon in 1928 and moved to Arizona, but returned after four years of debilitating financial hardship and failure there. Luther took a position as engineer with the Works Progress Administration during the Great Depression, continued social activities with his many clubs, and took up building and architecture again when the economy improved. He died in 1948, and Willie Doris died in 1978, both in Portland.

---

[19] *Upshaw Family Journal*
[20] *Love and Labor*, p20

The Bailey men at the Alameda house, 1925:
(back row) Rae, Luther R. Bailey, Joe; (in front) Jack.

Who's Who in the Doris Diaries

Family

Daddy: Luther R. Bailey, Doris's father

Mother: Willie Doris Upshaw Bailey, Doris's mother

Rae: Doris's eldest brother, 8 years older

Joe: Doris's brother, 2 years older

Jack: Doris's brother, 8 years younger

Ruth Crum: Rae's girl, to become his wife in 1930

Uncle Wood and Auntie Louise: Willie Doris's brother Woodson Upshaw and his first wife, in Arizona

Uncle Earnest and Auntie Marion: Willie Doris's brother Earnest Upshaw and his first wife, in Los Angeles

Mac: Doris's beloved horse, a male red roan

Patsy: Doris's female Pomeranian Spitz dog

Friends

Alyce (surname not given): One of Doris's good friends, attended Grant High School, same age as Doris

Claradell: Doris's only female friend in Arizona, about 2 years older than Doris

Crums: Andrew Virgil Crum, a Portland attorney, was business partners with Luther Bailey, and sat on the board at L.R. Bailey Co. Virgil Crum was with the firm of Lundberg & Crum at 721 E. 64th Street; his wife at the time was Beulah. Their favorite niece, Ruth, came from Montana to Portland for school, and then returned to live with Uncle Virgil and Aunt Beulah, who lived at 1262 The Alameda, very near the Baileys' home on that street. Rae and Ruth were married from the Crums' home in 1930.

Marjie Dana: Doris's best friend, same age as Doris

Danas: Marshall and Nora Dana, son Marshall and daughters Marjie and Mary; Doris lives in their home in 1928 and is close to the family for years. The Danas and Bailey parents were longtime friends.

Davidsons: More friends of the Baileys; Doris stayed with them in late 1929.

Evaline: Another friend of Doris's, Lincoln High School; same age. Her nickname is Eve, which indicates that pronunciation is EVE-aline.

Mathises: Family friends of the Baileys who also had a department store downtown in Portland

Meeds: Myra Meeds and her son Irving were longtime friends of the Bailey family.

Paintons: Friends of the Baileys; Willie Doris, Doris, and Jack stayed with them in 1928 before leaving for Los Angeles. Children include John (Doris's age), and younger sisters Elizabeth and Marjorie

Fanny Taylor: One of Doris's good friends, from a wealthy family; she attends St. Helen's Hall with Doris; same age

Van de Carrs: Irene and her son, Rēne, Van de Carr are old family friends. They live in Oakland, California.

Doctors/Around Town

Berg's: A department store in Portland

Bishop Walter T. Sumner: Episcopal bishop of Oregon from 1915 through 1935, a frequent visitor at St. Helen's Hall

Dr. Baird: Dr. Alvin Baird, Doris's doctor, probably a general practitioner

Dr. Harrison: Dr. Fred Harrison was Dr. Kiehle's partner; the other Dr. Harrison was an optician and shared office space with Dr. Eddy Laccell.

Dr. Kiehle: Dr. Frederick Kiehle practiced in Portland; eye, ear, nose, and throat specialist

Eddy Laccel: Dr. Edward Laccel practiced optometry in Portland

Dr. Scott: Abel David Scott was a young married intern, 28, at Good Samaritan hospital when Doris was convalescing there. He then opened his own office in Montavilla. Doris developed a crush on him and loved him from far and near.

Georgie Stoll: The organist and band leader at the Broadway; he sometimes played with his jazz trio, quartet or ensemble on the radio. See Appendix II for longer explanation.

Boys

Gene Rossman: A boy a year or two younger than Doris who lived on Culpepper Terrace a few doors away from the Baileys. Doris saw him occasionally after the Baileys moved away.

George Shade: A college boy she met on the beach in De Lake in 1928

George Tift: Friend of the Bailey family; introduced by Doris's parents. Doris fell madly in love with him in 1929.

Irvin: A young cowhand in Phoenix who worked at the stables where Doris boarded her horse

Jack Freidel, Jack Hibbard, Jack Kaplan, Jack Pillar: Various boyfriends of Doris over the years. Seemingly indistinguishable in her writings except for surname

Micky Stevens: Doris met him at Lincoln High School, and had a crush on him beginning in 1925.

Rex: Surname unknown, an adorable boy from University of Oregon

Richie: An Arizona cowboy and bronco-buster

Royal Oliver: Son of a wealthy haberdasher from Seattle; Doris's "Baking Powder Kid"

See Barnum: Related to P.T. Barnum, met at Alyce's college; see note in Appendix II

Abbreviations

Ariz.: Arizona

Cal/Cali: California

Chev.: Chevrolet

CE: Christian Endeavor, a youth Christian group

CS: Doris's private shorthand for (probably) her menstrual period

H—: Hell

HMA: Hill boys: Male students from the Hill Military Academy, Portland

L.A.: Los Angeles

M & F: Meier and Frank department store

MASC: [*sic*] Man on the streetcar

MV: Montavilla neighborhood or streetcar line

OAC: Oregon Agricultural College in Corvallis later became OSU, Oregon State University. See also **OSC**

OIT: Oregon Institute of Technology was located at the YMCA at 6th and Taylor. Business classes and night school classes took place there.

KO: OK

Oregon: University of Oregon in Eugene. See also **U. of O.**

OSC: Oregon State College; see **OAC**

OWK: Olds, Wortman and King store in Portland, which occupied the block of Morrison, Alder, Tenth and Park

S.A.: Sex appeal

SHH: St. Helen's Hall, where Doris went to school

Ss of Bs: Sons of bitches

SOL: Sure out of luck

U of O: University of Oregon in Eugene. See also: **Oregon**

WO: Westover neighborhood or streetcar line

YMCA: Located at 6th and Taylor

Oregon
(1927)[21]

[21] Doris is 16 years old when these diaries begin.

[on tag board cover sheet]

Here's hoping for some real excitement this year. Something thrilling, exhilarating, and all that sort of thing. Of course I made the usual resolutions, but I won't let them hinder me from having a good time. Maybe I'll rob a bank, or—who knows, I might capture a notorious criminal and become a heroine and maybe—just *maybe* I'll fall in love, or Micky will come back. Alas! No one knows, but I wish we could see into the future.

Monday, January 3, ~~1926~~ 1927

Came to the hospital[22] and I hate it, I hate it, I hate it. The nurses are so cross and I'm lonesome and I feel like hell and damn it when I think of spending a *month*[23] in this place I nearly go crazy.

Tuesday, January 4

The second day and it seems a year. I didn't sleep hardly any last night and tonight will probably be just as bad. My head aches and everything.

Wednesday, January 5

There was a delicious boy about 17 years old in the next room last night and boy! Could he swear. Gee, but I got a kick out of it. I hate this place more every day. They act as if they're doing me a favor to let me stay here. Bunk!

Thursday, January 6

Terribly long day. I decided to be real nice to that awful nurse and see what the reaction was. She was talking about a blanket some people gave her and I said, "My, they must have liked you." And she said, "Yes, nearly everyone likes me for some reason." Blah!

Daddy came down and brought me the *Saturday Evening Post*. Gee, but he's sweet. I think I have the nicest parents in the world. So self-sacrificing and etc. All the things I've done and the many times I've disobeyed them and they remain the same forgiving people. I'm going to turn over a new leaf and be good to them. I have been awful and I didn't realize how much I've probably made them suffer. They have enough business worries without bothering about us kids. So *I'm* going to be good when I get home!

---

[22] The 60-bed municipal Isolation Hospital at Kelly Butte was six miles from downtown and opened in 1920 to house contagious patients. It closed in 1960.

[23] Ten days was the isolation period for exposure to scarlet fever; in hospital for 30 days from onset of symptoms.

Friday, January 7

Feel much better today. The city is *beautiful* this afternoon. The sky is blue, blue, blue and the [Willamette] river just matches it. The mountains stand out so clear and white in the back ground. This is the kind of day that I would like to get into the little Chev. Just Marjie and me and ride, ride, ride across that Paradise of rugged mountains on into Eternity.

Later: [Eldest brother] Rae came down this evening, likewise Daddy and Mother. Rae's going to San Francisco tomorrow. Probably won't see him for a year or more. I'll miss him terribly. He's so sweet and nice. I *do* love him so.

Marjorie Dana, Doris's best friend, known as Marjie.

Saturday, January 8

Got a letter from Marjie. She's in love with James Worsehall. I don't see it myself. She picks on the funniest-looking boys. He's nice and all that, but when she could have had sunny, blue-eyed Ned, I don't see why she falls for a foreign-looking person like James. He doesn't *begin* to compare with my sweet, adorable, lovable, handsome Micky. And even Jack Hibbard has him beat a mile. It's a mystery but I *do* hope she doesn't marry some funny-looking, inconsequential person.

Later: This is the most dreary place I have ever been in. A minute ago I heard two nurses talking outside my door. One of them said, "Well, I doubt if Mr. Rags will live much longer. He's just about done for." And the other one said, "Well, we need the room for another patient anyway."

Don't they *realize* what death is? These hard-hearted creatures. How *could* they speak so lightly of a thing so deep? And when any of them get into a conversation with me, instead of being cheerful, they're gloomy and pessimistic. They seem to take a pleasure in telling me all of the patients that have died from Scarlet Fever because they caught cold or something. Why, the way they talk, it seems as if no one has gotten out of here alive. I'm beginning to doubt whether I'll ever get out, the way things look. The doctor says two or three more weeks, and when I'm in danger of catching a cold every day. I'm beginning to think my life is over and all that sort of bunk. They've got me scared stiff. Gee, but I'll appreciate home when (if) I ever get there.

Rae came down on his way to Frisco. Lucky dog! Mother brought me some oranges. Gee, but they tasted good.

Sunday, January 9

Sunday. That's all. Folks brought me the papers. Wish I was out of this Hell Hole.

Monday, January 10

I'm so bored. I'm ready to die. Nothing to read or anything. I just lie here and think, and I've about exhausted my resource. Haven't even anything to think about. Damn it! If I were in school I'd be in gym, playing Basket Ball, probably. Bah! I hate to think of going back to school and yet—it would kill me to stay here much longer. And I have two weeks or more left. Oh—

Wonder why I haven't heard from Jack Pillar. He probably doesn't give a damn whether I'm sick or not. He's the kind that will sing romantic songs to you, look at you with adoring eyes, make your heart go pitty pat, kiss you passionately and then forget all about you. Fickle, two-faced conceited men. *Oh, how I hate them.* The whole damn bunch. Girls aren't so hot, either. Most of them are either snobbish or cattish. All, of course, except Marjie. She's perfect beyond a doubt.

The nurse just came in and asked me if I had ever read *Right off the Chart*[24]. She said it was the diary of an actress that had to stay in the hospital four years, and that she saw the humorous side of everything. I don't see how anyone could find anything humorous in this dump. But anyway, her remark set me to thinking. I think I'll put my diary in book form. It has some interesting events and I could add some and make it really interesting. Especially my trip to Eastern Oregon. Maybe I'll turn out to be a well-known author, just like Anita Loos.[25] Who knows! I don't think I will, tho. I mean put it in book form. I'd hate to have the public know all my thoughts. Instead, I'll just write a separate story about the O-O[26] in diary form.

---

[24] Unable to locate said book

[25] Author of *Gentlemen Prefer Blondes*, 1926

[26] The O-O Ranch in Eastern Oregon, where Doris and best friend Marjie spent part of the summer, 1926. See *I've Got Some Lovin' to Do*, p. 98

Tuesday, January 11

Joe[27] got out today—lucky dog. Mother said she would come down about 10 o'clock. She didn't and neither did Daddy. I can't imagine why. I'm lonesome. Dr. Kiehle came by and brought me a book. Sweet of him.

Wednesday, January 12

Had a bath today, in the bathtub. I was awfully wobbly and I walked as if I were drunk. Mother came down and brought a bunch of my school books. Now for some good hard studying. Exams are at the end of this month. Gee, but I *will* have to work. Joe and Kathleen came by this afternoon. According to what Joe says, Alyce is taking advantage of the fact that I'm cooped up in a hospital and is flirting terribly with Jack. Guess she expects to make me jealous. Hell, I don't care if she has him. It's a compliment to me that she couldn't get him until I was safely away for a month. But just wait till I get out of here. I'll go after her Johnny and make her realize what a *fight* is. She thinks she can get away with anything but she can't. I'll show her. Damn her, anyway.

Thursday, January 13

A man died of Scarlet Fever last night. Encouraging, isn't it? Oh, well, if I get out of here alive, I'll say the day of miracles isn't over. The doctor came today. He just frowned at me. Also Kathleen. But the best news is—Daddy rigged up a radio set[28] for me. Isn't that scrumptious! It's cute, too, all shiny and new. Of course, I can only get Portland, but *that's* wonderful. *Hot diggity!*

---

27 Her older brother Joe, who was in isolation with her

28 A crystal radio set, which could receive radio signals without power or batteries; could be made from basic items including copper coil, antenna wire, a crystal receiver and earphones. Luther Bailey probably purchased the set.

Friday, January 14

Friday night. I wonder what the kids are doing. Got a letter from Evaline. She said that as soon as I was out, she'd have the kids over and have a big brawl. Not bad, that! She also said that Bob sent his "deepest regards." She wouldn't say "love" if her life depended on it. But I'll bet anything it was love that he sent. It's not like Bob to send anyone deepest regards. *Balongny*[29] [*sic*], or how ever you spell it.

Radio doesn't work for some reason but Daddy's coming down tomorrow and fix it.

Saturday, January 15

Radio is going fine and everything is hotsy totsy. Joe and Kathleen came down this morning. Gee, but he is crazy about her for some reason. I keep thinking about Micky today. Oh, my darling, sweet, adorable Micky. I wonder why I don't hear from him. I can see his firm mouth and laughing blue eyes as plainly as if he were before me now. Oh, I do love him so. I want him, I do, I do, I do. Fate isn't going to keep me from him forever. I know it isn't. Someday he'll appear before me in all his young handsomeness. Then the world will sing and I'll be happy once more. Life will hold forth its cup of pleasure and I'll drain it to the bottom.

Micky, my darling, I love you so.

Sunday, January 16

Folks brought papers up. Later, Joe and Bob came. They just left and maybe will come back later and bring the girls. Hope so.

(Later) Joe and Kathleen came up this afternoon. There's wild reports going around about Gene[30] getting drunk every Friday and Saturday nights and leading generally a *wild* life. I can't believe it myself. He's too much of a baby to get drunk. Joe says he looks terrible. Hollow-cheeked, dark circles under his eyes, and etc. Enough for Gene! Kathleen says that Johnny stopped her in the hall and asked her how I was and if anyone

---

29 Baloney/bologna
30 Gene Rossmond, Doris's neighbor on Culpepper Terrace

could see me. Maybe he'll come up! Hope not, tho. I don't get a chance to curl my hair here.

Tuesday, January 18

I'm convinced that in Marjie, I have one of the dearest, most loveable friends in the world. She came in this morning, couldn't stay but a minute, but she left a letter. *Oh*, how I love her. This afternoon, Bob, Joe, Kitty and Kathleen came over. They made a lot of noise and Bob looked adorable. He certainly is crazy about Kitty. She is cute, tho, and pretty as a picture.

Wednesday, January 19

This morning I woke up to behold a white world. The housetops were covered with snow and the streets were three inches deep with it. Even the air was white with a flying of fluffy white flakes. Oh, the spirit of restlessness that assailed me! Gone is my peace of mind. I can no longer sit still all day and read. I want to be out in it. Battling against the wind, trudging through the snow. Tonight the H[ill] boys will be up at Rayleigh [*sic*] Hill[31] sleighing and I'm *in bed, useless,* unable to be a participant in the fun. Damn, damn, damn.

I can't study, I can't read, I can't think. It kills me to sit here and see the rest of the world walk by my window, bundled up in furs and thoroughly enjoying themselves. Oh, Fate! Cruel Fate! Why does it pick this time to snow when I'm shut away from it? And there are so many memories connected with it (the snow, I mean). It brings so vividly to my mind a small car way out on the highway, with snow blowing around it, and snuggly inside, a boy, a girl. The boy singing romantic songs tinged with adventure, and the girl—happy, oh, so happy. Still another time, a toboggan, ~~speeding down a hill,~~ filled with 15-20 boys and girls. A breath-taking wind whipping their faces, an encircling arm, a stolen kiss—given and taken in the spirit of romance, an innocent flirtation, nothing more—but oh, the thrill of it.[32]

---

[31] Raleigh Hill in west Portland

[32] See *I've Got Some Lovin' to Do*, December 1926, for these stories.

Also, four happy people trudging up a hill, bursting into a warm house, laughing, talking, jesting—a hot cup of coffee, and then another kiss, a feeling of intoxication, of joy and anticipation, a dash into the biting air. A dare, adventure calls and they have gone for another spree. I'm silly to go rambling on like this. Anyone else would say I was crazy. But I shall never forget those days.

Later: A rather pitiful thing happened today. The operating room is right next to mine so I hear all the howls. Anyway, a baby 4 or 5 years old was operated on and died on the operating table. The mother was in there at the time. I never felt so sorry for anyone in all my life. Even tho I couldn't see anything. Later I saw her go out the front door, 10 years older than when she had rushed up the steps with the baby in her arms a few hours before. Oh, the grief that some are forced to bear. And to think I was feeling rebellious because I couldn't go out and play in the snow.

The snow, by the way, has turned into a regular blizzard, and no one but Daddy came to see me, tho the kids had said they were coming. I am isolated now. The paper said the snow had come to stay so I guess I won't have much company from now on.

Portland, Oregon, with Mt. Hood in the distance.

Thursday, January 20

I've never, in all my life, seen anything quite as beautiful as that which lies before me now. It's a cold, clear day. The sky is blue as topaz. But the city—oh, you *beautiful* city! I've seen it in the summer time, hot and sweltering. I've seen it in the evening, just as the sun is setting and it's all shadowy and mysterious. I've seen it in the early morning when the sun is rising in all its glory. I've seen it in 100 different moods, dresses and seasons and thought that each was unique and wonderful. But *never* have I seen it as it is now, clothed in a white, white blanket of snow. And behind it, the blue foothills, and above them, the snow-capped peaks. Oh, it is *useless* to try and describe it. Such beauty has never before existed. It is unreal, like some beautiful painting only no artist, however great, could paint that river, the beautiful Willamette, blue as the sky above, surrounded by white banks. I wish the whole world could see it as I do now. Heaven will have to be beauty *unsurpassed* to be at all interesting after looking at this. Personally, I prefer Portland, the Great West.

Later, as usual: There's a new girl in the bed next to me and she has two of the best-looking doctors, and young, too! Both of them struck up a conversation with me and flirted like hell. Gee, but it made the nurse mad. Also, Johnny asked K[athleen] how I was and if I needed anything to read. Guess his conscience is hurting him. Serves him right.

Friday, January 21

Gee! How I *hate* this place. I was talking to Joe today and the nurse and other girl's doctor came in and the nurse said, "Oh, you selfish girl, do you want this other girl to die? Shut that window!" And she slammed it in his face. The doctor gave me a nice friendly smile that said, "Don't mind her; she isn't anyone." I try not to mind her but she is impossible. And talk about partiality. She waits on this other girl constantly, calls her *dear* and *honey* while she glares at me and made me *make my own bed* this morning. I've given up trying to be nice to her. Three weeks is long enough to bow down to someone who is really your inferior. I return glare for glare now. Nine more days and I'll be away from this.

Joe said that he saw Hale and Hale sent me his love and said that the reason none of the Hill boys had been up was because Mr. Hill wouldn't let them because he didn't want any of them to catch it and start an epidemic through the school. So that's that!

Saturday, January 22

Another long, dry day. Oh, how I hate that girl in here. She talks to herself and whines all day long and groans all night so I can't sleep. Because I got her a blanket the other day she expects me to wait on her *all* the time. And when anyone comes to see me, she says, "Oh, I'm so chilly, I'm so chilly," all the time we're talking so that I usually end by shutting the window. But believe me. One of these days I'm going to say, "You damn little S of a B, shut your damn mouth and go to hell!"[33] And that's not all! The day before I go, I'm going to tell that ignoramus of a nurse what I think of her. And then I'm going to go home and eat all the cake and pies and candy I want and then I won't go to bed at 8. I'll stay up until midnight and then I'll go up to my little pink room and go to bed and then not wake up till I get damn good and ready. Oh! If I can live through the remaining eight days, I'll feel like singing, shouting, yelling, letting all the world know that I'm back in civilization again where there *is* no such thing as a pessimistic old nurse, a dreary ward, greasy food and *hostility*.

Sunday, January 23

Last night about 8 o'clock Bob, Gene, Joe, Kitty and Kathleen came up. Gene looked much older, decidedly handsome but, oh, so dissipated! He's traveling the downward path all right. Bob's in love with Kitty and she with him. Johnny's been inquiring about me again. Why the heck doesn't he come up and find out for himself? *I hate this place!* Oh, how I hate it! This girl's friends came to see her and oh, what friends! Cheap, loudly dressed and painted[34]! She gets on my nerves so I nearly go crazy, and I

---

33 This is as close as she comes to real profanity.
34 Wearing makeup was still fairly shocking to proper young ladies like Doris.

have a sore throat and a headache, and if I develop *pneomea*[35] (how do you spell it?) I'll have to stay here three more weeks and that would kill me. But I feel like hell and I want to go home! Oh, I do, I do! I *won't* stay here anymore than seven days!

The kids said they were coming up but I guess they changed their minds. Oh, I'm lonesome and blue and homesick and I wish I was alone so I could cry. DAMN IT!

Monday, January 24

Oh! Damn, damn, damn, damn, damn, damn, *damn*. Dr. Baird[36] came this morning and found some kind of spot on my lungs and pretty soon another doctor came and he took some kind of a test and if it proves negative, everything is nice, but if it proves positive (which it probably will), I'll have to stay *two* more weeks. I won't know until tomorrow for sure. I caught cold and it settled in my lungs or something and will probably leave me with a weak heart or consumptive lungs. And I try to be optimistic and say, "Oh, well, what's two weeks in a lifetime?" But two weeks is two weeks and I'll be way behind in my school work and it'll take a couple of weeks to get my strength back when I do get out of this hateful, unsympathetic place. They don't try to console me like Mother would, but instead they scold me as if it were my fault. As if I wanted to stay here any longer and eat greasy food and be nagged at.

[In heavy pencil] A horrible thought has just come to me. They think I have T.B.[37]

--An Enterlasps [*sic*] of three weeks during
which I was dangerly [*sic*] ill--

---

35 Pneumonia

36 Dr. Alvin Baird, with first-floor offices at the Medical Building, 729 S.W. Alder, also known as the Park Building. The Multnomah County Medical Society held its meetings there.

37 Tuberculosis — a death sentence at that time

Saturday, February 11

It's been nearly three weeks since I wrote last, and oh! What a lot I've been through. It was Dyptheria[38] [*sic*] that I had and I was delirious and had a fever of 105 and nearly died. Had to lie flat on my back and had a hell of a time. I'm home now, tho. At last! I'll have to stay in bed for a week or more and won't be able to go to school for the rest of the term. Damn! I'm awfully weak as it is. I can hardly walk and blah!

Wednesday, February 16

Johnny came up this afternoon. Stayed a long time. He's a cute kid but awfully juvenile. He made my fever go up to 100, tho, so he must not be so *awfully* bad.

Thursday, February 17

Oh! Oh! Oh! I can't think, I can't eat! I can't breathe! My heart is broken. My spirit is down. The long and short of it is that Micky is in Portland! But that is not all. He has been here for two months or more and hasn't made a single effort to phone or see me. Oh, what a let down! I've been a silly romantic fool. After all my dreams. But no, I still believe that he meant what he said that day, when he told me that I was the only girl for him and that he would always love me. He *couldn't* have been just playing with me. His eyes were too blue and truthful. The last night I saw him, nearly a year ago, he was so adorably romantic.

But if he did love me as he said he did, why didn't he come to see me as soon as he got back? Oh, death, where is thy sting? He must have met some other girl and fallen in love with her. He's probably pledged everlasting fidelity to her. Damn it! Boys are all the same. I always thought he was different but I guess he isn't. You can't trust any of them.

Alyce was over this afternoon and told me he was back. She saw him at Grant [High School] but didn't speak to him. Probably afraid he would

---

38 Diphtheria was once a major killer of children; however, childhood vaccines have made it virtually a non-issue in the United States.

snub her. But anyway, she had the pleasure of actually seeing his blue eyes and curly black hair. Oh, if I could only see him I'd be so happy. I do love him so and now that I can't have him, he's twice as desirable. But there's only one thing left for me to do. And that is—bury my love for him in the deepest corner of my heart and forget him. He's made it apparent that he doesn't give a damn for me (oh, how it hurts to admit it). But it's the truth, so goodby[39], Micky. You were sweet while you lasted but you didn't last long. Just like the rest. No more dependable than the weather. I'm never going to fall in love again. It doesn't pay.

Friday, February 18
Johnny came up again this afternoon. He looked awfully cute but why *doesn't* he grow up? He might be halfway exciting if he did. He's 18 but you'd never guess it. Anyway, he acted adorable and told me I had wonderful eyes. The same old blab but it's nice to have a boy flatter me again after being cooped up for so long. He brought me the [high school] paper, too. A fact which I greatly appreciated.

Saturday, February 19
Marjie came in today. She's in love with Ray Prescott. I don't see it myself.

Sunday, February 20
Well! My pride has received another blow. Evaline phoned and we were talking and all of a sudden she said, "Oh, say, I went out with your friend *Micky Stevens* last night and he was sorry to learn you had been sick and sent you his love!" Oh, the very fact that he would send it in such a nonanchally[40] way shows how indifferent he is and *he went out with*

---

39 Doris spells "goodbye" the old-fashioned way: *good by.* I made it one word but kept the spelling to retain the flavor of her writing.
40 Nonchalant

Evaline. That is what I can't stand. And he'd always told me before that he'd hated her type. But I guess he changed his mind. He probably kissed her, too. Oh, my sweet curly-headed Micky making love to that cheap, disgusting bit. She'll ruin him like she ruined Bob Styker and oh, I loved him so.

Johnny came up about 8:30 this evening. Daddy seemed to think it was perfectly terrible for Johnny to come up in my room when I was in bed. Oh, well! I guess parents are just naturally evil-minded. He stayed quite a while and was extremely interesting. You know what I mean. I don't think he likes Alyce quite as well as he used to, either. Now's the time to do my stuff. If I want him, it wouldn't be hard but I don't want him. I want my Micky. So I guess I'll keep our conversation entirely impersonal and unexciting.

Monday, February 21

Chauncey, Bob, Kitty and Kathleen came up this evening and since the folks were not home, I put on my robe and went downstairs. Enjoyed myself immensely but have a hell of a headache now.

Tuesday, February 22

Gee, but I'm tired. About 12 o'clock this morning [noon] Alyce came up. We talked and played Poker, and about 2 o'clock in walked Margie Schmol! Talk about your dramatic moments. Margie and Alyce haven't spoken for about six months and are deadly enemies. It was extremely awkward for about half an hour. Then they began to thaw out. After that, we had a good time until Johnny arrived. Then everything went blooie. Alyce fussed around Johnny and she knows he's been coming up here and I guess she didn't like it, and since the "war was on," I was determined not to let her beat me. So we were both sarcastic and mean and catty towards each other which of course ended in Johnny turning to Margie. It serves us right. I don't give a damn about Johnny but wanted him because Alyce did. I guess neither of us [has] him now, tho, but I don't care. All I want is to get well and to be able to go outside like a human being.

Wednesday, February 23
Fanny came up this afternoon. Dr. Baird's coming tomorrow to see if I can get up. Hot dog!

Thursday, February 24
Doctor came. My heart's all funny. Can't get up for ages yet. Maybe I have Bronchial Phenomea[41]. Fever of 101. Damn it! Feel like hell. Guess I never will get well.

Friday, February 25[42]
Feel like Hell.

Saturday, February 26
Sick as the Devil

Sunday, February 27
Will I *ever* get well?

Monday, February 28
Little better today but still in bed and I *do* so want to get well and be human. I've wasted over two months of my life in bed and I want to *live* but my crazy heart is all wrong. Damn it!

---

[41] Pneumonia
[42] Here she misnumbers the days through end of February

35

~~Tuesday, February 28~~
~~Still in bed. But gradually getting better.~~

Tuesday, March 1
The doctor says I can begin sitting up now and seeing people.

Wednesday, March 2
Dumn[43] day.

Thursday, March 3
When I get well—if I ever do—I'm going to California and stay with Mrs. V[44] for a month. Be fun.

Friday, March 4
It's spring time and the sky is blue and the birds are singing. Oh, *why* don't I get well? I'm so damned tired of being an invalid. Exactly two months ago today I went to the hospital and I'm still down and out. Oh, damn, damn, damn. But I won't stay in bed much longer. I can't. My constitution won't stand it; neither will my nerves. Being sick hasn't made me sweet and nice. It's made me grouchy. At least I am today. In a week I'll be 17 years old and after that I refuse to stay in bed.

Saturday, March 4
Marjie came in. Fanny came up.

---

43 She means *dumb*, but misspells it *dumn* for years.
44 Mrs. Van de Carr, a long-time family friend who lived in Oakland, California

Sunday, March 6

Walked around upstairs today. *Maybe someday* I'll get well.

Monday, March 7

Rain, rain, rain. Dreary day. In bed all day as per usual. Bored to death and longing in vain for excitement. Romance and Micky. And a star-lit night and a moon, a canoe and you[45]. I'm becoming incoherent now. I guess this inactivity is affecting my brain. But when I do get out? Oh, boy! Won't I stir up some entertainment! I feel as if I had been dropped from the world. I'm out of touch with everything.

Tuesday, March 8

Johnny came up this afternoon but I told Mother to tell him I wasn't feeling well because I didn't want to see him. My hair looked awful and besides, it'll do him good to know he can't see me every time he feels like it. (pen went dry)

[in pencil] Fanny came up this afternoon and looked adorable as per usual.

Wednesday, March 9

Another beautiful Spring day. I'm out on the balcony[46] getting a sun bath. I may dress tomorrow. Oh, how pretty the city is and I love life so. Everything's coming my way now, if I only don't get sick again. I made a resolve last night that I'm not going to sit back and let E. have Micky. He loved me once so he'll love me twice and when I get well, I'm going after him, and I'll get him, too, you just see.

Fanny and Alyce came up this afternoon. Had good time.

---

[45] Camp song, "A Boy and a Girl in a Little Canoe"
[46] Her bedroom in the house at Culpepper Terrace had a small balcony just off her window, which she sometimes used to sneak out. But she may be referring to the back patio with its broad view of the city from Westover.

Thursday, March 10

Fanny came up this afternoon. Just think — tomorrow I shall be seventeen. Seventeen. I'm grown up. It wasn't so long ago that I was 16 and now I'm 17. Gee, but life passes quickly. Anyway I'm glad I'm still alive and didn't die with Diphtheria. And I am getting better. I may get up tomorrow. And between now and this time next year I'm going to get Micky. I don't care—I am. I love him so!

Friday, March 11 [Doris's birthday]

Got up this morning just as usual. I mean woke up. Evaline came over about 1:30 and stayed till 4. Raved about Micky all the time. And she looked so fat! After she left I got up and dressed. Fanny and Alyce came about that time and stayed till 6:30. Fanny brought me a box of candy and Alyce, a flower for my coat. We talked and had a good time. It seemed so wonderful just to be dressed. Like other people.

After they left Marjie came and brought me a *ukelele*. Cute! Daddy gave me a cute clock for my desk, Mother a box of stationery and Rae sent me a "coolie coat."[47] And I can't get over the fact that I'm seventeen. Oh, yes, Evaline said that Bill Summers had gone to Annapolis. I'll miss him. And that Moody was going steady with some girl. Poor girl.

Saturday, March 12

Washed my hair this morning. Then got in car and went downtown to get it marcelled[48]. Just think! It was the first time I had been out and, gee, but it was nice. This afternoon Fanny and Judy came up. Judy cute as usual. This evening we all went to a show—Colleen Moore in "Orchids and Ermines." [*sic*] Very good. Gee, but I love life. It's so nice to be well although I'm awfully tired tonight.

---

47 Chinese-style jacket with Mandarin collar and loose sleeves. Rae may have bought this in Chinatown in San Francisco or Oakland.

48 Short bobbed and curled hairstyle, set with curling iron, popular in the 1920s; also known as a finger wave

Downtown Portland, Fifth Street north from Morrison, with streetcars.

Sunday, March 13

Dressed today and feel great! Marjie and I took the Chev[rolet] and went for a ride. Had lots of fun. Explored all of Old Portland[49]. Oh, yes! We passed [the] Hill [Military Academy] and saw Leo and Billy Ragsdale. They wanted us to stop but we didn't. I might have if Leo had been alone. But I *hate* Billy Ragsdale. Marjie left this afternoon.

Monday, March 14

Felt awful all day today. Have one hell of a cold.

---

[49] Downtown neighborhood where Portland was founded

Tuesday, March 15

Took car this afternoon and went for a ride. The folks went out for dinner so about 7 o'clock I took a hot bath and went to bed intending to break up my cold. About 7:30 the door bell rang and it was Johnny. I made Joe entertain him while I got dressed again. Then we played Poker, talked and had a good time. We decided to phone Alyce and not let her know Johnny was here and let Johnny listen upstairs and get her to talk about him and see what she said.

He did it just for a joke but I didn't know she was going to say what she did. She talked *terribly* about him. Said that the only reason she went with him was because he had the money and she hated him and oh, *awful things*. I couldn't stop her when she got started. Finally Johnny could stand no more. He let go a flow of eloquence, gave her the merry ha ha! Broke their date for Friday and hung up. Alyce will simply slaughter me when she sees me but it serves her right. Bet she doesn't have a chance to make a fool of him again.

About 9 o'clock Bob, Chauncey and Kitty came up. We had an awfully good time and Johnny became terribly affectionate all of a sudden. He has the leading part in the class play. Rather nice but it'll make him more conceited. I like Bob. He's cute.

Wednesday, March 16

I have an awful cold and it's raining and cold out. Mother has one, too. Fanny came up this afternoon.

Thursday, March 17

I did a foolish thing tonight. I don't know what possessed me but I was alone and lonesome, so phoned Jack Pillar. He was awfully congenial and asked for a date for this Sunday. So I made it. Hope we have a good time.

Friday, March 18

Went downtown with Mother and looked at coats. Bought a new pair of shoes this afternoon. Fanny and I went for a ride and when I came home, Johnny was here. We talked and had fun. We decided to have Jack come up tomorrow night instead and have Johnny and Alyce. Be more fun, and I won't be so bored.

Saturday, March 19

I hate Jack! I hate him! I hate him! I hate him! He's conceited, egotistical[50], and good-looking. But I hate him and I never want to see him again. We had quite a good time, tho, but I've never been so disappointed in a boy before. I HATE HIM. Micky for me.

Sunday, March 20

Johnny and Frank O'Conner came up this afternoon and we went for a ride. Had a fairly good time but I must admit, I'm terribly disappointed in men. Jack bored me to death last night. The poor little sap hasn't even a sense of humor. He's altogether too materialistic. Frank is Irish and supposed to be clever but I was terribly bored this afternoon. I'm through with boys. They don't even interest me. They're all the same. I can't imagine myself ever falling for a boy again. There's nothing about them to fall for, the conceited animals.

Animals, that's all they are. And girls are even worse. They're cats, everyone of them. I'm disillusioned in all ~~mankind~~ humanity and especially in Jack. Even Micky isn't worth going after. He'd probably turn out to be just as much of a flop as Jack. Damn it! I'm so bored with everything. I've got to do something unusual. I want to get away from the city. This city especially, with all its superfluity. Away from material things. Its men. Its egotistical men. Its women. Its sarcastic, jealous, immoral women. Its noise. Its bluster and confusion. Its pretense of being something it isn't. Its

---

[50] Psychological terms like "egotistical" came into conversational use after World War I.

petty trivial quarrels. Everything. I want to go away. Out in the desert or to the beach or away up in the mountains. Away from curling irons and powder puffs and MEN. Above all, men. I hate them, I do. OH!

Monday, March 21
Bummed around today. This evening we went over and bought the sweetest, most adorable Pomeranian Spitz[51]. I prefer a dog to a man any day.

Tuesday, March 22
Went downtown and bought a new coat and hat. Coat was $110 and the hat $12.50[52]. Both perfectly adorable. The coat is gray with gray fur. The hat is imported from Paris. Saw Jack Freidel. I guess he's home for Spring vacation. Had an adorable mustache. Went for a ride with Fanny this afternoon and saw Jack Kaplan. I put my hand out the window to turn a corner. I guess he thought I was going to wave to him. Anyway, he started to wave to me but when he saw that I was only putting my hand out the window he didn't want to be snubbed, so he pretended to be pushing his hat back. By that time it was too late to speak to him. It's funny about us. We never know when the other one is going to speak.

Wednesday, March 23
Went for a ride this afternoon. This afternoon Jack [Pillar] phoned and asked to speak to Joe but I told him Joe wasn't here. Then he tried to get into a conversation with me but I hung up. I didn't want to talk to that sap. This evening I went to the Music Box[53] with the folks. When we got back, Joe said he had talked to Jack and Jack asked him why I was so unsociable, and Joe said that I was sore at Jack because he had a date with Kitty. The big nut! Now Jack thinks I like him but I'm jealous of Kitty.

---

51 Commonly just called a Pomeranian today
52 Comparative cost in 2012: $1400 coat and $159 hat
53 Popular theater with Wurlitzer organ; see Appendix II

And I'm not. I hate him because he hasn't a sense of humor. Boys are so damned egotistical.

Thursday, March 24

Oh! Oh! Oh! At last after a whole year I have seen and talked to my darling, sweet adorable Micky! Micky! Himself. This is how it happened.

As I said before, I resolved to get him, so I took the car and went over to find his house. After I had located it, I went over to Grant [High School] and as soon as school was out Alyce and I went over to Franklin High School. Then we drove back and forth from his house to school about six times hoping to see him.

We didn't, tho, and had just about given it up. We stopped close to the school and watched some of the boys training for track. About that time two boys drove up in a Ford and we asked them if they knew Micky. They said they did but that we'd never find him at school. He avoided it like poison. We said, "Well, where is he, then?" And they said, "At the Mt. Tabor Apartments"[54] We asked them why he wasn't in his house and they said that his folks had gone to California and he was "batching" it[55] with another boy. We didn't quite believe them but we went to the apartment house anyway. Sure enough, his name was in the chart.

We didn't have the nerve to phone him, tho, and so we were going back. We had just gotten in the car when the boys in the Ford drove up and said, "S'matter, isn't he home?" We said we didn't know, and then before we realized it, they ran up the steps, called his [number] and then, oh, then, Micky himself appeared before us. My heart beat about 150 per [minute] and I didn't know what I was saying to him. Something dumn probably. He was awfully glad to see me and said how sorry he was that he hadn't had time to see me sooner and he said he'd phone me. And he's so damn cute and I love him so and I'm going to have him.

But I'll never forget how I felt when I first saw him. Why, it was terrible. My temples pounded and I felt hot and cold at once. And his

---

54 Possibly on SE Hawthorne near SE 50th Avenue

55 Living as a bachelor without a housekeeper or other woman (wife, relative, etc.)

eyes lighted up and he came towards me with outstretched arms and said, "Doris!" with that marvelous voice of his and I was so happy.

He's changed terribly, tho. Just like Jack H. When Jack first joined the Navy, he was sweet and unspoiled but when he came back he was so—I don't know. Micky's changed, too. His mouth has a cynical twist to it and he certainly doesn't look innocent. But he's Micky just the same and I'll always love him. He's thinner than he was and his face has a lean look. He looks as if he had been robbed of all his ideals. He's seen what life really is and I'm afraid he's decided to throw conventions to the wind and get what he can out of life. At least, that's the impression he gave me and if that's true, it's my duty to save him from himself.

Friday, March 25
Went to the doctor's office this morning. Fanny and I went for a ride. Had an especially good time. Met Fred Niche? Also saw Jack Kaplan and he smiled so cutely. I love Micky.

Saturday, March 26
Fanny and I took the car and started to a show this afternoon. But we changed our minds, called for Judy and went over to the East Side. We drove all over. Stopped by Evaline's a while. We saw Hal Paddock and he looked so cute. Also saw Sol Robinson, Frank O'Conner and several others including Moody who looked adorable. We were all feeling peppy and consequently had a good time.

After we had canvassed the East Side from Sellwood to Piedmont, we went to the dog show. Then we left Judy, and Fanny and I roamed around some more. Incidentally, saw Larry Lenate and talked to him quite a while. He isn't going with H.A. anymore and told me I looked simply keen. He wanted to know if I was still having my famous Friday night parties but, of course, I didn't have sense enough to invite him up. Gee, I'm dumn! He said that Bill Rummers had disappeared. Interesting, if true. After I had gotten home, Ed and Jack Pillar phoned. We gabbed for a long time and it ended in me inviting them up for next Friday. Damn! I don't want them. Now I suppose I'll have to get up a party. Went to a show this evening and saw Constance Talmage[56]. I'm crazy about her and I'm going to try and be like her.

After we got home, Bob, Chauncey and Billy came up. Nice kids. Forgot to say I saw Maloney—cute. I love Micky.

Sunday, March 27

Had the car today and went over to Alyce's. We rode all over town in search of excitement. But didn't find any. Once when we found ourselves in the vicinity of Micky's house we stopped under the window and looked up, in hopes he might be sitting in it. Just then a cute boy drove up and said, "No, Stevens isn't in." We asked him how he knew we were looking for him and he said, "Oh, all the girls do!" I don't like that.

Anyway, we rode around some more and Alyce insisted on going over to get Johnny. I didn't want to but we did anyway and bumped into Lunney Burkett and his Ford. He asked if he could go with us so we let him and the four of us went for a ride. Alyce kept wanting to park but "I'm not that kind of a girl" so we just drove all over the East Side. Lunney's cute. I like him and he acted like he liked me. We stopped in at Evaline's awhile and she had a cute blond boy [with] a mustache, so we didn't stay long.

Monday, March 28

Took Mother to a luncheon and got my hair waved. Went over to Grant and took Alyce for a ride. I saw Jack Pillar. He looked funny and acted terribly embarrassed. He even *blushed* when I spoke to him. Dumn! Also saw Frank O'Conner *and* Moody. He is so cute.

---

56 Could have seen Constance Talmage in either *Breakfast at Sunrise* or *Venus of Venice*, both released in 1927. Constance Talmage was best at comedy, even in her vampy roles.

Tuesday, March 29

Went to doctor's office this morning. That's all. Bob and Kitty came up this evening. But the big excitement is that the North Western Bank[57] went broke and everyone's all up in the air about it. M and F started a malicious report and caused a—[58]

Wednesday, March 30

Dressmaker was here today. Went downtown this afternoon and picked Fanny up on the way back. We bummed around. Saw Maloney, the cute little devil, and also Moody. I'm *crazy* about him. He has the sunshiniest smile. Gee, but I like him. Saw Billy Ragsdale but I snubbed him. Nearly bumped into Lunney Burchell and his Ford.

Margret Johnson had a party last Friday that lasted till morning. Everyone so damned stewed that they were lying around on the floor. Dick Marlet went to call on her Saturday at 3 o'clock and she came downstairs in her Pajamas. She was apparently still half soaked. Dick told Fanny all about it and she told me.

Thursday, March 31

This afternoon I went to the dressmaker's and incidentally saw Alyce. We went to LHS [Lincoln High School] and saw Johnny and Frank. Then I came home. After dinner Joe and I went over on the East Side. I left Joe at Micky's while I went to go get my dress fitted, then called for him. He said that Micky was the dirtiest, most disgusting, filthy-minded person he had ever known. That he had become common, cheap, immoral. Ugh! Oh, my

---

57 Doris's father's offices were in the North Western Bank Building at 6th and Morrison. The building still stands, overlooking Pioneer Square.

58 Entry is incomplete; however, the tale was true. Rumors that the bank was unstable began circulating in late March and on Monday, March 28, lines began forming before the bank opened. Anxious customers withdrew more than $2 million dollars. When the bank closed that night things were so hopeless that the bank went into liquidation. "M and F" could be Meier and Frank, but no way to verify.

Micky! My sweet adorable Micky! I was afraid you would be changed. Joe says that he isn't worth a damn and goes with cheap girls. Micky, Micky, I don't *want* to believe it. I want him to be like he was. Oh, my darling! He has it in him to be decent. It isn't his fault. He must have fallen into bad company.

Oh, I love him and don't want him to be bad. He's coming up tomorrow along with the rest of the bunch and I'll see how much of what Joe says is true. On the way back we saw Johnny, Lunney and Frank. Talked to them a while. Johnny tried to kiss me but I told him it wouldn't be fair to Alyce. Jack P. phoned after I had gotten home. Talked about 30 min.

The house on Culpepper Terrace where Doris lived in 1925-1928. The house was designed and built by Luther R Bailey. Doris's room was on the right, second floor, over the kitchen, and had its own sunny balcony to the right. The house has a large living room for entertaining guests.

Friday, April 1

The bunch came up tonight and gee, but there was a bunch. I expected about 10 and there were nearly 20. We had a wonderful [time] tho. And Micky! Oh, my Micky. I don't know what to think of him. I wonder if I really have loved him all this time or just thought I did. He was nice to me, of course. Told me all about his trip to the Orient and etc. When I'm talking to him I think—oh, he's not so wonderful. But the minute he looks at another girl I just boil inside. I can't stand it.

He's so different from what he was, too. He'd compliment me and flatter me and yet I'd feel as if he were doing it mechanically, as if he'd done it so much it didn't mean anything to him. I stood that for about half the evening and then I couldn't stand it anymore. If I can't have him wholly, I didn't want him at all.

So I turned my attention to Johnny and Lunney. Lunney is adorable and gave me his undivided attention so I played around with him. He kisses nicely, too. Another time Johnny motioned for me to come and sit on the stairs with him. We talked and it was awfully romantic. The light was out in the hall but a bit of moonlight drifted in. He said he was getting tired of Alyce and as my mind was all muddled about Micky I let him kiss me. Alyce hasn't any scruples about not hanging around my men so I decided not to. But he began saying things that I knew he would be sorry for afterwards. I guess the moonlight affected him. Anyway, I didn't want him to commit himself so made him come back in the living room. Micky looked at me kind of funny when we came in. Alyce was trying her best to flirt with him but it didn't have much effect. Then Micky came over and started to talk to me. But I couldn't stand to talk to him so impersonally when I wanted his love, so I made some flippant remark and left him. When everyone was leaving, he came over to me, took my hand, looked down in my eyes seriously and said, "Did you miss me so *awfully* much while I was gone?" Oh, his beautiful blue eyes and he was going to say something else I know but just then Lunney came and said, "Come on in the sun room, I've got to say goodby to you." Of course I didn't go but the conversation was interrupted. Everyone was saying goodby at once and everything was so confused and then out of the wilderness of hands came a big strong one that gripped mine intensely and through a haze of faces I saw a pair of blue eyes and a voice said, "I've *got* to talk to you. I'll phone you sometime, Doris," and then he was gone and I was smiling at Lunney and Basil and Jack and trying to talk sense. I don't know *what* I said.

Finally they all went away and I came up to my room to think and here I am! If he had something to say, why didn't he say it earlier? Oh, damn. I wonder if he meant it and what was he going to say when Lunney interrupted us and damn! I love him and I don't want to because he obviously isn't for me. And if he *had* said what he was going to say will he *mean* it? Anyway I'm going to try and forget him and let events take their course.

Saturday, April 2
Marjie came in this afternoon. We went to the Music Box this evening. Good.

Sunday, April 3
Johnny Bader was over this afternoon. He's a nut! Joe and I went to C.E.[59] this evening. Afterward I went over to Alyce's and left Joe at Lorraine's. Johnny L. and Frank O'Conner were there. We all went for a ride and had a good time. Alyce found out that Johnny kissed me and she was mad. But Johnny just laughed at her.

Monday, April 4
Took Mother to a luncheon. Came back and got Fanny and we went to Dr. Kiehle's. Dr. Kiehle was out so his pardner[60] [*sic*] took care of me. He's only about 32 and has an adorable mustache. Cute! Then we went over to Grant and saw the kids. Then we came home and saw some Hill boys on the way. Leo included. This evening we went to the Orpheum. Good!

Tuesday, April 5
Went to school today to see about my credits. It was good to see all the kids. On the way back I saw Lunney. He has a new Ford Roadster!

---

59 Christian Endeavor, a teen social group connected to the church
60 Dr. Frederick Kiehle and Dr. Fred Harrison were eye, ear, nose and throat doctors who practiced together at the Medical Arts Building. Later Doris mentions a Dr. Harrison, optometrist; not the same doctor.

Wednesday, April 6

Went to the doctor's office and he said my blood was low[61] so I couldn't go back to school. On the way home I skidded into a big Franklin [car] and bent the fender all up. Daddy's mad. Saw Leo and talked to him a while.

Thursday, April 7

Went to school today to see about exams. Fanny and I went for a ride afterward. Saw Lunney Burchell. Also my darling Moody and Johnny and Frank. Frank is as sarcastic as ever. Johnny said he came up here last Tuesday but I wasn't home. Interesting! Oh! How I long for Romance! Will it never come my way? I crave it, I long for it, I must have it. Am I so awful looking that I should be deprived of it? That reminds me. I saw Mr. Drew today and he said I was better-looking than ever. But that's all the good it does me! Damn!

Friday, April 8

Went downtown this afternoon. Bummed around and bought a new hat. This evening Evaline wanted me to come over there and since I had nothing else to do I went. I didn't expect to have an especially good time but I did. Met a boy from Seattle who has a Buick Roadster and his father's a millionaire[62]. He doesn't drink, smoke or neck, to excess. He has all the desired requirements and he fell in love with me. But as luck will have it, I don't like him at all. It seems to be impossible for me to like the ones that like me. If Micky ever looked at me like he did I'd be all up in the air. Anyway, I'm going to be nice to him and get what I can out of him. He has the cash and—oh, damn, that sounds like a gold-digger but dear diary, do you blame me? I would work my fingers to the bones if Micky would love me but he won't. He made me love him and then forgot me so

---

61 Anemic or low blood sugar, perhaps

62 Royal Oliver was the son of Edmond E. Oliver, a Seattle haberdasher and vice president of the Hatton-Oliver Co. The Olivers were prosperous enough to live in the North Admiral neighborhood of West Seattle in 1930.

I am going to shut my true self in and let Roy think I like him. I'll *make* myself like him. Alyce says I'm too particular and I guess I am. At any rate I'll try to stand him. His name is Royal Oliver. Dumm! Alyce calls him my Baking Powder Kid.

Saturday, April 9

Met Alyce downtown and we bummed around. Bought some sheet music[63]. On the way home I saw Charlie and stopped to talk to him. He said that Roy wanted a date but was afraid I wouldn't give it to him so he told C. to ask me. Crazy! I told Charlie that if he didn't have enough nerve to ask me himself I didn't want to go with him.

This evening Lunney Burchell and Johnny were coming up. About 7:30 Frank O'Conner called and asked if he could come. I said, "Sure, but you'll be odd." "Oh, no, I won't," he said. "Lunney's not coming." So he came up. After he had been here about an hour Lunney and Johnny drove up. I went out to talk to them and they said, "Is that d— Frank in there?" I said "Yes," and they got mad and said words to the effect that if we preferred Frank to them, they wouldn't come in. I said, "Well I don't see why you hate him so." And they said I wouldn't *look* at him if I knew what they did about him.

Frank and Alyce came out and the boys glared at him and we all came in the house. Lunney's cute and so is Johnny but, oh, how I hate Frank. We had a good time, tho, after Johnny and Lunney got over glaring at Frank. There certainly isn't any love lost between them. Frank is bad clear through and Lunney's headed that way if he doesn't be careful. He's a cute little devil and he's all right when he's with nice kids but the minute he gets around Frank or someone he becomes—cheap. But I *do* like him and I hope Johnny can keep him in the right path. Because he has it in him to be so nice. Roy phoned me this evening and wanted a date for tomorrow.

---

[63] The Bailey family had a piano and a music room and Doris sometimes mentions playing, although has never mentioned piano lessons.

Sunday, April 10

Daddy let me have the Chev. this afternoon to go to Evaline's, so Roy and I went over there. Charlie was there and they wanted to go for a ride. Daddy had told me not to go anyplace but there wasn't anything to do at her house so we went. We drove out to Oak Grove[64], bummed around, then went on to Oswego[65]. Stayed there quite a while and then started home. The kids wanted to bum around some more, tho, so I phoned Mother and asked her if I could stay a little while longer. She asked me if I had been at Evaline's all afternoon and I said yes and she said, "No, you haven't; you've been riding around. Come straight home and come alone!" Then I had to dump the kids, but Roy wouldn't be dumped so I had to bring him back to Hill. On the way home, he began making love[66] to me. But I wasn't in the mood to be pawed over and I was mad at myself for getting in bad with the folks so I treated him terribly. He'll probably never speak to me again but I guess it's impossible for me to be nice to someone I dislike, million or no million. I want my Micky.

Monday, April 11

The folks are [still] mad about the car and I can't have it for a month and I *hate* street cars. Roy phoned this evening and I despise him more than ever for phoning me after the way I treated him. He must not have *any* pride. He was so sugary-sweet and blah! Money doesn't make the man. I want someone with *character*.

Tuesday, April 12

This afternoon I took a long walk in the woods. Gee, but it was nice to get away from the city into the midst of nature. Everything was so clean and fresh and green. It makes you love life so. Roy called me again this

---

64 Oak Grove, where Marjie Dana lives, is ten miles south of Portland.

65 Across the Willamette River from Oak Grove, Lake Oswego is a popular place for water recreation. But there's no bridge at that spot, so Doris and friends would have had to drive five miles north or south to cross the river and get to Oswego; either way, it's another 12 miles in the car before heading back to Portland.

66 See *Glossary of Slang*, Appendix I

evening. He's leaving for Seattle tomorrow and wanted to see me before he left. I didn't want to see him, tho, so I told him I was busy.

Wednesday, April 13
Went to doctor's. Nothing else happened. Dull day. Oh, yes—Bob and Chauncey came up to see me but I sent them home early—tired.

Thursday, April 14
Went for a long walk in the woods this morning. Went to a show with Marjie this afternoon and out with the folks this evening. Some boy called me while I was gone but the maid[67] didn't get his name. Wonder if it was Micky. Dull life. But it's better than being in the hospital.

Friday, April 15 (Good Friday)
Met Alyce downtown, got my hair curled and helped her buy a hat. Then went to the doctor's office. Tired. The boys wanted us to meet them but I didn't want to.

**A view of Broadway in Portland, showing the Paramount (Portland)
Theatre and the Broadway, where Georgie Stoll conducted the orchestra.
The Orpheum and the Journal Building can be seen in the distance.**

---

67 The Baileys had at least one female servant as long as they lived on Culpepper Terrace.

Saturday, April 16

Met Alyce downtown and we went to The Broadway. Very good! Then met Johnny and went up to Frank's house. Bummed around and came home. The boys wanted to come up tonight but I was too tired so I told them not to.

Sunday, April 17—Easter

Went to church this afternoon. Afterwards I went up to Alyce's and Johnny and Frank were there. We bummed around and about 9 o'clock we went down to the store and got a Sundae. They left about 1 [a.m.]!

Monday, April 18

Gee, but this has been one eventful day. I stayed all night at Alyce's last night. This morning Johnny phoned and this is what Al[yce] said. "Hello, Johnny. How's my boy? What's the matter? Johnny, what *is* the matter? Did Frank say I said that? And you believed it? Johnny!" And then she began to cry. I didn't no [*sic*] what it was all about. But Alyce was crying so she couldn't talk, so I took the phone and lit in on Johnny. I asked him what he said to her and he said that Frank told him that Alyce asked Frank if Johnny really liked her or went with her for what he could get out of her—imagine it! Then I began to cry, mostly because Alyce was, and poor Johnny was so scared.

He said, "Well, what are you crying for?" and I couldn't convince him that seeing Al[yce] cry made me cry. Anyway, I finally made him believe that she *didn't* say it and he apologized for believing it and said he was coming up. He came about the time I was leaving. After I got home they phoned and wanted me to come over so I asked Mother if I could use the car and she said, "Phone your father." So I phoned Daddy and asked him if I could? But he said no. So I took it anyway, which I shouldn't have done. Anyway, we had a good time until I smashed into a Packard and bent my fender all up. Was I mad! There wasn't anything to do but take it to a garage and let them fix it.

Johnny, Alyce and I all managed to scrape up enough to pay for it. Then I took Alyce home. Johnny came back with me and I left him at 23rd. When I came in I went in the back way and asked the maid if the folks were mad. She said for me to go listen to them so I went in the hall and I could hear Mother and Daddy talking upstairs. Oh, boy! But they were mad. I went upstairs to face it and they just lit in on me. I can't ever have the car again and I can't go to Cal[ifornia] and blah! blah! Goodness! They were so mad about my taking it and keeping it out all afternoon, there's no telling what they would do if they knew I had a wreck.

About 9 o'clock Bob, Chauncey and Kitty came up. Chauncey and I went for a ride and he let me drive his Buick. Boy, was it fun! Then we came back and just Kitty and I went for a ride. Oh! I do love that car! Well—we rode all over. Met Lunney Burchell and took him for a ride. He's cute! Then we came home and bummed around with the boys. I rather like Chauncey!

Johnny phoned and wanted to know how I came out but I couldn't talk to him 'cause the folks were listening.

Tuesday, April 19

I phoned Marjie this evening and we blab[b]ed away. She said that Fritze had been talking about me lately and wanted to see me. He's a cute little devil. I like him. Rather dull day. Also—Ned proposed to her.

Wednesday, April 20

Alyce and Jean played hooky this afternoon and came up here to lunch. We went for a walk through McCleary[68] [sic] and two men followed us. They'd hide behind the trees. Crazy! We had an awful time getting rid of them. I'm not wild about going up there alone now. Damn it.

Johnny came up after we got back. The poor kid got kicked off the class play. I was so sorry for him. He nearly cried when he told us. Roy phoned

---

68 Macleay Park is a forested park with trails not too far from the Baileys' Westover neighborhood.

me this evening. He got back from Seattle last night. Said he thought of me all the time and blah! blah! He's a nice kid, tho.

Thursday, April 21
Went to a show with Marjie. Saw Johnny down at 23rd and talked to him. He feels terrible about getting kicked off the class play staff. Chauncey came up this evening and he let me drive his Buick. We drove all over. That car hits 60 as easily as 30, and I hit it, to[o]. We started to Seaside[69] but that's all. Gee! how I *do* love that car.

Friday, April 22
Went to the class play with Alyce. It was unusually good. Saw Jack Freidel. Gee! I don't see why I was ever so crazy about him. He's a nut. Afterwards we were riding home on the street car, being bored to death, and a car drove up behind us, and Bob Grandie, Bob Freitag, Phil Manning and Frances Pilkington were in it. They motioned for us to get off the street car so we did. We bummed around and went into an eating place. Then we went out towards the Alderwood Country Club[70]. It was a marvelous evening and the kids were all so full of pep, and Bob Freitag sang and he has a wonderful voice and a smile like Micky's and I like him. We didn't get in until nearly 2 o'clock. Folks were mad but—what do I care? We had a good time.

* * *

---

[69] Oceanside resort town about 78 miles northwest from Portland up State Highway 26

[70] A golf club seven miles from downtown, near the Columbia River; it closed in 1953. It hosted the 1937 US Amateur golf tournament. Designer Vernon Macan considered Alderwood his greatest golf-course design.

Thursday, August 18

It's been over three months since I've written. Terrible, isn't it? Oh, well, lots has happened to me.

I saw "Don Juan" [the movie] tonight and I hate men. From now on I'm going to be different. Beginning tonight I'm not going to kiss or be kissed. The next boy that kisses me is going to feel as if he had accomplished something. I'll be cold and aloof. I'll make them fall in love with me, and then give them the merry ha-ha. Men and boys are all the same. Conceited, egotistical creatures. They have acquired the idea from somewhere that we should cater to them. Nothing doing—I'm going to give them a taste of their own medicine and never, never, *never* will I fall in love again. I'm going to have them at my feet, pledging everlasting fidelity. I'll steal their hearts and then trample on them. Laugh in their faces. They deserve it. Damn them. I'm going to hurt them like Micky hurt me.

Never again will I be in a position to [be] hurt like that. Speaking of Micky, I wish I could make him fall in love with me and then turn him down. Then everything would be nice.

Friday, August 19

Had a crowd in tonight. Jack Pillar was among them, also a cute little Irish man, Jimmy Morgan. We really had an *awfully* good time. Everyone was full of pep and Jack was a little too full. Jimmy kissed me. The dirty little devil, and only last night I resolved never to be kissed. But I really couldn't help it. We were dancing on the porch and before I knew what was happening he'd kissed me. And when I objected, he kissed me again so I thought I'd better not object anymore. And you can't get around the fact that the Irish do know how to make love. But I hate men.

Saturday, August 20

Haven't anything but a pencil so I won't write. Nothing much happened except Bob C. called up a couple of times. That's all.

Sunday, August 21

The folks took Joe and Chauncey to Mt. St. Helens[71] [*sic*] this morning. They're going to climb it. This afternoon Bob and John Haney came up. John Haney's father is well known and has *loads* of money. I might like him if Mother would quit raving about him. She must have social ambitions for me or something. This evening Eve[line] phoned and said there were some Grant boys over there and she wanted me to come. But I couldn't, so they came up here. And boy, were they cute! And full of pep. There was the cutest brunette who played the uke [ukulele] all evening and sang marvelously. His name was Eddie Morgan. Also there was a boy named Mickey. He was so different from my Micky as he could be. Blond and even sported a mustache. I stuck to my resolution and was cold and aloof. It went over heavy and I didn't let any of them kiss me. Not even Mickey although it was a temptation.

I hate men, tho. When you stand away from them and look them over, they're not so hot. And I absolutely refuse to fall in love with the brunette. Altho it would be easy. He'd be just like the rest, tho, and I HATE MEN!

Monday, August 22

Went downtown this morning to see Dr. Harrison [optometrist]. He's cute! He's a bachelor and isn't 30 yet and belongs to the University Club[72]. I wore my new sweater and he said I looked nifty. I like bachelors. They're so sophisticated and nice. But I still hate men.

---

71 The active volcano in Washington state about 70 miles northeast of Portland that famously erupted in May 1980; Mt. St. Helen is visible from the Baileys' back windows and patio at the house on Culpepper Terrace.
72 The University Club, at 1226 SW Sixth Ave., was for college-educated men, and eventually, ladies as well.

Tuesday, August 23

Stuck around home all day. Fanny's gone to Crater Lake. Patsy [Doris's dog] had a romance today. The Gay Cavalier was an Irish Setter and named Micky! That's Fate for you. "It won't be long now."

Went to the Heilig tonight. "The Goose Hangs High." Very clever. Arthur Churghly was one of the ushers. Looked tough.

Wednesday, August 24

Alyce came home this morning. Nice! Marjie's coming Monday. Went up to school and arranged my work. Gee, but I'm going to take a heavy course. I'll have to work like hell to get through. Jack got stuck in the garbage can tonight and all the neighbors were in the backyard trying to get him out. It was funny but serious, to[o]. It took us nearly an hour to get him out[73].

Thursday, August 25

Met Alyce downtown and we went to Dr. Laccel's[74] office. He's only about 25 and cute. We stayed there quite a while and then went to Dr. Harrison's. And, oh, boy! You know the rest!

On the way home we saw Bob and Lunney Burchel. Lunney's bleached his hair or something. After dinner we went to the Columbia and saw "Metropolis." It's a show about the way the world will be 1,000 years hence. They make people and everything. It's a marvelous show but makes you hate civilization. It was only about 9:30 when we got back so Alyce and I went for a walk over the hill. On the way home we met John Haney and Clarence Digman on their way up here. They had an adorable Roadster

---

[73] The garbage can may have been the type that was buried in the ground with a foot pedal to open the lid. Little brother Jack was 7 at the time.

[74] Dr. Laccel (named spelled variously in diaries) is evidently a flirty Portland optometrist, but he is not listed in the city directory. He seems to share space with Dr. Harrison, who is also not listed in the 1928 Portland City Directory. There were just two optometrists listed at the time; D. Chambers and Sons in the Pantages Building (171 Broadway, now 743 S.W. Broadway) seems the more likely office.

so we went for a ride. Then they came back here and stayed till about 12. I like John. He's full of pep and clever.

Friday, August 26
Nothing much happened today. I intended to go swimming but it rained. And that's that.

Saturday, August 27
Stuck around home all day. Darrel won the poster for the fall opening. Wasn't that nice? His picture was in the paper and everything. He's a promising young artist and all that sort of thing.

Sunday, August 28
Alyce came up this morning. This evening we decided to go to a show so we told Mother we were going for a walk in [Macleay]. We started down the hill and were about half way there when we met Bob. He took us for a ride and then left us at the show. It was late when we got out and we didn't have time to walk clear up the hill and we only had eight cents between us. So we walked to where the W.O.[75] car goes up a dark street. When it came, Alyce got on the car. I waved goodby to her and walked to the back of the car. Just as it started up I jumped on the back steps and rode up the hill. Several people looked at me but didn't recognize me. Thank goodness. When the car got to Culpepper I jumped off and we proceeded on our way. It was fun.

Monday, August 29
Marjie came back this morning. It rained all day long. Evan phoned me and made a date for next Thursday. I don't think I'll keep it, tho. I haven't

---

75 Westover street car line ended on Culpepper Terrace, just a few houses away from the Baileys.

seen him for two years and I don't know what kind of a crowd he goes with or anything. He may be terribly fast and he may be slow. I might like him and I might not. Anyway, I don't want to take the chance.

Tuesday, August 30

Went out to Marjie's this afternoon and we went to Rotary Club[76] picnic. Had an awfully good time. It was so good to see Marjie again and everything. We went to the dance in the evening and Bud Whiting was there. The boy we met last year, and hadn't seen since. That's all.

Wednesday, August 31

Marjie came in with me today and we played Poker all afternoon. Broke that date with Evan. Went to a show this evening. Dull life.

Thursday, September 1

Marjie and I both baked cakes this morning. This afternoon we saw a show and about 4:30 Bob came up in his *beautiful* Cadillac. He also came up this evening and we went for a ride. And—he can sing! Oh, boy.

Friday, September 2

Went to The Broadway and saw Clara Bow in "Hula." It was exceptionally good. I also went to see Mr. Laccel. He kept calling me "Doris" and so when I left he said, "Goodby, Doris," and *I* said, "Goodby, Eddy," and went out. I don't see why I shouldn't call him by *his* first name if he calls me by mine. I like him. Chauncey and Kelly came up for a while this evening. Also Bob.

---

[76] Luther Bailey was a Rotarian.

Saturday, September 3

Met Alyce downtown. I got some sheet music and $11.50[77] worth of school books! We also went to all the steam ship companies in Portland and got information about boats going to Alaska. We're going to bum our way North next summer. Believe it or not. Gene is home from his vacation. Cute as hell, of course, but wilder than ever. Went to a show this evening.

Sunday, September 4

Met Alyce downtown and went to see "Beau Geste." It's a marvelous show. Then we went over to her house and bummed around. We decided to go to Alaska next summer and when and all about it. In about two weeks we're going to save $10 and go down to the coast on a boat just for the fun of it. Round trip ticket is only $3 and we can easily do it over the weekend. We're going to, to[o].

Monday, September 5 (Labor Day)

It rained all day long. I love this time of year. It makes me think of Micky. It was just about this time ~~last~~ *two* years ago that I met him. Oh, the darling! *Two whole* years and I still love him.

But that's all the good it does me. Damn! I haven't seen or heard from him in nearly five months. I have no reason at all to hope. And yet I do. Every time the phone rings I think *maybe* it will be he. But it never is and probably never will be. Damn! Damn! I say it again, DAMN. I can see his laughing gray eyes, his strong chin, and his frank, pleasant smile as plainly as if he were here. I love him. I love him. And yet he has passed from my life as silently as the fading of day. He probably never thinks of me. Never dreams how I yearn for the sight of his tall, muscular form. Oh, Micky! How little did I realize when you were here, how much you meant to me. I took you as calmly as night and day. But now that you are gone—life is but an empty bubble.

---

[77] Those books would cost $150 in 2012.

If I only knew *where* you were. Maybe you are in trouble—and need me. But again—you may be dancing, flirting, with another girl. But whether you need me or not, I am *sure* that I need you. Oh, Micky, my darling! Can't you here [*sic*] me begging, imploring across the continent? Surely you *must* care. Just a *little*. Fate couldn't, wouldn't be *that* cruel. Maybe you have done something which you think I would disapprove of and are *afraid* to see me. But *nothing, nothing* could altar [*sic*] my affection for you. Even if you were accused of murdering a Chinaman[78]—I'd love you ~~as my life~~ till my dyeing [*sic*] day. All this sounds dramatic. But it *is*.

It's a funny world. The chances are I'll *never* see him again and yet I'm pledging everlasting fidelity. To what? A gambler, a drunkard, a fool. Little *he* cares whether I live or die. But I can't help it. I can't. I love him! Love him! Love him!

And *someday*, Micky,
you'll cry over someone,
as I have cried over you.
Teardrops will dim your eyes.
and then you'll realize
that while you're crying
my tears will be drying
although my love was wasted
I can't regret
just mark my words, sweetheart
and don't forget
that *someday* you'll cry over someone
as I have cried over you.[79]

---

78 She means "kill" a Chinaman; she'd love him even he'd killed a "Chinaman." The unfortunate phrase "to kill a Chinaman" was used to explain a run of bad luck. "It appeared as though someone in the Battalion must have killed a Chinaman, as the weather continued rough and stormy, with strong wind." —1925, L. M. Newton, *The Story of the Twelfth: A Record of the 12th Battalion*, p 132
79 Doris's own poem.

And now that I have this out of my system, I make a solemn resolve to *forget* him. The dirty, lowdown, drunken fool. Oh, but I love him. Sweet adorable darling Micky. I love you, love you, love you, worship you, idolize you, adore you.

Tuesday, September 6

Rain, rain, rain! School starts tomorrow. Damn. Gene came over this evening for a little while. Gee, but he's got a wonderful tan. He looks like a Greek God and acts as if he owned the universe. But he doesn't and he makes me mad. Darn him. Went downtown today.

St. Helen's Hall, where Doris went to school, was an all-girls parochial school in the Episcopal diocese, run by the Anglican Sisters of St. John Baptist. It was located in Portland Heights, in the Goose Hollow area, at 13th and Hall streets. It later became Oregon Episcopal School, still extant today. This building, however, was knocked down to make room for the freeway. Only one building from SHH remains, as a private home.

Wednesday, September 7

Started school today. Gee, but I'm taking a heavy course [load]. Evan phoned this evening and wanted a date. Didn't give it to him, tho. He's a sap! And that's that.

Thursday, September 8

Oh, gee! Oh, gosh! Fate seems against me. Just when I had made a solemn resolve to forget Micky, I see him. It was on 5th and Washington and we were crossing the street (Fanny and I), and my eyes beheld a gray suit and a mop of curly hair and my heart started to race and my knees became weak and I felt hellish. Simply hellish. And before I could get over the effect, he had gone and Fanny said, "Say, what's the matter with you? You look like you're going to faint." And I was brought back to Earth. He'd disappeared in the crowd and that was all. After five months I saw him for just one fleeting instant. For the next five months I'll live on the memory of his bronzed face and black hair amidst a crowd of people. Oh, I love him, love him, love him. But I *shall* forget him.

Friday, September 9

Had a gang up tonight and had fun! Oh, boy. Darrel didn't get through [with] work until 10 and so Jimmy Morgan, Ed and I went to get him. We were early though, so we rode all over and Ed tried to kiss me and I said "Try and get it!" and Jimmy stopped the car. And they held my hands down and first Ed and then Jimmy kissed me. I was between two fires but they both kissed nicely. Then we went to a funny little place and had milkshakes.

Then we went to get Darrel and brought him up here and he was nice and attentive and danced with me all evening. But I don't like his nose and he's too dignified and I felt terribly kiddish all evening. Jack was here and so was Jerry [Jenny?]. But Micky wasn't and I love him. Oh, if I could only have him. Instead of Darrel and Jimmy and Ed. Damn!

Just to think, after waiting five months for him. Dreaming, praying, longing, and then when my dream comes true, I'm absolutely void of all reason. Haven't even sense enough to speak to him. Just stand like an idiotic fool. As if I were 13 or 14 years old. What's the matter with me, anyway? And I'll probably be the same next time. When I think of him I can plan the most marvelous things to say. But the minute I see him I'm struck dumn. Damn it. Oh, Micky, darling, sweetheart, just you wait. I'll get you yet if I have to die to make you notice me.

Saturday, September 10

Met Marjie downtown and went to a show. I've got to study now.

Sunday, September 11

Church this morning. Alyce phoned this afternoon and said that Darrel was simply crazy about me. He showed it in everything he did or said. Talked about me constantly and looked at me with his soul in his eyes. I'm not saying this. Just repeating what she said. I don't believe it but it's nice anyway.

Monday, September 12

Felt like hell all day.

Tuesday, September 13

This sure was the 13th. Missed my [street]car and flunked a quiz and have a headache. Evaline said that Frank Fisher wanted a date with me. Interesting—if true.

Speaking of Fate—Micky is in Joe's typing class at O.I.T.[80] and goes to night school and works during the day and lives at 22nd and Everett[81] and I love him.

Wednesday, September 14

Lindbergh[82] was here today. We went to the Stadium to see him, and besides seeing him, I saw Micky. He was two aisles away, but I saw him. Oh, he's adorable, but looks awfully tired and discouraged. Didn't enter into the fun at all; just sat with his head in his hands and frowned. Oh, I love him, love him, love him. I wish I could help him. It's terrible to be

---

80 Oregon Institute of Technology, at the Portland YMCA on 6th and Taylor
81 Micky has moved from the Mt. Tabor apartments.
82 Charles Lindbergh; see Appendix II

able to see him and know that he's worried about something and not be able to do anything about it. Damn! That's Fate—

I also saw Bud Whiting and bumped right into Frank, so I *had* to speak to him.

Thursday, September 15

Micky's lost his job. Oh, how I wish I could help him.

Friday, September 16

Guess who's in town—Johnny Leaverton. Will wonders never cease? He's going back Monday. Oh, yes! Charles Ford was killed in an accident last week. Isn't that awful? He was racing a freight train and was killed instantly.

Saturday, September 17

Went to The Broadway with Marjie this afternoon. Had a date with Frank Fisher this evening. I like him. He's cute and full of pep. Lots of fun and sophisticated enough to be interesting but not too sophisticated to be boring. All in all, it was a very pleasant evening.

Sunday, September 18

Went around The Loop[83] with the Halls. Had an awfully good time. It was a perfect day and Mt. Hood was beautiful. Didn't get back until 11. Studied till one (a.m.). Sleepy.

---

83 The Mt. Hood Scenic Loop connects parks along the Columbia, Sandy and Hood rivers in a 146-mile loop of roads, trails and meadows.

Mother (Willie Doris) seated on the log with unidentified friends. Rae took this photo on a drive around the Loop in about 1918. His caption says "On Mt. Hood Loop; White River glacial detritus, Oct. 19."

Monday, September 19

After school, Fanny and I went up to Darby's[84] to get something to eat. Saw Leo and Billy Ragsdale and talked to them quite a while. Leo's cute as hell and just as full of pep as ever. The little devil. It was good to see him.

Tuesday, September 20

Studied hard all day. Lost my glasses yesterday and I'll have to tell Dr. Harrison and I hate to because he'll raise hell. Micky has a job in a jewelry store. Gee, I'm glad. The folks are talking about boarding me at the Hall but I'm not doing it. I'd run away first. It's bad enough to be a day pupil.

Wednesday, September 21

Went to see Dr. H[arrison] and Dr. Laccel. Had a nice time—of course. Sleepy and tired.

An hour later—Oh! Can I stand it? I can't. My hands are shaking so

---

84 There's a Derby Cafeteria at 9 E. 28th North (NE 28th).

that I can't write. I had just undressed when Joe came home and Micky with him. He's downstairs now and I can hear him talking. Hear his darling voice. But I can't get to him. Oh, this is misery. To have him so close I can hear his chuckle and not be able to get to him. They're in the kitchen and if I lean over my balcony[85] I can see him move, see his hand fixing the root beer. Oh, Micky darling, sweetheart, I'm such a little way away. Damn, my tears are blotting the paper [ink is blotched]. I'm bawling like a baby. Why, I don't know. Oh, God! I can't stand this. He laughed just now. His deep, throaty laugh. Oh, Micky, Micky. Why am I undressed?

Two hours later—Some way, somehow, I mustered up courage to dress and go downstairs. Oh, boy! Did it take nerve! I casually said, "Well, hello, Micky," and he said, "Well, well, well, how are you, Doris?" And my poise was required. Then I sat down and we talked and talked. He told me about his trip and about everything he's been doing all summer. For my own self-defense, I was rather sarcastic, I guess. Anyway, he said, "Say, what have I done to deserve this sarcasm?" And I said, "Well, that's merely self defense." And he said, "What do you mean by that?" and I said, "Oh, actions speak louder than words." And he looked surprised and said, "Gosh. You act as if I had passed you up on the street or something. What's the matter? I'm sorry." And just then Joe said something and the subject was dropped. But when he left, he said, "We're going to straighten this out later, Doris!" And he was gone and we hadn't gotten any place. And I'll probably never see him for another six months and damn it all, anyway. But I can live on the memory of this wonderful evening. Just about two weeks ago I said he had passed from my life. But he hasn't. He's come back. All the time he was talking to me, I sat and kept saying to myself, "This is Micky. Here he is, right in front of me. So close, I could touch him. It's him—flesh and blood. Now he's smiling at me. Smiling directly at me. His blue eyes are twinkling. I can see his wavy hair, just as I have always dreamed of it. This, at last, is Micky himself. I can see the little scar on his upper lip. The scar I have dreamed of kissing."

And so forth. I don't know what we said half the time. Oh, I love him so. Oh, yes! Once he said, "Gee, I was surprised when you didn't turn

---

85 Her room is above the kitchen, at the front of the house.

around and go right upstairs when you saw me." And I felt like saying, "You darling. As if I could live away from you when you're so close." But instead I said, "Oh, that would have been impolite." And he said, "Yes, that's probably the only reason you didn't do it." And it took all the will power I possessed to smile back and say something flippant. When I could see his eyes frowning I wanted to kiss him. Love him. Say, "Oh, my darling, can't you see! Don't you know how I love you?" I couldn't look at him in the eye all evening. I was afraid he would see something in them. See that I worshipped him from the bottom of my soul. I can't look at his eyes, his hair, his mouth without feeling like a leaf. It's a wonder that I lived through the evening.

Thursday, September 22
Got excused at noon today to see Dr. Laccel. My glasses weren't ready yet so I had to wait half an hour. Had an awfully good time. He's cute! What I mean—he said that Dr. Harrison said that I was "some kid!" Not so worse! Only it sounds as if he thought I was little. Oh, well.

Friday, September 23
Worked like hell at school today. Saw Larry Lenate down on 23rd. He looked nice. But he said that Moody was married! Imagine it! He got married this summer. I wonder what the girl is like. Dick Marlet and Chuck Coffin brought us home in Dick's Cadillac. Fun! Went to the fashion show and saw just oodles of marvelous clothes. When I marry I want to be just smothered in furs and shimmering evening dresses. Some of those clothes just made me long to be rich. I've always wanted money but I've never longed for it like I did this evening. Oh, if I could only have all the clothes I wanted. Blue velvet dinner dresses and gray carricul[86] [*sic*] coats and an evening wrap of silver and gold with big white fox collar. A sky-blue Roadster with a rumble seat and a musical horn and a checkered radiator and fancy radiator cap.

---

[86] Caracul: Persian lamb; a curly fleece

Saturday, September 24

This afternoon I went down to see Dr. Harrison and had a *very* good time. He said, "You know, you're awfully pretty, but you know it!" Wasn't that cute?

But! Listen and ye shall hear[87]. This evening I was deeply engrossed in my work and the door bell rang. I went down to answer it and it was Micky! My poor little heart. I wish he would give me warning. My heart will give out if it has many more sudden shocks. Anyway, well, he asked me what I was doing and I said studying and he said, "Well, come on, we'll go out." So I changed my dress and we went. Betty Bane was having a party so we tried to find her house but couldn't. We had an awful good time looking for it. He is just the same, at heart, as he used to be and we both acted silly. We rode all over—East Side, West Side, all around the town[88]. I understand him better than I did, and love him more. The poor kid works like a slave and is getting disgusted with life. He says that he thinks he ought to find what he's looking for pretty soon. He's wandered all over the globe and lived every type of life. Trying to find what everyone so obviously waits for. I wanted to tell him that it was love he needed to pep him up. But I couldn't. When we got home we drank some root beer and then he read me Emerson's ~~Contemplations~~ "Law of Compensation." I really love him. I do, I do. I sat and watched him. Oh, he is so handsome. I talked to him rather seriously about drinking and dissipation and he was really interested. I told him that he was making himself common and he said he knew it but he had to do something and we had a long discussion and I think I came out [the] winner. At least he thought about what I said.

I wish I could remember it. It was really quite a good speech. Oh, the darling! He is trying so hard to figure life out. I wish I could help him with all his little problems. He needs someone who will *believe* in him.

---

87 Longfellow's "The Midnight Ride of Paul Revere"
88 From the 1894 song, "The Sidewalks of New York," long considered the theme song of New York

Sunday, September 26

I left my hat in Micky's car last night. This morning I drove by his ap[artment] and he was so cheerful and he said, "Oh, you don't want it now. I'll bring it up this afternoon." So I took him at his word, but he didn't come. I don't know why. He sounded as if he really wanted to come. And he didn't. And naturally I'm perfectly miserable. Why do I love him so? And I almost wish he hadn't come back if he's going to hurt me. Oh, why can't I have him? I thought all my worries were over but they obviously aren't. He's just given me a taste of what I've been wanting and now he's taking even that taste away. Why did he say he was coming if he wasn't? He said it so convincingly. I naturally didn't doubt him. Oh, Lord! How I love him.

Monday, September 26

Three test[s] today. One right after the other and I flunked them all because my mind was on Micky. Ye Gods! Why can't I forget him? I was serious before I saw him and I can't live now. Joe said that Micky brought my hat to school this evening and Joe said, "Gee! It's lucky you brought that. Sis was raving this morning because you didn't come up." He *would* say something like that. Big sap. Of course it had just the wrong reaction on him and he said, "Well, if that's the case, then you take [it] home. I'm not going up there to get bawled out!" Damn it! Joe hasn't the slightest idea when to say the right thing. The big fool.

The reason he didn't come was because he had to go out with his folks and he thought he'd get back in time but he didn't. Oh, damn! I feel like crying, but I've cried so much over him it's getting monotonous. Why are people made to love? It just results in heart-aches and unhappiness and tears. *But I will have him.*

I won't give up now. They say if you want a thing badly enough you always get it and the Lord knows I want him. And I'll have him. I will, I will. He needs someone to love him, to comfort him, to smooth away the frown from his for head [*sic*]. And *I* was chosen to do it. Fate chose *me* to love him and care for him and because I'm meeting a few difficulties is no reason I should drop out, give up. Ruin his life and mine. When he realizes, he'll love me as I love him. And we'll go thru life together. Helping each other. Comrades! I *will* have him.

Tuesday, September 27

I *know* that eventually I shall have him. Altho every minute when I'm not with him, when I'm not doing something to progress, I feel hopeless, futile, useless. Absolutely. I live on hope—and dream and I know that *someday* we shall meet at the altar. And go from this to a "cottage small by a waterfall"[89] and live in peacefulness, live with love. But why, oh, *why* doesn't that someday *hurry*?

I've just been reading over the six weeks that I was in the hospital. I feel like a new person. Here I've been bawling and feeling sorry for myself because of a man. Hell, what's a man anyway? I'm not in the hospital. I'm well and alive and I have my life before me. To live as I choose to live it. I'm free to come and go as I please. I don't have to eat greasy food and I can go places. I'm not shut up in a 2 x 4 room. I've all of Portland to roam around in. I'm well and oh, how I love life. I'm going to devote the rest of my life to helping others. I have two feet and an ample amount of intelligence. I'm not a hunch back or a maniac. I haven't a deformed nose or false teeth. I'm whole—and I'm going to live. I've got lots of studying to do and I'm glad to do it. Glad that I'm capable of studying. That I have an opportunity to go to the best school in Portland and associate with the nicest girls. I'm *alive* and I love life and I'm happy! Happy I'm *not* in the hospital.

Wednesday, September 28

Worked like hell at school. Taking six subjects is *no* snap. Saw some of the H.M.A.s[90] after school.

---

89 A popular song written in 1925 sung by John McCormack; popular for ukulele
90 Hill Military Academy boys

Thursday, September 29

Work, work, work. It's just *plain hell*. Met the boy D. Rogers goes with. He's as cute as you make them. How some of these women rate the good-looking men gets me down.

Doris and her brother Jack on a horse in Oregon, about 1924. Jack is about 6 years old.

Friday, September 30

On the Deficiency list for Eng[lish], of course. There's a crazy man up on the hill and they have two policemen up here trying to get him. The folks have gone out and even Joe isn't here. This evening about 9:15 the door bell rang. I was upstairs and Grace[91] and [little brother] Jack were in the kitchen. They refused to answer the bell so I krept [*sic*] down and cautiously opened the door. It was only Jimmy Morgan and a car full of kids. They came in and there was an *adorable* new boy with them. We had a *very* good time, needless to say.

---

91 Probably the maid

Saturday, October 1

Went downtown with Fanny. We went to see Dr. Harrison. Gee, but he handed out compliments today right and left. I'm crazy about him. He's so—oh—metropolitan. Then we went to The Broadway and saw a marvelous show. Gee, it was hot. Saw Bob Cunningham on the way home. Nice kid. Evaline phoned this evening and wanted to bring Bob Swan and Frank up, but the folks are down on Evaline so they wouldn't; they made me tell her Daddy had a headache. Isn't that just plain hell?!

Sunday, October 2

Drove the car to church this morning. We went to F.P. [?] and saw all the old kids. This afternoon Johnny Leaverton drove up and went into Catlin's[92]. Can you beat it? S'funny life.

Monday, October 3

Wet, wet day, but I love it. I love rain. I love Portland. I love Oregon. *I love life. And* I love Micky. I'm glad I'm not insane. Glad that I know what's going on around me. Glad that I can't have Micky without a fight. Glad that I *can* fight. I've had a certain number of heartaches, but I'm only 17. I'll live through them. I have 50 years of life, if not more, to do as I please[93]. To get all I can out of this existence. And I'm going to. My life is going to be worth while. It *is*. I'll make it so.

Later: After I had written this the door-bell rang and my heart began to thump-thump-thump and I went down to answer it and it was Joe and Micky. I turned to come upstairs again and Micky said, "Oh, don't go up. Stay down and talk." So I did.

As usual, we argued all evening. Mostly about love and life and religion. He says that he is going to get *all* that he can out of life. He's going to get

---

92 The original Catlin-Gabel school was called Miss Catlin's School and was located on Culpepper Terrace. The Hillside School Building was completed in 1926 on Culpepper.
93 Doris lived to be 101 years old.

a taste of everything before he dies. That he is going to look after himself and no one else. He excuses himself with the theory that "Nature is kind to the race, but careless of the individual."[94] *He* wasn't going to get in a rut and decay. He was going to look after himself and let the rest of the world go to hell. "We live but once," he said, "and there is no hereafter—so why worry about other people?" He put up a pretty strong argument but I said, "Micky, what you need is to fall in love. To meet someone who you would like to devote the rest of your life to. To get joy out of making them happy. You wouldn't think only of yourself then."

He said, "Maybe you're right but I doubt it. Love wears off and becomes tiresome, the same as anything else."

"Oh, but it doesn't," I said. "Love *is* life, and when you do fall, you'll fall hard. I know you will. You're not the kind that does things by halves."

He said, "Well, you must be in love, else you couldn't say that so convincingly." He doesn't know how near the truth he came. But he still persisted that life was a series of episodes and that the climax was death. I argued that everything he had been doing was an episode leading up to the climax which is love.

After an hour on that we branched off to religion. The age-old question. How much of the Bible is true? What is right and wrong and what is God? Is there a life hereafter and how did the world begin? An inexhaustible subject and terribly absorbing. It was late when we finished. He said that he liked to argue with me. That I had so many arguments and etc. About 12 o'clock the folks came home and brought my costume[95] from Marjie's. I came upstairs to try it on and it looked surprisingly nice. So I went down to show them. Micky said I looked "wonderful." Pitty-pat-skid-skid. It's funny how a compliment counts if it's from the right person.

And he thinks I'm in love with someone else and that's why I believe so implicitly in love. And he acted just jealous enough to be natural. Oh, I'll get him. I will. I'll keep these same impersonal tactics and make him fall in love with me. He will, he must, he can. He has said flatly that there

---

94 Seems to be a cross between Darwin (*Descent of the Species*) and Alfred, Lord Tennyson's thoughts ("In Memoriam")
95 For the dance at St. Helen's Hall on Oct. 13

isn't such a thing as love and he knows he'll never like a girl better than himself. Of course, that's rather discouraging but I won't let his prejudiced ideas stop me. He'll change his mind and everything will be nice. Oh, I love him, love him, love him. Surely my love won't be wasted.

Tuesday, October 4
Worked awfully hard today. Test and all that sort of thing. Met Alyce downtown. Johnny's back and she has a date with him Sat[urday]. Dear old Johnny. An adorable man rode up on the W.O. car this afternoon. Gee, but he was sweet, and flirt—oh, boy.

Wednesday, October 5
Did I work today? Oh! And I'm still at it. Joe says that Micky said that I knew a lot and was interesting to talk to because I was *intellectual* and had *sense* (?) and didn't try to flirt with him all the time. And I could concentrate and *knew* things. Isn't that *scruptuous*? [*sic*]

Thursday, October 6
Got A in an English test! Whoopee! I love Micky. Oh, I do, I do, I do.

Friday, October 7
Studied all evening.

Saturday, October 8
I had it planned that Bob and Eva[line] and Frank were to come up this evening. But Joe wanted me to invite H[arriet] A. for him, so I did. But when Harriet got here, Joe decided he didn't like her and ignored her. Of course, that made her odd. Neither Frank nor Bob liked her and treated her terribly. It was awful. About ten o'clock Frank and I went into the kitchen to get some root-beer. In about 10 minutes Harriet came out and

said, "I've got to go home, and Frank, you're coming with me." Frank said he came up to see me and he wasn't going so early. But Bob said, "You're staying all night with me and we've got to take Harriet home so you've got to come." What could he do? He took me off in a corner and said he'd get rid of H. and come back. When the discussion was becoming heated, a car drove up with a whole gang in it. So one party left while another came. The other was cute as *hell* and we had a marvelous time. Full of fun and so forth. And Al Plarson [?] came for me so that's that. Frank never did show up again, tho. Funny.

Sunday, October 9

Evaline phoned this morning and told me that when they got below the hill last night, Harriet said, "Let's not go home. That was just a gag to get out." Frank let out an oath and commanded Bob to let him out of the car. But Bob said, "Wait till we get Harriet home and we'll go back." But H. refused to tell them where she lived and they wandered all over, looking for the house. It was 11:30 when they finally got rid of her and Frank said, "Come on, we're going up to Baileys'." And Bob told him he couldn't because it was too late. And Frank said "Let me off at the car-line, then. I told Doris I'd come and I will. She'll never invite me up again." Evaline said they had to practically hold him in and kept him from coming back with the promise that the four of them would come up today.

But I was going over to Alyce's so I told her they couldn't. And that's the long and short of it. That little *cat* Harriet. How I hate her.

Monday, October 10

Snubbed Harriet today. Frank phoned this evening and said how sorry he was that things hadn't turned out as they should [have], that he tried to come back but they wouldn't let him and next time he would "stay put." I told him he left his hat up here and he said—"Good! That's an excuse to come up." He said he'd come sometime this week. He's cute and *awfully* nice. I like him.

Thursday, October 13

Daddy and Joe left for California[96] tonight. Lucky dogs.

We had the school party this evening. Had a marvelous time. Madge Mason was dressed as a boy, and handsome! She had on light trousers and a dark coat and cane and derby hat. She carried a light overcoat over her arm and had a mustache. And was she popular! She looked so much like a boy that it actually thrilled me to talk to her. And I danced twice with her. She had to sing a song in front of everyone. She stood with her hands in her pockets and looked so damned sweet. I've never met a popular girl so unaffected. Gee, but I've got a crush on her. She told me about the time she took a girl to a dance and made love to her and the girl fell for her and then she let her know that she wasn't a boy. Gosh! but she's adorable.

Fanny and I rode home on the st[reet] car with our costumes on. It was fun. Some curfew officers nearly picked us up, but we alluded [*sic*] them. Ha! Ha!

Friday, October 14

Wasn't on Deficiency! Madge looked adorable today. Crazy about her.

**Doris, circa 1928, in a sophisticated black dress,
perhaps the new one she had made.**

96 Possibly scouting for business ventures. Luther Bailey had changed his business offices from the North Western Bank Building to the Kraemer Building at 242 Washington Street, as a money-saving decision in September.

Saturday, October 15

Mrs. Shaeler made me a new coat. It's adorable. And I'm having a black velvet dress made. Rhinestone buckle and terribly sophisticated.

I haven't heard from Micky for nearly two weeks. Now that Joe is gone, I'll probably never hear [about] him. He'll forget me again. I'm nothing to him. I wish! Oh, I wish he hadn't come back at all. Those few blessed nights when I had him to myself were heaven. Oh, I love him, and I will have him. Oh, I will, I will.

Bob phoned this evening and talked about 30 minutes. Nice boy. I asked him if he'd seen John Haney and he said, "All the time." And I said, "You have my sympathies." And he said, "Johnny's right here," and then Johnny talked for a long time.

Sunday, October 16

Dumn, dull day! Bob and Kitty and John Haney came up this afternoon for about two hours. I had a raging head ache and sore throat. Felt like hell and treated them coolly. Which was mean because they didn't know I was going to feel so hellish. Of course, when I'm feeling peppy, nothing ever happens. It must be Fate.

Monday, October 17

Just as I got off the 23rd Street car this morning and was waiting for the 13th a st[reet] car passed with Micky in the front. He smiled so sweetly. I was glad I had on my new coat. Oh! How I love him!

This afternoon I went to see Dr. Harrison. Gee, but he is a-dor-a-ble. Hot Diggity Dog! Did I have fun! Well, I should say! He hands out compliments by the bushel, and his eyes! We were in a little dark room and he was testing my eyes and his face was so close to mine that his eye-lashes touched my face. Speaking of hot doctors—wopee! [*sic*] More people killed[?]—I'm becoming incoherent. My paragraph lacks unity, euphony, and emphasis, but a lot I care. I'm in love—with a blue-eyed Irishman named Micky[97].

---

[97] Micky has gray eyes in other entries.

Tuesday, October 18

Virginia called this evening and said that next Friday she and Gil were going to a party and from there to a midnight matinee at the B[roadway]. She wants me to get a boy and go with them. I'd love to, of course. But who would I get and how? I'd love to ask Micky—but I hate to. I might ask Darrel or Frank Fisher. Who, oh, who will be the victim?

Later—Somehow, some way, I summoned up courage to phone Micky and ask him! At first he agreed—smack off—and then he said he had some wild nights and ought to stay in and study. Finally he said, "Doris, I'll have to tell you. I'm in love." I took a big breath and said, "Congratulations, Micky. Who is she?"

"Dot Finely."

"Well, wasn't I right about *love* being the climax?"

"I think you were, Doris. In fact, I'm sure of my side of it, but not so with her. I'll wait a while and see if she lasts. I'll let you know from time to time how it's coming on."

"Yes, do."

"And if it isn't the real thing, I'm right. And if it is, you're right."

"Well, I wish you luck." Oh, the courage it took to say that.

"Thanks, Doris. You're a real friend—and if she turns me down, [call] me for all the wild party [*sic*] you can give."

The long and the short of it is she'll turn him down and he'll tell me about it and I'll sympathize with him and I'll get him on the rebound. Oh, well. My fighting blood is up. See if I don't!

In the meantime, I'll look up this Dot person's credentials. I wonder what she's like. Damn her.

Wednesday, October 19

Got a h— of a cold.

Thursday, October 20

Stayed home from school. Decided not to go to V[98]. To[o] bad of a cold.

---

98 Virginia's house or party? Unclear

Friday, October 21
Studied all evening.

Saturday, October 22
Patsy has some puppies! They were born at 10:30 this morning. Five ugly little brown pups. They *might* turn out to be cute but I doubt it. Baked a cake and sent it to the boys [her brothers]. Then went downtown and Mother and I saw a play. Then we met Marjie and went to the Chamber of Commerce[99] dinner. Then to another show and then home. Wild night—

I love Marjie. She's broken off with Ned. Damn. I love Micky, to[o]. As I've said before. Oh, but I do!

Sunday, October 23
Slept late and after dinner Marjie and I went to a show[100]. Which we shouldn't have done. Money's all gone.

Monday, October 24
[blank]

~~November~~

~~December~~

~~January~~

---

[99] Luther was a member.

[100] Going to the movies on a Sunday was considered sinful or, at least, naughty.

Oregon
(1928)

[front cover, new diary]
Do what thy manhood bid thee do—
From none but thyself expect applause
For—he nobless [sic] lives and nobles [sic] dies
Who makes and keeps his self made laws.[101]
The conflict is infinitely greater
Than the victory—or the defeat.

---

101 "For — he noblest lives and noblest dies..." from *Kasidah of Haji Abdu El-Yezdi*, by Richard Francis Bacon, 1870.

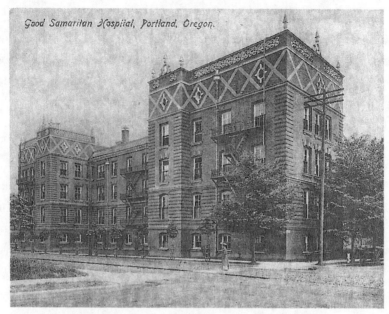

Good Samaritan Hospital, Portland, Oregon.

Doris had her operation at the then-Episcopalian hospital, Good Samaritan. It is still in operation today.

Friday, January 6

It's been nearly three months since I last wrote. And oh! What a lot I've been through. This is it!

Just after I had written my diary [on] Oct. 23 I went to bed. About 12 o'clock I woke up with a terrible pain. I went into Mother's room and fainted. The next day the doctor came but didn't know what was wrong with me. For two weeks I was in perfect agony. Then it dawned on the doctor that I might have appendicitus [sic]. They took me to the hospital and operated. The appendics [sic] had ruptured and for a week they didn't know whether I would live or not. They had five tubes in my side draining out the poison. I stayed a month at the H[ospital]. Then they brought me home. Let me stay two weeks, decided to operate again and took me back. When they got me there they decided to have a consultation with Dr. Rockey. He told them not to re-operate so they didn't. In about a week I went home. Xmas Day was the first day I could get out of bed. Then I had to learn to walk all over again.

When I first got sick the doctors said I ought to go to Southern California [for her health]. So Daddy sold our house and dis-continued his business. Then I didn't get well as I was supposed to. The people who bought the house wanted to move in and the firm Daddy was going to be with in Cal[ifornia] wanted him. So the day before New Year's, Daddy left for Cal[ifornia]. Last Wednesday the ambulance brought me over to [the] Paintons'[102] and here I stay until I get well. Jack, Mother and I have a suite of rooms.

Forgot to say that when I was in the hospital I met a young Intern[103] and he came to see me every day. Sometimes twice a day. The second time I went back, he was even more devoted than the first. It was very interesting and relieved the monotony. He was awfully nice. Black hair, gray eyes and everything. For a while Micky was in danger but he's still on top. Even tho he did only call once or twice while I was sick.

Saturday, January 7
Went downstairs to dinner. Fun!

Sunday, January 8
I dressed today! For the first time since Oct. 23. Ate dinner downstairs and felt like a human being. Raymond Dutton came to see John[104] for a while. He's a little bit cute—but not very. John really isn't a bad sort. Evaline came to see me and brought me some presents. Perfume, etc. Nice!

---

102 They stayed at the house belonging to Englishman Charles A. Painton, who ran a palm and olive oil business in Portland, and his family. They lived in the Irvington neighborhood, on NE 16th Avenue.

103 The intern was Dr. Abel David Scott (not his real name), and the hospital was the then-Episcopal Good Samaritan, where Scott was on staff for several years.

104 The Painton children were John, same age as Doris (17), Elizabeth, 15, and Marjorie, 13.

Monday, January 9

Dressed again. John's cute and he knows a lot of cute boys. I like the girls, to[o].

Tuesday, January 10

This evening I was phoning and the most adorable boy walked in the booth[105]. He didn't know I was there. We shall await further developments. Alyce and Virginia came over this aft[ernoon].

Wednesday, January 11

I'm getting well, feel fine. Went for a ride this afternoon with Marjie—fun.

Thursday, January 12

Alyce came over this afternoon. She's madly in love with Earl. Dumn.

Friday, January 13

Went to the beauty parlor this afternoon and walked back. Gee, but it was fun. We had a good time at dinner this evening. Everyone was so full of pep.

Saturday, January 14

Bob, Chauncey and Fanny came over this afternoon. It was so good to see them all. Fanny brought me a [box] of candy. We played the Victrola and then went for a ride in Bob's nice blue Cadillac. Drove all over. Bob said I looked "sweet enough to kiss!"

This evening I put on my new black velvet dress [from October] and

---

105 The telephone nook in the house

went to the Mathis['s][106] for dinner. I was the guest of honor. Then we came out to [the] Danas' to spend the night.[107] Gee, but I love Marjie.

Sunday, January 15

We all went for a long ride this afternoon. This eve[ning] Ned came down. And is he cute! Oh, boy. His hair is so nice and curly and his eyes are so blue. He's clever, too! Marjie's too damn lucky, that's all I've got to say. Oh, well, he'll be in Los Angeles when I am. I wish Marjie didn't like him so well. My conscience would hurt me if I had any fun with him. Darn it! The cute boys are always claimed. Darn it! I say it again. *Darn it.*

Monday, January 16

Mrs. Dana drove us in this morning. This afternoon. I got my hair reset. This evening we all went to the show. Gee, but it was good.

Tuesday, January 17

Went downtown this afternoon and bought new shoes, hat, dress. We are leaving Portland Friday. Oh! How I hate to think about it. Leave everyone I know, and I do love Portland so. Marjie doesn't like Ned anymore. Isn't that nice?

Wednesday, January 18

This afternoon Alyce came over and I persuaded Mother to let me go up and stay all night with her. Earl was in town and Chauncey came over. We all went for a ride. Earl bought us some ice-cream and we had one H— of a good time. Said goodby to Kitty, Kathleen, [illegible], etc. Gee, but I love Alyce and oh! How I hate to leave Portland. But it will be fun to go to

---

106 Family friends Charles and Mary Mathis; he was a "proprietor of men's clothing" and had a successful store, Mathis Men's Wear, downtown at Fifth and Morrison.
107 The Marshall Dana family lived in Oak Grove, 10 miles from downtown.

Cal[ifornia]. It's like entering a new life. We're leaving everything we know and will start life anew. I'm even leaving Micky and all he means to me.

Thursday, January 19

Went down to see Dr. Harris but he has the Flu so I saw Dr. Kiehle. *Tomorrow* we leave. *Leave* the *only* city I've ever been in and start for the great unknown. Gosh! And tomorrow—I leave Micky. Forget him!

"Tomorrow"

"Although tonight I weep alone
Tomorrow I shall rise
And put on a robe of scarlet silk
And paint my mouth and eyes.
And I shall throw away my woes
For feasting and for wine
And break the hearts of a score of men
Because a man broke mine."[108]

I resolve never to mention his name in this diary again. He shall be gone—dead—forgotten. I shall start this new era of my life without him. Tonight I shall bury my first love. Goodby, my darling. Fate has decreed that I shall not have you.

---

[108] "Tomorrow," by Dorothy Dow, circa 1920s

California
(1928)

Friday, January 20

We are on our way—Oh, Fanny and Marjie came to see us off. Alyce was to come but she was late. I waited as long as I could. Then kissed the girls goodby. We stood on the observation car[109] and just as the train started, Alyce came dashing up. I stood outside until I couldn't see them anymore. Then came inside. It's night now and I'm sitting in my berth writing. Gee, but I'm happy.

Saturday, January 21

We came through the most wonderful scenery today. No wonder they call this heaven. Life is wonderful. We arrive in L.A. tomorrow. I wish the train wasn't so wiggly. I can't write.

Sunday, January 22

Arrived in L.A. this morning. Daddy and Uncle Earnest[110] met us and took us to Daddy's [apartment]. This afternoon we drove around and looked at houses. Just about decided on one. Gee, but this is the *biggest* place I've ever seen. We drove at least 30 mi[les] without getting out of the city limits. The weather is perfect. So balmy and nice. This evening Uncle Bert and Aunty Louise[111] came in and got me and brought me out to Long Beach. Just *two* blocks from the *ocean*. I'm going down to the ocean tomorrow. Lie on the sand and bask in the sun. I'm just going to stay here until the folks decide on a house. Then back to L.A. Happy? Well *I should say*.

---

109 Last car on the train, with a very small platform at the back
110 Earnest Upshaw, Willie Doris's youngest brother, sold real estate in Los Angeles in the late 1920s and into the 1930s. His wife was Marion and daughter was Patricia, age 5 at this time. They lived at 158 South Oxford Ave., in Central L.A., currently Wilshire/Koreatown area.
111 Family friends Bert and Louise Weatherby

**Doris stayed at Long Beach with friends for several
days until her family found a new home.**

Monday, January 23

This morning I awoke to behold—Paradize [*sic*]. The sun was shining like
June. I walked down to the beach. Oh, it's wonderful. I feel as if I'm in
another country. I've never seen so many beautiful mansions. They take
your breath away. Wonderful gardens with swimming pools and beautiful
statuary. A garage big enough for 4 or 5 cars. Palm trees every-where, birds
singing. Oh, it's heaven! I feel like I'm in a dream. There isn't a shack in
the whole city. I haven't even seen a Ford. It's a play ground of the rich.
Marvelous cars with a liveried chauffeur dash by. Cars of every hue: blue,
green, yellow, red, purple, etc.[112] Everything is bright. Even the sky. Who
wouldn't be happy in a city like this? There is no rain, no clouds, no tears.
Nothing but sunshine and blue skies and laughter.

---

112 Henry Ford famously said in 1909, "Any customer can have a car painted any
color that he wants, so long as it is black." Twenty years later, there were still more
black cars than colors.

Tuesday, January 24

This afternoon I walked to the beach again. It was a marvelous day. I sat in the sand and wrote letters. It was so warm and nice. Then I walked down the beach and came upon two boys in bathing suits. They smiled and because I was happy I smiled to them. We talked and they had a blanket on the sand and we sat down. This sounds bad but it isn't. Everyone is so friendly. Besides the cute one used to live in Portland. They had both been sailors and gave me an entirely different version of the Navy. They were really *awfully* nice. You can tell the difference in being cheap and in being just friendly. They asked me to come down tomorrow. I'd like to but I really shouldn't. It wouldn't be techniche [*sic*]. Still, if I haven't anything else to do. I love California.

**Doris was astounded by the beauty of Los Angeles,
and the apparent wealth everywhere.**

Wednesday, January 25

Some girl name[d] Margaret *Something* came to call on me this afternoon. She stayed late. I went down to the beach but he had evidently left. It's just as well. I'm going downtown tomorrow so won't see him until Friday which will be to my credit. Folks came out this evening. They rented a house in Hollywood. I hope it's cute. Wonderful day. I love California. Sleepy—

Thursday, January 26

Another marvelous day. We went downtown this afternoon. Gee, but this is a beautiful little city. Then we went to the "Pike"[113] which is like the Oaks only twice as big. Then we came home, ate dinner, and went for a ride this evening. Met a lot of nice people. Everyone is so friendly and nice.

Friday, January 27

I spent all afternoon on the beach. The ocean was so blue and the sun so bright. And the sand was so warm I nearly went to sleep. I'm beginning to be bored, tho. Everything is beautiful and all that, but I'd like to *do* something. I think when we get settled I'd like to go to school. I won't feel like I'm wasting my time so. I feel so adrift as it is.

Saturday, January 28

I went to return this Margaret Somebody's call today. The shades of the house were all pulled down and I didn't think anyone was home but rang the bell anyway. She answered the door and was clothed in a very decided *neglize* [negligee]. Also her hair was down[114]. I thought she must have been taking a nap until I perceived a man's head over the back of a chair. She introduced him as Jack *Something*. I said I would call later when she didn't have company and she said, "Yes, do." So this is the way the Cal co-eds entertain. I found out later that this man had lots of money and she was trying to get him. She has a queer style. We drove up on Signal Hill[115] this eve. And saw the oil derricks. Thrilling.

---

113 An amusement area near Long Beach with arcades, rides, roller coaster, and a bath house

114 In 1928, a woman who wore her hair loose and flowing (in public or during the day), rather than chopped short or pinned up, hinted at a lack of morals, i.e. a "loose" woman.

115 Signal Hill, in the Los Angeles area, is an oil town; petroleum was discovered there in 1921, and a city of oil derricks and industry grew there. The town of Signal Hill is completely surrounded by the city of Long Beach.

Sunday, January 29

We took a long drive today, 190 miles. Half of the way was along the coast, beautiful. Then we visited an old Spanish mission[116]. One of the oldest in California. A monk conducted us through it. He wasn't bad looking. It was awfully interesting. The folks were here when we got here [Long Beach]. The furniture hasn't come yet so I [will] stay here a while longer.

Monday, January 30

This afternoon I had a haircut and manicure. Also spent a couple of hours on the beach. I love life! Went to a wonderful show this evening.

Tuesday, January 31

This afternoon we went downtown. Did some shopping and went to a show. Mother phoned that the furniture was here so I may go in tomorrow.

Wednesday, February 1

Came home this evening. The house is adorable[117]. My room has running water in it and big closet with full length mirror. There's a cute little terrace off of the dining room and a big back yard. Daddy has a den and there's a big breakfast room, so that's that.

Thursday, February 2

I fixed my room up this morning. This afternoon I went with Daddy to hear a man lecture about Real Estate. On the way home we came by Hollywood High School. I've decided to start Monday. I'm homesick for

---

116 There are 21 historic missions in California, one day apart by mule, founded by Spanish missionaries. Near Los Angeles, there are several, but perhaps she means San Juan Capistrano, famous for its nesting swallows, near the California coast.

117 The house the Baileys rented was at 1926 North St. Andrews Place, now in the Hollywood Grove Historical Preservation Zone. It was near enough to walk to Hollywood High School.

Portland tonight. I don't know why. Everything is so big here and I don't know anyone. I feel so lonesome and left out of everything. Gee, but I'd like to see Fanny and Marjie and Alyce. I love them all so much.

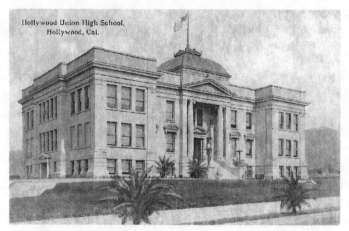

Hollywood Union High School,
Hollywood, Cal.

Doris registered to attend Hollywood High School.

Friday, February 3
Went to school this morning to arrange about my credits. The school is composed of five [buildings], a campus and a million people I didn't know. I felt so small and useless. I start Monday. Got a letter from Alyce. Bless her heart. I love her.

Saturday, February 4
This afternoon I got my hair curled. After I returned home [Uncle] Earnest and [Aunt] Marion came by and we went for a drive. Through Beverly Hills and out to Santa Monica to the ocean. Bought hot dogs and started home. Had a wreck on the way home. Not bad. That's all!

Sunday, February 5
This afternoon Daddy went to the [real estate] tract and while he and Mother were listening to the speech, Jack and I took the car and drove all

over. Gee, but it was fun! I'm going to start school tomorrow although I feel rotten. My side hurts.[118] Damn.

Monday, February 6
Went to school. Gee, but it's an enormous place. I'll bet I walked miles just going from one class to another. I was walking down the hall and who should I see but Buck[119]. It was good to see someone I knew. I didn't even know she'd left Grant [High School]. Went to the doctor's when I got home. He opened me up some more. I like him.

Tuesday, February 7
I was walking down the hall today and who should I see but Victoria Stuart. I hadn't seen her in at least five years. I hardly recognized her. She introduced me to some girls, no boys. Damn. Had dinner at Aunt Marion's. Good.

Wednesday, February 8
School is so damned *big*. I'm going to drop French. It's too much. My side hurt today. Got a letter from Fanny. Made me so damned homesick for good old Portland. I wish I could see it again.

Thursday, February 9
Feel like hell. A cute boy sits across from me third period. Things are beginning to brighten.

---

118 Indicates that the infection has not healed; Doris will have ongoing issues with her appendix wound for years
119 Unclear who Buck is

Friday, February 10
I didn't go to school today. Fixed the house up and took a walk on the Boulevard[120]. Bought a new floor lamp.

Saturday, February 11
Oh, this wonderful weather! It's sublime. We drove all over Beverly Hills and accidentally got into one of the estates. We got out, tho, before anyone saw us. Then we drove to Santa Monica. Went to show this eve.

Sunday, February 12
Uncle Bert and Aunty Louise came out and we went for a ride and then they stayed to dinner. That's all.

Monday, February 13
Had a rather good time at school. Became acquainted with some girls.

Tuesday, February 14
I'm going to get my English class changed to Mr. Booth. He's only 24 and good-looking. *Fun.*

Thursday, February 23 [in purple ink]
I'm so homesick I could cry. Actually I'd give up all most anything I possess if I could go right back to Portland. Dear old Portland, with its cool refreshing rain. And its hills and conventionalities. I love it so. Here I just don't seem to fit in. We had a party after school to get acquainted. I was introduced to a number of girls, but I just can't be natural. I hate to meet new people anyway. If only Marjie or Alyce or Fanny were here. I don't seem to belong. I just seem to have lost my tongue and when I meet

---

[120] Could have been Sunset, Hollywood or Santa Monica Boulevard

anyone I just can't think of a word to say. I feel so hicky. At home I was always so self confident. I had some what of a social position. But here I'm not anybody. Oh, damn! What did we ever come for? I want to go home. Can I stand it? I can't. I get so tired before the day is over. Oh, death, where is thy sting? If I could meet someone like me. But I can't. I'm dumn and no one likes me. Oh! For the joy of being in Oregon. Surrounded by people who know, appreciate and look up to me. Who like me for what I am. *I hate California!* I do! I do! I do!

But I won't let it beat me. I'll conquer somehow. I'll prove my worth. Doggone it, I'll *make* a place for myself. I'll be someone. Starting Monday, I'll *make* myself talk and *make* people realize who I am. Yes, I will. See if I don't.

Friday, February 24

I went to the doctor's and he probed around in me. I've lost two pounds. I don't know why. From here on I make a resolve to stuff myself until I weigh 110. I'm just 100 now. I'm happy tonight. I don't know why.

Saturday, February 25

I got my hair curled this morning. This afternoon Daddy had to go to Arizona on business. I drove him over to Uncle Earnest and Earnest drove him to the [train] station and I drove back alone for the first time in L.A. traffic. It was thrilling and exciting. The traffic is overwhelming. Cars to the right of me, cars to the left of me, etc. This evening Mother, Jack, and I went to a show and I managed all right driving. Fun!

**Traffic was much heavier in Los Angeles than in Portland,
but Doris says she navigated well despite the crowds.**

Tuesday, February 28

My credits came from the "Hall" today and they put me way back. Just mere babies in my classes. It's so damn dumn. At the Hall they didn't do me that way. I may quit. I hate high schools. If I can't go to a private school or have a tutor, I won't go. Damn it! That sounds like a quitter but what else can I do? I don't like to be just anybody. I've got to get through some time. But how? And when? My life is all muddled up. Why did I have to have an apendic [*sic*] anyway? Damn it!

If we were only rich! Then I could have a Roadster and scoot around and I wouldn't mind being inactive. But I can't just sit around the house and twirl my thumbs. I've got to have something definite to do. Daddy let me take the car and go to a show tonight. Nice of him.

Wednesday, February 29

Didn't go to school. Quit! Got two letters from Marjie. I love her so. Went to the Chinese Theater[121] this evening. Most expensive in the U.S. and too beautiful to be true.

Thursday, March 1

Oh, boy! Daddy has to go to Portland on business. He's driving the car as far as Frisco. Going from there on the train. I'm going with him as far as Frisco and stay with the boys [her brothers]. Oh, boy!

Friday, March 2

Got my hair curled. Nice day.

Saturday, March 3

Going tomorrow. Oh, boy.

Sunday, March 4

We drove all day today and reached Oakland by night. The boys have an adorable apartment and it was so good to see them. They gave me my birthday present because I saw it accidentally. It's an adorable fountain pen set for my desk. But this is the big surprise. Daddy decided to let me go on to Portland with him. Isn't that scruptuous [*sic*]?

---

121 Grauman's Chinese Theatre opened on Hollywood Boulevard on May 18, 1927, and has since become famous for the handprints of Hollywood movie stars in the cement forecourt.

Monday, March 5

Daddy and I went over to San Francisco this morning. Marvelous place. Left about noon time and are staying at Redding[122] for the night. I have a cute room furnished in walnut and a private bath. Fun.

Tuesday, March 6

We're spending the night in Albany[123]. Tomorrow we'll drive in to Portland. Hot Ziggity Dog.

Wednesday, March 7

Oh, I'm so happy. It's so nice to be home. It's raining, of course, but I don't mind. Marjie nearly had aploxey [apoplexy] when she saw me. Her mouth dropped open and her eyes popped out. Guess she thought she was seeing thing[s]. She has the lead in the class play. Nice! I phoned Alyce this evening and she nearly fainted. I guess I shouldn't surprise people *quite* so much. I'm glad they appreciate me. Anyway. Staying at Marjie's.

Thursday, March 8

Came in to see Alyce. Went to Grant [High School] and saw all the kids. Gee, it was fun. As I went down the hall, all I could see was gaping mouths. It's fun to have people make a fuss over you. Al[yce] has second lead in the class play. I'm proud of her. She acts awfully well, to[o], and seems quite popular.

I phoned Fanny this evening. She was also surprised. This evening Frank Roberts and Chauncey came up. We went for a ride and visited all of our old haunts. Went up on the hill and peeked in the windows of our old house [on Culpepper]. They have it arranged nicely but not very homey.

---

122 Northern California town about halfway between San Francisco and Oregon border

123 Albany, Oregon

Pat jumped all over me[124]. She's grown inches. I hope that I can take her back with me. I love Portland. And I'm so darned happy. Forgot to say I saw Ned yesterday. He looked cute.

Friday, March 9
Left Alyce's about 10 o'clock. Came downtown, got a marcel, stockings, brassiere. Then came out to Marjie's. Went to an oratorical contest up at school. Met Marjie's Oscar. Dumn. After it was all over, we all washed dishes. It was fun. And I became well acquainted with Oscar. Fritze was there but I ignored him.

Saturday, March 10
Marjie and I stayed home all day and baked a cake. It was fun. I love Marjie. Daddy came out this evening and Marjie, Daddy and I went to a show. I drove.

Sunday, March 11 [Doris's birthday]

Today I am 18. Just think. I feel so funny. Daddy let Marjie and me take the car and we went for a drive. Also this afternoon, Dad and I were in town and went by Alyce's and saw Patsy. Bless her heart.

Monday, March 12
I love Marjie. Ned's gone to California. I'm happy. I'm alive. I'm not in the hospital. I'm in Portland.

Tuesday, March 13
Came into town and got a marcel. New underwear, lipstick, flower for my coat, hat, and music for Alyce. Was supposed to go to the doctor's but I

---

124 Doris left Patsy with Alyce.

lost my nerve. Going tomorrow. Went to a show with Marjie and came out to Alyce's. I love her. I love Patsy. I love Portland. I love the whole damn world, so there! This evening Alyce and I went for a walk. Bought some Coors[125] and ice-cream. Flirted with a garage boy and acted generally silly. I'm in love—with life!

Wednesday, March 14

Went to the doctor's. Bah—he nearly killed me. The brute! But my blood is a lot better. And I've gained. Honest. Daddy came over about 6 [p.m.] and gave me some money. He wants to start home. But *I don't*. No siree. Bob came over for a while this evening. He's awfully dumn. I was loved to death. After he left, Alyce and I walked five blocks to the drug-store in the cold. Got a Coca-Cola and walked five blocks home. We nearly froze. But I don't care. I'm alive [and] happy. I'm going to Fanny's tomorrow and I may—[if] I have the courage—drop by and see Dr. Scott. Hot Ziggity. My heart beats about 50[126] when I even *think* of him.

Thursday, March 15

I *did* have the courage and I went. And I *won't* be in love. I won't. ~~That's all.~~ This is how it happened.

When I got to 23rd I mustered up my courage and went into the hospital. I went up to the 5th floor and asked a nurse where I could find him. She said in Ward 24. So I went down. I peeked in the door and saw the back of his head. I went to the end of the hall and I waited for him. That was one hectic 10 minutes. I powdered my nose, combed my hair, refreshed my lips and did all over again. All the time my knees were shaking and my heart was thumping. Then I saw him coming towards

---

125 When Doris got a Coors, she bought malted milk. The Coors Brewing Company survived Prohibition by converting the brewery into a malted milk and near-beer production facility. Coors also sold a lot of the malted milk to the Mars candy company.

126 "Doin' 50" was an expression of speed, as in 50 miles per hour.

me. Oh, my heart. I walked up to him and he didn't recognize me for a minute. But when he did! His eyes lighted up and he held out his hand and it's a wonder I didn't have St. Vitus Dance.[127] Anyway, we talked and he said I was looking *marvelous* and *oh!* His smile. I had on Bob Freitag's Frat[ernity] pin and he said something about it and I said "Not so bad, considering what it represents," and he said "Are you serious?" And I said, "Well! I'm eighteen," and he said, "You're not thinking of getting *married*, are you?" And I said "You never can tell." And he said "Well, *you'd better* not," and looked straight into my eyes and added, "I finish interning in July." He said, "I'll see you tomorrow." And I said I was all dated up and I was, damn it. Oh—

I don't *want* to be in love and I won't. I'll never see him again and besides, he's too old, twenty-eight, but adorable. *Gosh*, what's the matter with me? Even Micky never made me feel this way. I feel as if—oh, well.

Friday, March 16
Stayed at Fanny's last night and came downtown this afternoon. Went to luncheon and The Broadway. Good show. Good lunch. Lots of fun. Saw Dr. Laccel and bought some stuff. Saw a lot of Hall girls downtown. Had dinner at Alyce's and Daddy took us to the Portland.[128] It's a beautiful theater. Peg's giving a party for me tomorrow night.

Saturday, March 17
Went downtown early this morning. Visited doctor's offices. Met Marjie and we went out to the Flying Field[129] and were going to go up in an areoplane [*sic*] but it was to[o] windy. Peg couldn't have the party at her

---

127 Sydenham's chorea ("Saint Vitus Dance") is a disease causing rapid, spastic movements of the face, feet and hands.
128 The Portland Theatre is located at 1111 SW Broadway in Portland, still extant today as the Arlene Schnitzer Concert Hall, Portland Center for Performing Arts.
129 The flying field was a landing strip in former farmland outside Portland that had just been recognized by the U.S. Dept. of Commerce in 1927 as the Stroudwater Flying Field. It grew and was renamed the Portland Airport in the 1930s.

house so we went to Evaline's. Had a blind date with an adorable boy in a taxi. I love taxies. The party was inclined to be wild but I had a good time. Chuck had some gin which was atrocious to taste but heavenly when it was down. Chuck was terribly attentive and kissed divinely. I'd sworn off cheap petting. But this wasn't cheap. Just nice. I met Bob Heitkemper, Evaline's latest. He's fat. Chuck was thrilling on the way home. It may have been partly due to the gin. But he was nice. And oh, that goodby kiss. It's been so long since I've been on a good party like that. They all teased me about Cal[ifornia] and tried to persuade me not to go back. Dumn.

Sunday, March 18
Left Alyce's this morning. Had dinner at the Parkers'. Gene sure's cute and we went for a drive. He's sophisticated and just back from Chicago. Came out to Marjie's. Made pop-corn and candy. Read. Tired. Forgot to say we saw Harold North downtown yesterday. He's gotten rather cute.

Monday, March 19
I had the car this morning and Fanny and I went for a ride. Out to the Flying Field and around. Had a good time. Then we bummed around her house for a while and I came downtown about 11. Saw Dr. Laccel who is perfectly sweet. I like him. He was so friendly and nice and kept calling me Doris. He gave me Dr. Harrison's address and told me all about him. He's gone back to Pennsylvania to take care of his old dad. Isn't that nice of him? Then I bought some stuff and had lunch and went to a show and came out to Marjie's. We made fudge this eve. Beautiful day. I hate to go home.

Tuesday, March 20
Marjie and I went downtown and saw *The Student Prince*. It was awfully good. Afterward we had three Coca-Colas and felt like hell. This evening Marjie went to rehearsal and I went with her. Talked to Fritze quite a while. He's dumn. We leave tomorrow. Damn!

Wednesday, March 21

Left early this morning. Gee, but it took all my will power to make myself leave. Spending the night at an adorable hotel. Patsy is with us.

Thursday, March 22

Arrived in Oakland this evening. It was good to see the boys. I think that we will take Joe back to L.A. with us.

Friday, March 23

Went to S.F. this morning. It was fun going over on the Ferry. Bought Mother some things and started for L.A. We're staying at Paso Robles, an exotic-looking town, and sophisticated men. Oh, boy! Is it fun—and how!

Saturday, March 24

Arrived in Hollywood this afternoon. It's good to be home and everybody's happy. The light went out and I'm working by candle light. Headache? Gee, but I'm glad I'm alive. Got a letter from Miss Butler. Nice.

Sunday, March 25

Mother and Daddy have gone to Phoenix, Arizona, for a week, and left me in charge of the house. I have to order the meals and cook and everything. Gosh! And on only eighteen dollars[130].

Monday, March 26

Life is fun. I'm alive. Bought groceries today. Fun. Made dinner. Fun. I'm happy.

---

[130] The value of 1928's $18 has risen to $238 in 2012.

Thursday, March 29

Too lazy to write. Sleepy. Wrote a letter to Dr. Scott. Hope he answers. Side hurts.

Friday, March 30

Dumn, dull day. Went to a show this evening.

Saturday, March 31

Folks came home this afternoon. Cooked a big dinner for them. I don't know what's the matter with me. I never feel like writing anymore. Spring Fever, I guess.

Sunday, April 1

April Fool's Day. I just looked back to see what I did last April 1. Had one hell of a good time. Guess what! We're going to *Arizona* to live, in maybe a week[131]. Gee, but this family is temperamental. A year ago, Ariz[ona] or even Cal[ifornia] was as far out of our minds as Europe. But it's pretty definite. We'll go in a week or two and I'll have a *horse!*

Monday, April 2

Went downtown today. Bummed around in all the stores. Ate lunch and went to the "Metropolitan." It's a beautiful theater.[132] Also a good show.

---

131 Another Upshaw brother, Woodson, and his wife Florence, had just moved to Phoenix from Tucson, where he was the editor of the *Tucson Daily Independent*. He took a job as the editor of the *Arizona State News*, but soon after, formed a real estate company with Luther Bailey. In 1929, he's listed as the vice president of the Bailey & Upshaw Realty and Trust Co.

132 The Metropolitan, at 323 West 6th Street, Los Angeles, was one of three theatres designed for Grauman by architect William Lee Wollett. It opened January 26, 1923, for vaudeville acts and film.

William Hanes [*sic*] in "The Spart Set [*sic*]"[133] He's cute and clever. I like him. Then I went to the doctor's and he injected some bismuth[134] in my side. Then I came home. And that's all.

Tuesday, April 3
Bummed around house.

Thursday, April 5
Just another day wasted away. Doggone it, I've got to do something. If I would only get well. Damn! We're leaving for Arizona Monday. Oh, well, if Daddy will buy me a horse or a car as he has promised, conditions might be more faborable [favorable]. Hell! Mother gave a dinner party tonight. Left lots of dishes.

I wish Marjie or Alyce would write. But mostly Dr. Scott. Gee, but I'd feel cheap if he didn't answer my letter. And I do like him so well. He's so kind and sweet and nice and sensible. Of course, he isn't the least bit romantic but for some reason I keep thinking about him. Which is very silly because he's 28 years old and really doesn't look like a Romeo. In fact, he lacks a lot of being my ideal but he has charm and damn it! I wish he'd write. Altho I really don't care if he doesn't. He'd probably write awfully dumn letters. No, he wouldn't. They'd be nice, just like him. He has such a nice smile, but— Damn! What's wrong with me? I don't like him and I don't care if I never hear from him again. He's nothing in my young life. Just a hard-working intern born in *Tacoma*! Hicky and country-fied. Used to milk cows. Why, the man of my dreams is going to be born in Boston or some-place and be care-free and handsome and rich. Why should I waste two pages on a man that wears glasses, takes himself so seriously and is poor?!

---

133 William Haines, in 1928 MGM silent film, *The Smart Set*
134 Bismuth was used to treat infections before antibiotics. Its properties are similar to aspirin; Pepto Bismol is used for ulcers and stomach ailments today.

Friday, April 6

[in pencil] Lost my fountain pen. Sorry. Went to doctor's. Don't like him anymore. He's mercenary. Also went to a show.

Saturday, April 7

[in pencil] Got letter from Marjie. Hate to write without a pen.

Sunday, April 8—Easter

Went to church, came home and packed all day. Leave tomorrow for Ariz. Happy? Well I'll say—

Arizona
(1928)

Monday, April 9
Left today for Phoenix. Staying at a hick town tonight. Full of Mexicans.

Tuesday, April 10
Arrived in the Metropolis of Phoenix. I haven't quite gotten my equilibrium yet. It's a little town surrounded by sage-brush and cactus and miles and miles of desert. We looked at houses and may get one out of town. So that I can have a horse. Most of the houses are awful-looking dumps but we may find a nice one. Let's hope for the best. We went to a nice eating place this evening. Dance orchestra n' everything. Joe and I danced. First time I've danced for just ages. Staying at a hotel until we find a house and this town is *hot*. I mean warm. Not unsophisticated [*sic*]. I nearly died with the heat and it's only April. The worst is yet to come.

A new house built in the Arizona sunshine, just like the ones Luther planned to build and sell. This one is Uncle Wood Upshaw's house in Tucson before he moved to Phoenix to go into business with Luther in 1928.

Wednesday, April 11
We found a house today[135]. It's not in the country. The country houses were impossible. This is rather nice, tho. Big two story with lots of ground. I

---

135 The 1930 census puts the Bailey family at 1516 E. Almeria Road, Phoenix, a two-story house that's currently in the Coronado Park neighborhood, but was definitely on the edge of town in 1928. A 1928 map shows open fields and corrals to the north and east.

can either keep a horse in a pasture about 2 blks away or else join a Riding Academy and rent a horse. I haven't decided yet. We'll move tomorrow.

Thursday, April 12
We moved in today. Lot'sa work and no pay.

Friday, April 13
Worked some more. The house really looks awfully nice.

Saturday, April 14
Oh—! Oh! oh! oh! I got a letter from Dr. Scott. *Ten* delicious pages in his very own hand writing. And *such* a letter. He gave me a regular sermon about life and said that I was a girl to be admired and would make a wonderful wife for some nice man who would make me happy. And that he knew I was inclined to be wild, and if I couldn't be good, to be careful. And that he was busy and he was becoming serious about life. He sounded rather morbid. He needs someone to pep him up. Oh, yes! He told me to be skeptical of men—that I wouldn't regret it. Oh, I'm *crazy* about him. I've never received a letter like that. It's simply divine. I read it and re-read it and got more out of it every time. Oh, he's *wonderful*. What I mean—he has so much sense and he's so characterful [*sic*] and—well—*nice!* I wonder if he likes me. He must—just a little, or he wouldn't be so concerned about me. But I *won't* fall in love. I just *won't* have my heart broken again. *Damned* if I will.

Sunday, April 15
Went out to look at a horse today. Found a pretty three-year old colt for $25[136]. I'll go out next Friday and try her out. The only trouble is I don't know where I'll keep her when I do buy her. But I'll find a way.

---

[136] The $25 horse would cost $331 in 2012.

Monday, April 16

Started a letter to Dr. Scott. Hot day, and everyone says the worst is yet to come.

Tuesday, April 17

Finished his letter and sent it this evening. Now I wish I hadn't. I should have waited at least a week longer and not written the kind I did. I'm afraid I was rather sarcastic. I *know* he won't answer. I just have a feeling that he won't. I don't dare. Yes, I do. Oh, damn.

Wednesday, April 18

Wish I had some decent clothes and I wish I didn't think about Abel David Scott, MD, so much. It really isn't good for me. I went to the Drug Store this evening. A good-looking boy was there. We gave each other the once over. After I left, he did, too. Jumped in a cute blue Roadster and passed me, then he went around the block and passed again. He kept doing this and was just ready to stop when I reached our house. The folks were sitting on the front porch so I had to come right in. Worse luck. But it was fun anyway.

Midnight—I went to bed but can't sleep, so I got up. I can't get my mind off of Dr. Scott. I keep reviewing the days in the hospital when I first met him. Oh! He was wonderful. Every day I'd look for him and he'd come in and smile his wonderful smile and hold my hand. When I couldn't go home Thanksgiving, he was so sweet. And when I came back the second time he was so nice. I never could have lived through those 3-4 weeks if it hadn't been for him. Oh! He's darling. And I'll have to go to bed because it's cold sitting by the window. Gee, but I wish I could forget him.

Thursday, April 19

Went downtown and bought a dress, shoes, stockings. Goofy about my dress. It's green and makes my hair look blonder. Shoes are beige-colored kid[137]. Sent a telegram to Alyce tonight. She's in her play tomorrow. Happy! Marjie's coming over this summer. Hot Dog!

Friday, April 20

I cooked the dinner this evening. All by myself. Grilled veal chops and green peas and mashed potatoes and fruit salad and lemon pie 'neverything. I feel so virtuous. While I was cooking it I pretended that I was getting dinner for my husband and me in a little house. Gee! it was fun. And strangely enough, his face took the frame of Dr. Scott. Tho, of course, that just happened, but it was nice. I'm afraid I'm falling in love and I don't wanna.

Saturday, April 21

Felt like the devil all day today. Uncle Wood and Aunt Florence here for dinner. I wish I would get entirely well. Darn it! It's so discouraging.

Auntie Florence and Uncle Wood at their Tucson house, circa 1924; the 1928 directory shows them living in Phoenix. Wood left his job as a newspaper editor to go into real estate ventures with Luther.

Sunday, April 22

Church this morning and horse-looking this evening. I tried out everything from a scrub to a thoroughbred.

---

137 Soft, fine leather

Monday, April 23

I bought a horse today. He's a dark roan—five years old—full of pep and is gaited. He can single-step, canter, lope, etc. Cost $35 and his name is Mackay. I don't know whether to keep it or not [the name]. Sounds too much like a certain person's name that I'm forgetting. Or trying to. I'll keep him at a stable about 12 blocks away. They'll feed him and curry[138] him and deliver him for me for $10.50 a month[139]. I don't want him delivered too much, though. I like the atmosphere around the corral. It's so horsey. There's one funny old Mexican cowboy who's a real Paul Bunyan character. Then there's a young one—that's nice.

Tuesday, April 24

Went for a ride this afternoon. I like my horse, although he's inclined to be stubborn. Rears up on his hind legs when things don't suit him. George—the young boy—rode him for about 10 minutes and afterwards he was as meek as could be. Also took a ride in the evening. Gee, but it was nice. I love desert evenings. They're sublimely beautiful and then I rode back under the stars. Oh, it's heavenly.

Wednesday, April 25

Went to doctor's. I like my new eye doctor. He's cute and not slow. Saw Harold Lloyd in "Speedy." This evening Jack and I went to the Drug Store. And that cute boy—that tried to pick me up—was there. And I had to have Jack[140] tagging along. Damn. Such is life.

---

138 Brush and clean

139 The horse would cost $463 to purchase in 2012, and cost $139 per month to keep him.

140 Jack is now 8 years old.

Thursday, April 26

Gee, but it was hot today. I rode this evening. Too hot to ride in the day time. I wish I had someone to ride with me. It would be lots more fun. Got a letter from Marjie today. If she were only here. I wish I knew somebody. I haven't been kissed for so long.

Doris (white shirt) and Marjie on horses in Arizona, 1928. That may be Mac that Doris is riding.

Friday, April 27

Got up at 5:30 [a.m.] and rode until 8:30. I drove the car down and caught my horse and saddled him. Gee, but it was nice today. I mean this morning. It was hot as hell this afternoon. I went to see Dr. Swartze,[141] my eye-doctor. Lottsa fun.

---

[141] Dr. William Schwartz had offices at 14 N. Central Avenue.

Saturday, April 28

Rode again early this morning. I didn't feel so much in a riding mood so after I had ridden an hour, I took the car and drove over into the desert. Sage brush and cactus n'everything. I'm homesick for Oregon today. This town is so damned hot and I don't know anyone. I wish some of the old bunch were down here. Boy! We'd show this [burg] how to have a good time. We'd paint the old town red. Damn it, if Marjie or Alyce or Fanny were here. Or Bob or Chauncey or some of the H[ill] boys. Someone that talked the same language that I do. I've got to have an out-let pretty darn quick or else I'll go goofy! Damned if I won't. And how.

Roosevelt Dam

Sunday, April 29

We went to Roosevelt Dam[142] today. It's simply wonderful. I've never seen such superb scenery in all my life. Simply undescribeable [*sic*]. We also went swimming and I got a terrible case of sun-burn. Oh! Does it hurt! Also fished and Joe caught a big bass, 5 lbs. There was a rather nice man along, 25 years old. Lived in Tucson. Blond and laughed like Jack Pillar. We got along fine.

---

142 The dam was completed in 1911. The Baileys probably took the Apache Trail east of Mesa to the dam and swam in Roosevelt Lake.

Monday, April 30

Gee, but I'm sore! Couldn't ride today. I can hardly walk. But it's a great life. Got a card from Marjie. It had a picture of a person sitting in a tent on a rail road track and said, "Some-how my world is up-side down, Since you packed up and left this town. I think I'll camp on the rail road track and greet you first when you come back." Nice.

Tuesday, May 1

Joe and I saw the "King of Kings" tonight. It's the story of Jesus. I won't attempt to describe it. I can't. But I'll say this. No radical or Atheist could see that picture and still remain skeptical. It's wonderful. It makes you feel as if you lived then. It makes you see things in a different light. People get in the habit of thinking of Jesus as a myth. And this picture made him so real, so human, it makes you feel as if there is a reason for living and a purpose for dyeng [sic].

Wednesday, May 2

Went downtown and saw my doctors. Looked at hats.

Thursday, May 3

Bought a hat and went to see Dr. Swartze. Then I went out to ride. Mackay hadn't been ridden since Saturday. He was soft. Reared up and even bucked. Had an awful time with him. He nearly threw me a couple of times. I let the boy ride him and [Mac] did throw him. He's going to take him out for me every day and ride him till he's hard[143].

Met an interesting old Englishman (friend of Dad's). He's a Baron and everything. Been in a lot of wars. He said there's only two times when he's perfectly happy. When he's on horse-back and when he's yachting. Isn't that thrilling? He's going to ride with me some time.

---

[143] Broken in

Friday, May 4
Tried to ride Mac again tonight. He's wilder n'ever. Regular little Bronco, had a terrible time with him. Mr. Kaigler[144] wouldn't let me ride him. Said he was dangerous. He's going to take him on a trip tomorrow and try and break him. It's a great life! Dad rode him some but even he could hardly hold him.

Saturday, May 5
Went to a Bridge-party today. Terribly dumn. The girls, I mean. Their [*sic*] so small-townish and goody-goodish. Got a long letter from Alyce and also Fanny. Gee, but I wish I was in Portland. It's *so damned* hot here and I'm so homesick. I wish Marjie were here. I wish I'd get a letter from Dr. Scott and I wish something exciting would happen. *Damn,* it's a Hell of a life.

Sunday, May 6
Rode Mac this morning. I used spurs on him and he behaved wonderfully. Hellishly hot day. I mooved [*sic*] my bed downstairs. It's a little bit cooler, but not much.

Monday, May 7
Rode this morning. Got my hair curled this after-noon. Was going to ride some more this evening, but the family intervened. Said I had to wash the dishes before I went and after the dishes were done it was too late. I don't know what's the matter lately. I can't get along with the family at all. They object to everything I do and say. I'm almost afraid to speak for fear they'll jump on me and say I was disrespectful. I can't even be natural. The minute they see me, they find fault with something. It's discouraging.

---

144 Otto Kaigler was a 54-year-old trader in horses and cows. He hailed from Texas and lived about 12 blocks from Doris's house. Stable may have been at his house on North Eighth

They've become so antagonistic. I guess they're tired of me. Got a long letter from Marjie. Gee! I love her.

Tuesday, May 8
Rode this morning. Also this evening. Gee, but it's a wonderful life! And how. I love to ride in the evening. I feel so peaceful and serene. The stable-boy brought me home in his car. He's rather cute and it was fun, and then some! Gee! I'm glad I'm alive.

Wednesday, May 9
Rode this morning. It was a marvelous day! Not too hot. Regular Oregon weather. Went to the doctor's this afternoon. He darned near killed me. Felt too hellish to ride this evening, although I wanted to. I'd like to take a long trip tomorrow if it would be cool and if my side felt all right and if I had some-one to ride with. *IF.*

Thursday, May 10
Rode about 20 miles today. "Over the hills and far away"[145] beyond Camel Back[146] into the desert. I'm tired—and how!

---

[145] Traditional English/Scottish song

[146] A mountain near Phoenix which resembles the head and hump of a kneeling camel; popular for hiking and recreation

Camelback Mountain

Friday, May 11

I went down to take my usual morning ride this morning about 6:30. When I got there, Mr. Kaigler and Irvin were going on a long ride to get some Broncos that they were going to ship to Prescott for the rodeo. They asked me to go along. At the last minute we discovered that Mac was lame. We had to take his shoe off and cut into his foot. Found a big nail in it. It bled terribly and of course I was unable to ride him. But I rode Palomar. It was thrilling. Catching the horses and separating them. Gee, but they were wild. Irvin the stable-boy is so nice and interesting. We had fun. He's going to the mountains Tuesday to ride wild horses. Damn! Also—they have a new Dapple grey. Big and aristocratic. They asked me to name him and I named him Micky. I shouldn't have—but I couldn't help it. Gee! I'm tired. And sunburned.

Saturday, May 12

Gee, but I was stiff and sore today. I went down this evening to see Mac. He's much better and I may ride him tomorrow. We brushed him up and he looks fine. There were a bunch of cute boys down there and I had a good time. There's another horse they want me to name. I'd like to name it David.

Sunday, May 13

Rode this morning. Also this evening. Irvin was there this evening. I was cold to him. I don't know why. Dad says I can't go riding tomorrow but I am.

Monday, May 14

When I got to the corral this morning there was a whole gang there, including a new cowboy, 24, named Richard[147]. He started out of the corral on a big sorrel horse just as I started out on Mac. Mac took it into his head to be temperamental and rear up. He nearly fell backwards a couple of times and Richard said, "Let me try him." So I got off and started to get on his. I had just put my foot in the stirrup when she began to buck. Up and down. Everything was whirling around and I kept saying to myself, "I won't fall, I won't." But I did! She threw me about ten feet and I landed on my head. Crash! Bamn! [sic] And everything was black.

Then through the haze I heard voices. "Is she killed? Get some water." "My God! Bring her over in the shade!" A pair of strong arms lifted me up and carried me to the car. Then things began to clear up and I realized I was sitting on Richie's lap and there were [sic] a crowd of cowboys around. When he saw I was awake he put me down and everyone began talking at once. I finally discovered that that horse had just been broken. He didn't know I was going to get on her or he wouldn't have let me. He's a Bronco Buster. Can ride anything and has won some prizes at the rodeo. He was so sorry and kept asking me if I felt any better and gee! He was nice.

Then he said, "Let me show you some Bronco ridin' to cheer you up." We went around in another corral where he had two 2-year-old colts. He put the one in a stall—like this.

---

147 Doris calls him Ric in *Love and Labor*.

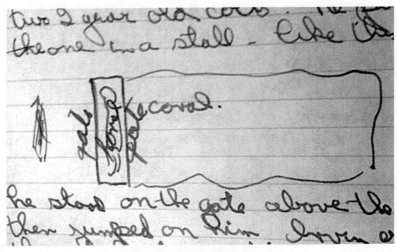

Doris's sketch of the corral.

He stood on the gate above the horse, then jumped on him. Irvin opened the gate leading into the corral and away he went. I've never seen a colt buck like that little Bronco could. Afterward I came home. My side is bruised all to pieces, my wrist is strained and I had a raging, splitting headache. Oh, it's a great life.

Tuesday, May 15

Rode this morning. Richie was down there. Pitty pat skid skid. He *is* so nice. Also rode this evening and had a good time. The boy from next door came over to ask us over to play Bridge. I was getting ready for bed. Just my luck! Mother answered the door. Joe wasn't here. He said he'd come again.

Wednesday, May 16

Rode this morning. Both Richie and Irvin were there. Fun! Got a new pair of spurs this afternoon. Mr. Jack came in the office[148] while I was there this afternoon. He's nice.

---

148 Luther Bailey had an office at 134 W. Adams Street, in the Title and Trust Building; Doris often helped her father or visited him at work, the Bailey & Upshaw Realty and Trust Company.

Thursday, May 17

Richie was there when I got down this morning and we went riding together and talk about fun! He has a smile like Micky's. His eyes crinkle up when he laughs and smiles. 26 years old [not 24]. He held the world champ[ionship] for three years. He's a marvelous rider and has a di[a]mond studded metal [sic].

I also rode this evening and did another Prince of Wales[149] act. I was riding peacefully along, thinking of Oregon, when all of a sudden Mac shot ahead. It took me by surprise and I landed on the ground. On my head, as per usual.

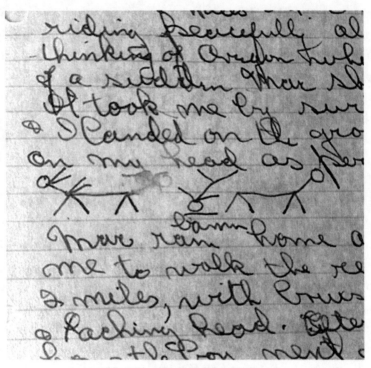

Doris's self-portrait in action.

Bamn! [sic] Mac ran home and left me to walk the remaining two miles, with bruised side and aching head. After I got home, the boy next door came over again. And I was going to bed. *Of course.*

---

149 Fell off her horse

Friday, May 18

Didn't ride this morning although I went to the corral. My wrist was too sore. Went downtown. Mr. Jack came in the office. He's dumn! [*sic*] But—as I was driving down Central I had to stop at a traffic signal. I heard a honk beside me and there was Richie, all dressed up. He asked me how I felt and I said rotten and showed him my wrist. I told him I got thrown yesterday and he said, "Shame on you." And then the traffic lights changed and I had to go. He—is—cute—

Saturday, May 19

Mac was mean today. Disgustingly so. I *do* wish he would behave. Richie wasn't there. What's the matter with the sap? I had the car for a while and a dumn boy in a red Ford Roadster followed me. Nut! This is the deadest, damnest [*sic*] town. I'm thoroughly disgusted with it. Dum [*sic*] people. Blah! I want some excitement. I'll go goofy if something doesn't happen. I wish Marjie were here.

Sunday, May 20

Went down this morning to ride—as usual. Irvin and a girl about 20 and a man were just going out. They asked me to go along. The girl is nice and we had a good time. Went down to the river[150]. She told me a lot of things about the boys at the stable—one of which is that Richie is married. Damn! Just my luck. He didn't act it, tho, the other day when he picked me up. We swam (or rather, our horses did) in the river. Mac is a regular water dog. Lots of fun and I got *wet*. It's beautiful down by the river. So cool. She (Claradell) got caught in some quick-sand. Exciting! This afternoon we all went to the horse-races[151]. Gee, but it was thrilling—and hot. She is nice and we're going to ride together lots.

---

[150] The Salt River is about two miles south of Doris's house and the stables.

[151] Probably at the state fairgrounds, which were located by the railroad tracks where the Veteran's Memorial Coliseum is now; west of the stables

Monday, May 21

Mac was mean this morning. Didn't do much of anything all day. This evening I went over and played Bridge with two boys and a lady next door. The boy, Chuck Galliger [*sic*], is blond and cute. We really had an awfully good time. They were a jolly bunch.

Tuesday, May 22

Last night there was an ad in the paper that read like this: *"Attention Boys-Girls. Collegiate types wanted Betw. Ages 18-21 to work in pictures. Apply Mr. [Whorler?], Universal Picture Co. Jefferson Hotel, 9 a.m."*

I didn't have anything else to do so I ans[wered] it. I hadn't meant to do anything rash, but he looked me over. Said, "You'll do," and hired me. I'm to be at the stadium tomorrow at 8. They're going to shoot some grandstand scenes to go in the picture, "Trooping Co-eds." I get $3 a day. I hardly know what to think.[152]

The Jefferson Hotel

---

[152] The movie is not listed in IMDB (Internet Movie Database).

Wednesday, May 23

Didn't take the role. Various reasons. Wish now that I had. Baked a cake today. Not bad. Have been reading Dr. Scott's letter over. I can't understand why he hasn't answered my last letter. His other one was so encouraging. He even asked me to write again. It isn't like him to just be impolite. There must be a reason. I wonder if he's sick or anything. I'm almost tempted to write again if I could be sure he wasn't just not answering because he was bored. Have decided to write a book about Arizona. I'm serious and I've got to do something. I'm so bored.

Thursday, May 24

Bummed around the house today. Hot as hell. Went riding with Claradell this evening. Had a keen time. We went over to the race track and raced our horses. Mac can run like the wind and doesn't heave at all. He's the fastest runner of the two. Gee, but I was proud of him. I like her [Claradell]. She's a good sport.

Friday, May 25

Went downtown and bummed around. Bought a new compact. Got letter from Marjie. I love her so. Also went out to the corral to see about my bill. Irvin was there and, oh boy! Took Mother to the train this eve. She's going to Georgia. Grandfather's sick.[153] A girl fainted at the station. Exciting!

Saturday, May 26

Went to the office today to help Daddy. Fun. Miss M. came over this evening. Played Bridge. Fun!

---

153 Doris's grandfather, William James Dallas Upshaw, a Baptist minister, died June 9, 1928.

Sunday, May 27

Well! Well! Well! I rode with Irvin this morning. Went to the race track and had one heck of a good time. This afternoon he and I went to Mexican Town[154] to watch the horse races. One of the men said, "Why don't you enter your horse?" They all took up the chorus and asked me to run him. But Irvin talked against it and wouldn't let me. Later I was sitting on the engine of a car talking to one of the men and I looked up and who should I see but Richie. He came over and I told him about Mac and he said, "Why don't you run him?" and I said I didn't have the cash and Irvin wouldn't let me and he said *he'd* bet on him and run him for me.

So we matched him against a beautiful black horse—Oh! The thrill when he started down the track. He won by about two lengths and Richie won $2[155]. I was so happy I could have cried. They all swarmed around Mac and wanted to race with him but Richie said, "No." He said, "I'd never be able to hold him." Then we talked for ages and someone said "Is that your horse?" He said, "No, he belongs to this girl, but this is my girl."

He wanted to give me half the winnings, but I wouldn't take it. So we got in a Black Jack game. Squatted down on the ground with a bunch of Mexicans and played for cash. He kept his arm around me all the time and—oh—we lost the two dollars but even that was fun.

When I got on Mac to go home, he ran wild and ran for one mile before I could stop him. I had to let Irvin ride him home. Also Richie said if he could, he'd go riding with me Tuesday night. I hope he can. He's wonderful and acted so conspicuously attentive. The only trouble is—he's married.

Monday, May 28

Worked in the office today. A lot of cute men came in. This evening Claradell phoned. "Congratulations on your race horse," she said. I asked her how she found out and she said she went to the stable last night and they told her. She asked me what I was doing tomorrow night and I told her

---

154 South central, east Phoenix toward the Salt River, across the railway tracks

155 The $2 bet is worth $26 in today's money.

I was riding and like a fool I asked her to go along. Damn it! He'll think I think I need protection. Of course, he *may* not be there.

Tuesday, May 29

So much has happened, I hardly know where to begin? Joe and Claradell went with us. We went to the Fair Grounds and monkeyed around. Raced our horses and boy! How Mac can run. Anyway, it was a simple matter for Richie and me to lose the others. Then we talked! Impersonally at first and gradually the talk became more daring. We were talking about my being thrown off that day. He said how scared he was and how well he liked being the one to pick me up. He said, "Didn't you notice how nicely I held you? I would have kissed you if there hadn't been such a crowd around!"

That was the beginning. Later we got off to change horses. It was just growing dusk and everything was so beautiful. Somehow or other I was in his arms and oh! The sublime exstasy [*sic*] of that kiss. Then we rode some more. So many times after a kiss, I feel embarrassed and am actually tongue tied. But tonight I was witty. I can't figure it out myself. But I had something clever to come back with at everything he said. Then the others caught up with us and we decided to go down Canyon Road. Richie and I loped our horses and it was so thrilling. The wind in my face and the wonderful sensation of galloping down a moonlit road beneath the stars. About 9 o'clock we started back. He was more romantic than ever but my conscience hurt me. After all, he *did* have a wife. So by careful maneuvering I got on the subject of her. At first he didn't want to talk about her. But for some reason my mood had changed from reckless daring into a slight contempt for him.

For a married man really shouldn't say the things he said to an unmarried girl. And I told him so. I told him that when I married, I was going to be true to my husband. That marriage was sacred and should not be desecrated. He said that there were a lot of things that went on in married life that outsiders couldn't understand. But still I blamed him.

I said he could have made a go of it if he'd been made of the right stuff. And then he told me, he said:

"My wife is a beautiful girl. She is tall and slim and dark. But *terribly* spoilt and used to having her own way. She was sick when I married her but *she* was the one that wanted to get married. She was willing, she said, to start from the bottom with me. I bought a house in the mountains and we started a cattle ranch. She planted roses around the house and everything was fine. In two weeks she moved to Prescott. She couldn't stand the isolation. I lived with her in Prescott. Got up at daybreak every morning, fixed her breakfast and went to the ranch. I worked all day. Came home at night. Made dinner and washed the dishes. I waited on her hand and foot. I had ambitions that some day we would be rich. But she couldn't stick it out. She wasn't willing to work with me. She wanted a mansion to start with. I finally had to sell the ranch and we came here. I may make a million eventually—but I doubt it. If we had stuck with those cattle I would be rich now.

"She is a little better than she was but is still spoilt. She isn't willing to undergow [*sic*] hard ships and tho I still love her, it isn't anything compared to the way I used to love her. Now I'm out for a good time. This 'being faithful' business is the bunk. She isn't willing to give up personal comfort for me so I won't give up personal freedom for her. You'll come down to earth when you marry and see that it isn't all love and kisses and romance."

That's practically what he said only in more detail. Oh! I was so sorry for him. And I couldn't tell him so. A man *hates* sympathy. I wish I could help him. Oh, that damn little fool of a girl. Hasn't she any sense? I'd live in a hovel if a man was willing to do so much for me. She'll wake up some day to her mistake and when she does, it will be too late. He will have left her. At least—his heart will have.

Wednesday, May 30

Claradell and Irvin and I went riding today. We went to the Dog Chow[156] where they cut up horses and make hamburger. They had a lot of beautiful wild horses that they'd driven in from off the range. Claradell bought a

---

[156] Best guess for this is the Brown Hide Company, once located at South 15th Ave at the Santa Fe Railroad tracks, now the intersection of North 15th Avenue, Grand Avenue and W. Roosevelt Street

beautiful 3-year-old black mare for only $10[157]. It's never been broke. We're going to have Richie break it for her. We're going Sat[urday] to get it.

Thursday, May 31

Had the picnic this evening. More darn fun! We found the prettiest spot way off by itself. There was a full moon and no mosquitoes. The river was simply splendiferous and it was all so thrilling. Irvin and I raced on the way back. Fun! I'm crazy about Arizona. Everyone is so friendly and nice and it's so darn beautiful. We got back about 12:30 [a.m.].

Friday, June 1

Claradell, Irvin and I rode this evening. I raced Irvin's little Pinto. Mac beat [him], of course. There was a man at the stable that wants to match his horse against Mac Sunday. I may do it.

We went to a Holy Roller meeting that was being held out in the open. They yell and stomp their feet and roll on the ground. It's all so—weird and fantastic. They keeping [*sic*] yelling "Praise be the Lord" and "Hallelujah." Claradell and I got the giggles and had to leave.

Saturday, June 2

We went to get Claradell's horse today. And boy, it was wild. It took *four* hours to catch it. When we finally did get it, it fought like a young hyena. Broke the rope twice. Just imagine trying to catch a young bronc [*sic*] that never even had a rope on its neck in a big corral with 300 other wild horses. It's hell!

When we did get it and started home, it bucked and kicked until we were exhausted. It got mired in the river and balked. I spurred it until the blood came but that's all the good it did me. We got back at 8:00 [p.m.] but had intended getting back at four. Eight hours it took to bring it in. It got loose on Grand Avenue and we had to lasso it all over again. Some wild ride

---

157 Her cheap horse would cost $132 today.

and were we tired! And thirsty! It was something of an accomplishment, tho. The men bet we couldn't bring it in. They said it took experience[d] riders. But we did! The three of us. Where there's a will, there's a way.

Sunday, June 3

Went to the Mexican races today and raced Mac. He [won]! And I won 50 cents. Had an awful good time. Micky, Irvin and Jerry were there. Hardly anyone would bet against Mac. They know a good horse when they see it. Dad came down and he says I can't go anymore.[158] Demoralizing influence, I guess. But I like it.

Afterward, Irvin, Claradell and I went to the river. Fun. I love life. Irvin raced his gray horse and won. Irvin and I are going to match our horses next Sunday if we can.

Rae took this photo of a horse race when he was in Phoenix in about 1924.

---

[158] Doris retells this story in colorful detail in *Love and Labor*, chapter 1, "My Strawberry Roan."

Monday, June 4

I went to the corral this morning. I was sitting in the car talking to Irvin and Richie drove up. It was the first time I'd seen him since Tuesday night. We talked and he wanted me to take him for a ride. I wouldn't, tho. He was awfully nice. He rode the little bay colt we brought in Sat[urday]. Gee, but it was wild. And buck! Oh, boy! We were sitting on the fence once and he said— so seriously—"Gee, but you have beautiful eyes." He put his arm around me and I thought he was going to kiss me before Irvin. Glad he didn't. Walter and I matched a race between his gray colt and Mac for tomorrow morning. Everyone is betting on the gray. Gee, but I'd be in seventh heaven if Mac would win and show 'em up. He probably won't, tho.

Claradell, Irvin and I went riding this evening. I'm sick of them. The[y're] childish. Claradell gives me a pain. She hinted around until I had to ask her to go with us tomorrow. Damn!

Tuesday, June 5

We went down this morning. Richie was late—but he brought me a box of candy. Claradell started flirting with him for all she was worth as soon as she saw him. Damn fool! I can't stand her. Richie rode the gray and I rode Mac. It was a fast, thrilling race, but Mac won. They were all so surprised and I was hilarious [*sic*]. Claradell acted funny when he won. She wanted the gray to win because Richie was riding it. I hate her and I don't like Richie very well anymore. She can have him. He's nothing in my young life and if he can see anything in a tall, lanky, pusilaminous [*sic*] prune like her—it's his funeral. I *hate* him. Oh! He's awful. Got a funny nose. *I hate him*. I never want to see him again. *Never*!

Later: I went to the corral this afternoon to see about shoeing Mac. Irvin said that Walter said that the race wasn't fair. That Richie held the gray horse back. The devil with him! I told him to tell Walter that we'd race it over. I insisted that we have a crowd to witness it and I'd *prove* that Mac could win. Damn him. Jim was there and wanted me to go swimming. I think he likes me. He's always nice to me and he isn't hard to gaze at. Guess I'll be in love with him for a while. That'll show Richie. On the whole I'm glad I'm through with him. I couldn't let a flirtation like that go on much longer. It just isn't done. It had to end sometime and the sooner the better.

Wednesday, June 6

Got a letter from Alyce today. I feel homesick tonight. I don't know why. I didn't ride today. I guess that's why. I've had too much time to think. If I'm doing something all the time, I'm happy. But when I'm not doing anything, I feel blue and lonesome.

Thursday, June 7

Got some new riding boots today. Gee! They're *hot!* Went riding with Claradell. We had a lot of fun. I like her when she's alone. We didn't mention Richie. Went to the race track and loped our horses. Mac has the easiest canter. He can go for half a mile without puffing a bit. I'm crazy about him.

Friday, June 8

Worked downtown today. This afternoon I went to the corral. Jim and Micky were there. Talked to them a long time. Went swimming this evening. Got letter from Marjie and Fanny. Marjie's left for Arizona. Whoopee! Fanny said Betty Bryant and Ida got expelled from SHH for getting drunk. Evaline came darn near it.

Saturday, June 9

Irvin, Claradell, Micky and I went riding this evening. Lots of fun. Micky told me all about himself. He and Jimmy have been bumming their way around the U.S. They've been all over. California, Colorado, Mexico, Kansas. Every place. They're going to Canada next. Oh! I wish I were a boy!

They have so much freedom. Jim's been married but divorced and only 21. Oh, they're seeing life. Jim's going to sell my pups for me. I like him.

Sunday, June 10

Raced Mac again against the gray. They were all so sure the gray could [win]. Irvin rode the gray and Micky rode Mac. Mac beat [him] by about 10 feet. Gee, but I'm glad! I'm goofy about him. Irvin, Jimmy and I went swimming this afternoon. Went in at the same spot we had the picnic. It was fun. We undressed in the bushes and then dove and ducked and swam under water all afternoon. The boys were so nice. Didn't try to get familiar with me because I was the only girl or anything. I know a lot of boys in Portland that I wouldn't have dared to go swimming in a lonely spot. But not these he-men. They've got more breeding and deep down gentlemanliness than any pamy wamy Hill boy. They respect you and don't think about sex every minute. It was 8:00 when I got back. Boy! Was I hungry!

Monday, June 11

Oh, what a wonderful day! What a wonderful life. What a wonderful world. I'm brimming over with happyness [*sic*]. My cup is full, etc. Gee, but I'm glad I'm alive. Marjie's coming day after tomorrow. Just think—.

Went riding this evening with Irvin, Claradell, Leslie. Lottsa fun. Raced Babe and Mac. Babe won first prize at the rodeo last year. But she didn't beat Mac. They finished neck and neck. Afterwards we went to the Holy Roller. They yelled and cried and moaned. One old lady fell on the ground and groaned and shook like a leaf. Then all of a sudden she jumped up and danced up and down with tears streaming down her cheeks and called, "Jesus! I see you, I see you, oh, take me with you, Jesus." Then she grabbed the Bible and cried all over it. They were all blubbering like maniacs. When we got back, Jimmy and Micky were there. Jimmy said I have pretty eyes. I like him.

Something about Arizona and horses seemed to bring out the silliness in the Baileys. Here is Rae performing a circus trick.

Thursday, June 12

Gee! I'm happy. Marjie's coming this evening. Whoopee! At 11:10. I can hardly wait. Have just come back from a ride. Raced Mac and gray. Mac won. The whole gang was up to see the race. Jimmy, Micky, etc. After they had all gone, Claradell, Irvin and I were riding around the track. A car drove up and it was Richie. We talked and he said he had some good Whiskey at the barn, for me to come with him and we'd get it and bring it back to the others. But right there I let him know I wasn't his slave and I said "Let Claradell go." That suited her fine. She jumped off her horse and into his car. Then Irvin and I rode around. In about five minutes they were back.

Richie sat on the fence beside me and we drank it and boy, it was good. It made me feel so nice way deep down in. Then Irvin and Claradell went for a canter around the track and Richie and I were left alone in the gathering dusk. He started saying how much he loved me and pretty soon I was in his arms. Oooh la *la*. He knows how. I guess the whiskey made me more responsive than usual to a mere kiss. Anyway I felt as if I were floating away on a haven of bliss. Or else it's the way he goes about it. I feel all jumpy inside as if I could drift away to paradise in his arms. Oh, it's wonderful. Just when I was so thrilled I thought I'd bust we heard the patter of horses' feet and in a minute we were back on the fence. Talking as if my whole world hadn't been turned topsy turvy. Gosh—And Marjie's coming in an hour ten minutes. What could be sweeter?[159]

Later— Marjie's here. Gee, but I love her.

Wednesday, June 13

Marjie and I went to the corral this afternoon. Irvin was there and he said he'd go with us to hunt for a horse. We'd just gone a little way when Richie drove up in a Ford coupe with another man. We told him our troubles and he said he knew where we could get a horse. So we went back to the barn and we left our horses and he left the other man and the three of us (M., R., and I) went in the Ford. He let me drive so he could sit between us. He had his arm around me all the way but he had it around M., too. But it was thrilling just the same. We drove into the desert and lost the road. Ach! What a wild ride. Bumping over bumps and around sage brush. Fun, tho. We couldn't find the horse but he said he'd let us use one of his until we found one. So we drove out to where it was and I had to ride it home and Marjie got to [ride] home with him. Just my damn luck, but I don't like him as well as I did anyway. So there are no lives lost. He made a date to ride with us tomorrow evening and bring another boy. *Who isn't married.* Be fun.

In the evening we rode some more, just Marjie and I. Down by the river in the moonlight. Stopped at the Holy Rollers on the way back. They were acting like maniacs as per-usual. Micky and Charlie and Irvin and Claradell were there. Irvin and Claradell acted funny. Claradell's probably jealouse [sic] cause of Richie's made a date to go swimming. Fun with Jim and Micky. Tha's all.

---

159 Handwriting and diction indicate she's still tipsy at this writing

Thursday, June 14

Marjie and I rode all over this afternoon looking for a horse. It was hot and I'm tired. This evening Richie and Ross didn't show up. Damn fools. Bought a saddle. S'nice.

Friday, June 15

Gee! So much has happened. I got a letter today in Dr. Scott's handwriting. I tore it open and what I saw made me feel like a fool, an idiot and an imbecile. I didn't know whether to laugh or cry. No—it wasn't a wedding announcement. I might have stood that. It was a card announcing the birth of an 8 lb. baby boy to Dr. and *Mrs.* A. D. Scott. I felt *awful,* and to think he's been married all this time. Even when I was in the hospital he knew he was going to have a son. Oh! I can't believe it. I'd like to think it wasn't true. *Married, a father.* [160] Oh, why didn't he tell me? I've never had such a shock before. I wonder what his wife is like and if he loves her and she loves him. He makes love so nicely. I wonder if he kisses her every night. Oh, death, where is thy sting?

Went swimming with Jimmy, Micky, and Irvin tonight in the old swim hole. It was so romantic and thrilling. Marjie likes Irvin. Jimmy kissed me. It was nice. He's nice. I like him. There's a lot to him below the surface. He has character even though Marjie *does* say he has a weak face.[161] She doesn't know him. Got back at 10:30 [p.m.]. Folks had waited two hours for us and were naturally furious. Daddy says he's going to sell Mac tomorrow. More power to him.

---

160 Dr. Abel David Scott (not his real name), born in 1899, is listed as a married intern at Good Samaritan Hospital in the 1928 Portland City Directory. The 1930 census shows him as married with a daughter.

161 A reference to the then-popular idea of phrenology, wherein the shape of a person's head indicated his intelligence and weaknesses.

Saturday, June 16

Marjie and I went swimming this afternoon. Fun. Richie came down. He and Ross and M[arjie] and I are going riding (auto) tomorrow.

Sunday, June 17

Went to the races with Jimmy and Micky. Richie was there. Raced Mac twice and he won both times. Won 50 cents. Whoopee! I like Jimmy. We talked and talked on the way back. He knows so much.

This evening—Richie and Ross. Ross was awful. Funny-looking and cheap, vulgar. Oh! I hated it! Drinking and necking by the side of the road. I feel so inferior. Oh, this isn't life. I hate that sort of thing. Passion—ugh! It's so animal-like and degrading. I didn't let him kiss my lips. I couldn't. I would have felt degraded. But he slobbered all over my neck and heaved like an old horse. Oh, I hate him. Richie did the same thing to Marjie. She likes him—oh, how could she? *A married man.* I don't see how I ever let him kiss me. I never want to see him again.

Oh! Somewhere, some place is the man I love. The man who will love and cherish me. Who will keep me and make a home for me. And I will not cheapen myself just to satisfy some dirty low-down [fish—oh]. I'll meet him soon. And I'll meet him with a clear conscience. I shall never (and I mean this) never, never, never let a pusilaminous [*sic*] idiot pet and feel and heave over me again.

Love is devine [*sic*]. Love is sacred. And kisses were made for a man and woman whose souls are entwined with love. A kiss is immortal. A kiss was not meant to be given to anyone. A kiss, yes, a mere kiss, was meant for love. A kiss is a symbol of truth and faith and everlasting fidelity. A kiss is a promise for a greater thing yet to come, and marriage is sacred. It is a wonderful institution but, oh, how easily it can be made into a farce.

Damn it! I wish I could say all that I'm thinking. But I can't. Words are so futile. But oh! My lover, who I have yet to meet. I pledge now that never again shall I cheapen myself by giving my body to another. I shall keep myself *clean* until I meet you. Clean and pure and virgin. *Oh!* I mean what I say. *I do.*

Monday, June 18

Oh! I feel awful. I can hardly stand it. My heart cries out in sympathy and understanding to a tall gray-eyed boy. This morning I received a card edged in black. I opened it and it said, "With regret—Abel David, Jr., on June 13. Dr. and Mrs. A.D. Scott." Oh, the poor kid. A few days ago he was a proud father. A father with a fine baby boy and only four days later it died. He's the kind that would take a thing like that so much to heart. He's so serious and honest. He works so hard. He deserves to be happy. Oh, Fate is cruel. I ought to write him. But I hardly know what to say. Oh, I'm so sorry for him.

Later: I wrote Dr. Scott. Gee, but it was hard. I'm afraid I was too formal but under the circumstances I could hardly be anything else. Went to the doctor's this afternoon. He darn near killed me and I feel like hell. Jimmy called this evening and wanted me to go riding but I felt too rotten. Doctor says I may have to have another operation. The *hell* with him but my side *does* hurt. Damn it all anyway.

Tuesday, June 19

Went out this morning to get Marjie's horse. I drove the car out and she rode her horse back. Jimmy went with us and after I left Marjie we were alone. Fun. He bet me he could kiss me even if I didn't want him to and he said he'd show me this evening. Marjie and I went swimming with Irvin and Micky this afternoon. Really had an awfully good time. The boys are good sports and a lot of fun. This evening six of us went riding. Mac acted crazy and nearly threw me off. Had an awful time with him. Jimmy was romantic. He can say the nicest things. About my eyes and lips. He kissed me but he had to fight for it.[162]

Wednesday, June 20

Went to doctor's and he hurt. Didn't go riding today. Jimmy phoned this eve. Bought a new dress. Doctor says I shouldn't ride or swim. But I'm going to anyway.

---

162 Doris seems OK with "fighting" for a kiss.

Thursday, June 21

Marjie's horse went flooey today. So we couldn't ride. Went swimming this afternoon. This evening I went to the corral alone. Was going to have a horse race but the man didn't show up with his horse. Jimmy was there and tried to be romantic. He gives me a pain.

Friday, June 22

Took Marjie's horse back to where we got it. Irvin went with us. It was a long hot ride but I enjoyed it. I love the sun. This aft[ernoon] I went to the doctor's. I hate him. He says I shouldn't ride. He tries to see how discouraging he can be. To *hell* with him.

Saturday, June 23

Went to the horse auction this afternoon. Also raced Mac against a thoroughbred. He won! The darling. Gee, but I love him. This evening Jimmy, Micky, Irvin, Marjie, and I all piled into a hay wagon and went to the river and had a weenie roast. Talk about fun! Gee! It was thrilling. The moon was so pretty and the bon fire so picturesque and romantic. Oh, I love Arizona. I don't like Jimmy, tho. I wish I did because he likes me, and it would be interesting. But I've tried and I don't and that's all there is to it. He's common.

But, oh, you Arizona! I rather think I'm going to hate to leave. It's so wild and free and untrammeled. I never would have dared to sit in a riggedy [sic] wagon full of hay and rattle down to the river in Portland. But here! Oh, anything. It's all so unaffected and easy. So free from restraint. I love it, I tell you. Love it. I *mean* that!

Sunday, June 24

This afternoon Irvin, Micky, Marjie and I went for a ride. We were going to go to the races but there weren't any. It was hot, about 115 [degrees] and we all felt the urge to go swimming. But alas! We had no bathing suits.

So the boys said we could have the good swimming hole and they'd take another about a mile down—and we'd go in without our suits. All went well until some pusilaminous [*sic*] prunes invaded on our private pool. Two girls and one boy. We saw them coming but didn't have sense enough to say anything. Just stood with water up to our necks and stared. That is, until they reached the edge of the pool. Then we yelled, "Hey! Don't come in here!"

"Why not?"

"Oh—it's muddy and stagnant. It isn't very deep, either."

But they insisted and we desisted [*sic*]. The truth came out finally but that didn't squelch them. They merely told us to stay under cover and they came anyway. I never felt so ridiculous in my life. About that time Irvin and Micky appeared, thinking we would be out. We were in a heck of a mess but the others eventually made themselves scarce. And we dressed in a hurry. All unmindful of wet backs and sandy feet. Oh! It's a great life but that's the last time I go swimming without a suit.

This is what downtown Phoenix looked like to Doris.

Monday, June 26

Went downtown this morning in our riding clothes. Big Rick rode this evening. Mac was all right till we got to the race track. Then he went crazy.

I couldn't control him so I let Irvin have a try. He ran and reared and got caught in some wire and fell, Irvin underneath. Oh! It was awful. It hurt him, of course. He leaned against the fence and cried. Poor kid. He was so brave. I cried, too. I couldn't help it. It's so darned pathetic to see tears in a boy's eyes. The others wanted to take him back in the car but he wouldn't. Rode with the rest of us, tho his arms must have killed him. Micky and Jimmy brought us home.

Tuesday, June 26
Went swimming this afternoon. Got a nice case of sun-burn. Bunch of funny boys at the tank[163]. All acted like half-wits. Irvin, Marjie and I drove out about seven miles to look at a horse. Really a beauty. Think she'll buy it.

Wednesday, June 27
Marjie bought a horse this morning. I'm bored. I shouldn't be. I'm in Arizona with a horse and the big wide world to ride in. But I feel restless nevertheless. Guess it's because I'm not in love. Jimmy's faded out and Irvin's too young. Damn it! If I'd only meet someone new. Someone tall and lean and romantic. I can't stand this in-between stage. But I guess I'll have to. There doesn't seem to be anyone in Arizona who makes the eyelids flutter. This is a land of horses. Not Romeos.

But just the same—I can't help but hope that the tide will turn and Fate will throw me a man. At least someone to be interested in. If only something terribly dramatic would happen. But nothing ever does. I'll just have to content myself with Mac and Marjie. These Arizona nights are so devine [*sic*]. So romantic and fascinating. I feel as if I'm letting them go to waste.

There is something so electric and magnetic in them. As if an unseen force is charging them with voltage [in] breathless stillness. Like the lull before the storm. The million, million stars like a multitude of tiny lights in a sea of blackness. Or better still—like a thousand precious diamonds

---

163 Water tank, probably near the train tracks

sewn on a cloth of rich black velvet. Infinitely big and over-powering. And the moon—oh, was there ever a moon such as this? Why does it seem so unlike the moon I have always seen in Oregon? What is it about it that leaves a breathless feeling in your throat and an ache in your heart? A desire for a hearth and a home. A craving to love and be loved by the man of your dreams. A wish to do and be something worth while. A desire to give, give, give and make the world happy. Perhaps it is the happy contentment of these Arizona native[s?], reflected in its light ~~Perhaps it is the solitude and wide open desert~~ that makes the observer feel the want of a home. Or perhaps it is the reflection of the solitude of the great unending desert that leaves the ache in your throat. But whatever it is, no one can look upon it night after night without being cast into its spell. Without longing and wishing for that intangible something called love. And I'm not *in* love. So I feel as if I'm wasting these nights.

Thursday, June 28

Feel good tonight. Rode this evening with the bunch. Mac acted temperamental as usual. But I love him just the same. Jimmy and Micky rode home with us and we all sat on the front lawn in the moonlight and ate watermelon. That is—they did. I drank lemonade. It would have been fun if it had been any other boys. But *those* saps. They're all right in their place, but they don't know it. Oh, well, they mean well so I shouldn't kick.

Friday, June 29

Marjie and I went for a long ride today into the desert. Billy [Taylor, Marjie's horse] became tender-footed because he hadn't been shod[164]. Refused to walk. Balked as firm as the Rock of Gibraltar. There was nothing to do but tie him to Mac's saddle horn and lead him. So we did and naturally felt ridiculous. In the middle of the desert, with two horses, and both of us walking. It's funny now but was serious then. To have to walk under the burning desert sun. Not so good. We didn't have any water, either. Started

---

164 Billy Taylor did not have horseshoes.

out with a thermos-bottle full but we dropped it—and it broke[165]. So you see, we were waterless. And oh! Boy, did we get dry. Got back about 6:30. Ate dinner and went to Holy Rollers.

There was a boy there from Chicago. Funny? Oh, my! He had a high forehead and starry brown eyes. Terribly effeminate looking. And the way he talked! And the things he said! He said that he'd never been that close to a horse before and that people here were terribly queer and informal. And he went downtown last night about 12:15 and—what do you think? "I saw girls out—*alone*. Why, in Chicago, if a girl is out after 10, unchaperoned, she'd be *kidnapped*. Attacked and thrown in the gutter. Oh, my goodness, gracious me!" Blah! He's going to get that knocked out of *him* before long. He's here for two years because his mother is ill. Says he used to be on the stage and impersonate women. He *looks it*!

Saturday, June 30

Went downtown this afternoon. Fun! Like Mr. Norton [?] better than I did. Marjie had stomachache so didn't go riding. Just went for a walk. Full moon tonight. It's beautiful. So big and white. Wonder if Dr. Scott's looking at it. Now I wonder why I wondered if *he* was looking at it? Dumn. But I do, I think about him so much. Why—I don't know. S'Fate, I guess. He's so darned sweet and sympathetic, and such a mixture of childishness and sophistication. Poor boy—to think his clear gray eyes have witnessed the death of his son. He's probably smiling still—as ever. Undaunted and undiscouraged. People may deem him hard and cold—but he isn't. He's brave. Brave and hopeful and full of determination. In a few weeks—he will start his career alone. And oh, I hope—I pray—that he will be the success he deserves to be.

Sunday, July 1

Went down to the corral to go riding but Marjie's horse was too tender-footed. Jimmy and Micky have left town for good. Funny, they didn't say

---

165 Thermoses were made of glass inside at that time.

goodby. Oh, well. Irvin's gone to Prescott for the Rodeo[166]. We're going Tuesday.

Marjie and I had the car this afternoon. Fun—rode all over. Beautiful evening. "The stars [*sic*] are starry and bright, and there is no one in sight—under the moon."[167] I positively love moonlight and oh! The moon is so glorious tonight. A big white Orbe [*sic*] making of the world a sea of shadows and mystery. Romance and kisses. Making the sad, happy—the frivalouse [*sic*], serious; the restless, contented and the lonely—(Damn! I can't think of the opposite extreme of lonely—) Well, anyway, they're not lonely anymore. They feel as if the world is kin. (There!) A feeling of fellowship and friendlyness to all mankind. There! How's that?

Monday, July 2
Bummed around the house all day. Lunched on bread and butter. Ah ha! Now why did I say that? Dumn. Going to Prescott tomorrow morning at 5:30 [a.m.]. It's 10:30 [p.m.] now so I'm going to bed.

Downtown Prescott in about 1930. Doris went to Prescott to see the famous rodeo in 1928.

---

166 Prescott, about 100 miles north of Phoenix in the mountains, has hosted a rodeo annually in July since 1888, the oldest and longest-running rodeo in the world. It includes contests of skill, a dance, and a parade.

167 Annette Hanshaw's signature song, "Under the Moon," with the lyrics, "The skies are starry and bright. The birds are sleeping at night. And there is no one in sight, under the moon."

Thursday, July 5

Oh! What a lot has happened. Life is so much fun. I'll start at the beginning. We left for Prescott early Tuesday morning. Reached there about noon. It's a beautiful little mountain town nestled in among the hills and pine trees. Of course, it was fairly bustling with excitement. A Rodeo come[s] once a year and they make a real celebration of it. They had a parade—and a good-looking cowboy on horse back lassoed us and pulled us down the street together. Fun! Then we went to the Fair Grounds. Sat on the trunk on the back of the car and flirted. The rodeo was superb. Broncs and steer-throwing and horse racing. Everything—including a man hurt and taken to the hospital. Oh! How I love to see these "devil may care" cowboys get on a wild bronco and try to break it. It's such a contest of strength. The horse—nostrils quivering and eyes dilated with hate. The men strong and determined with set mouths. Sometimes the horse wins. Sometimes the man.

After the Rodeo we drove out about five miles to our camping place: a beautiful little spot by a stream. We ate dinner and then—to the dance. We wore our riding cloth[e]s and felt perfectly at home. It was a wild, wild dance. And we came in for our share of popularity. Of course, it was because we were new. But was fun just the same. Met a lot of cute people. One man looked like Dr. Harrison. Danced with him quite a bit. Everyone was about half shot. I'd barely get around the floor once when they'd say "Shh! I've got something good to drink in the car." Of course, we didn't. It was an advantage not to. We had the upper hand. Some college boys brought us home—at two o'clock.

We slept like true children of the West on the hard ground with the sky for a roof and the moon for a light. And oh! How we did sleep. The next day we went into town and bummed around. Looking people over and being looked over. That evening (the evening of the 4th) was the big dance. We were just as popular as before and everyone was just as free with the liquor. About the same crowd was there and so we felt among friends. Really some awfully good-looking boys—and *not* slow.

Richie was there. He's a marvelous dancer. So smooth and rythmetic [*sic*]. His wife was there also—not so good. I don't like him, tho. Afterwards, Hershal McBride and Tommy Philip took us home—only we detoured and oh, boy! Tommy had a broken nose and an operation so we got along spiffy. We parked on a pretty little dell and Tommy and I took a walk in the moon light. He's cute and kisses nicely. In fact, it was thrilling at the time. But I managed to escape without falling in love. Damn it! I wish I could. Life would have more purpose to it. Marjie fell for Hershal. So she's happy. Anyway we got back at 3:30. We decided not to go to bed so packed the car and left about 4. Slept all the way in. Arrived here about 7:30. Feeling hot and dirty and tired. Took a bath and slept most of the day. Went swimming this evening.

Friday, July 6

Damn it! I knew I was too happy for it to last. Went to the doctor today and he said I have to have another operation. *Within the next two weeks.* That means the hospital and I can't ride anymore the rest of the summer. I'm going to Portland and have Dr. Baird do it. I'll have to stay in the hospital for 14–18 days. Dr. Scott won't be there and oh, hell! I suppose I should do it here, but much as I love Arizona, it would be just plain hell if I couldn't ride. And he says I couldn't ride or swim for two or three months after the operation.

So you see—but darn it, I don't know how I can make myself go back to the hospital. No one knows the horror it holds for me. Those drab gray walls and dumn nurses and greasy food. And the awfulness of death all around me. The surgery—with its green tile walls and white masked doctors. And oh, to have to take ether, and the folks won't be there and I'll feel so lost and alone and friendless. One minute I want to go—and the next, to stay. One is as bad as the other. Oh, damn it! What have I done to deserve this? Why can't I get well like other people and be human, instead of having lumps on my side and operations.

Saturday, July 7

Went downtown today and saw a show. Really splendid. I can't get my mind off the hospital. Damn it! I don't know whether I can go through with it or not. All day long, lying inertly in a narrow white bed. Dr. Baird's rubber gloves and drainage tubes—oh, hell! Why do I torture myself like *this*? If I could only forget until the time comes. But I can't. I keep going over it. Detail by detail. The way I feel going under the ether—that awful smothering sensation. That feeling that I am being slowly exterminat[ed]. I try to hold on—I try to think and keep my mind active—but I'm falling against unseen forces. Little by little my brain is numbed. The bottom drops out of everything and I am sunk into oblivion. And then—years later it seems—centurys [*sic*]—eons—I'm struggling again. Trying to grasp that intangible something. I barely reach it—and I'm thrown back again. I fight. I yell. I exert my will power. Every fiber in my being is streaking toward it. In a dim haze I am conscious of life around me—but I'm too weak to get it. It's too far away. I try to talk—to tell them to help me, but my vocal cords, too, have deserted me. And then—after eternity of suffering, I seem to step on a ledge. Vague figures become familiar faces. People talk—and I am once more among the living.

And so—I die a thousand deaths. Merely in my imagination. I suffer untold agonys [*sic*]. Even the thought of it all leaves me weak—and the real thing is a thousand times worse. Damn it! I'm the biggest doggone coward that ever was.

Sunday, July 8
Raced Mac this morning against Babe. It was awfully unfair. Irvin rode Babe with a 10-pound racing saddle and he only weighs 130. Charley rode Mac with a 25-pound bronc saddle and he weighs 160. And Mac is the smaller horse. I wanted to ride him but they wouldn't let me. Mac lost by a little. Oh! But it hurt my pride. Damn! Hershal appeared, from Prescott, about 9 this morning. He's dumn.

Got telegram from Dr. Baird and he said not to do anything about operation till we got his letter. So we don't know yet whether we're going to Portland or not.

Monday, July 9

Monkeyed around—slept nearly all day in basement. Letter from Alyce—Chauncey and Kelly have made up. Earl's getting married. Picnic tonight at Tempe. Fried chicken and plenty of fun. That's all.

Tuesday, July 10

Well! I'm not going to be operated on after all—that is, not till the middle of August. That means another glorious month of swimming, riding, and maybe even the Grand Canyon. Hot *Damn*!

Herschel [she corrects her spelling] and Tommy didn't come. That's a Bell Hop[168] for you. Dr. Scott opens his office today. Dear—Darling—Dr. Scott. Like a small boy trying so hard to be independent and sophisticated. I have a feeling his marriage isn't the success it ought to be. He's the type that would make a wonderful husband and father if he loved his wife. He would be faithful and sincere, *not* indulge in foolish flirtation—IF he loved his wife. But I don't think he loved her, else he wouldn't have acted as he did. He probably doesn't consider it as a real marriage because their souls are not united. Oh, damn it! Why am I always thinking and wondering about him—it merely wastes paper. I'm going to quit.

Wednesday, July 11

Gee! I'm happy. Rode this evening and Mac nearly killed us both. Jumped in front of a car. He gets so darned crazy when I don't ride him. I'm going to get a Martin gale[169] [*sic*] for him.

Thursday, July 12

Went downtown this afternoon—bummed around. This evening—ride with Herschel and Johnny. Awfully dumn. Herschel is so childish and

---

168 He worked as a bellhop in the hotel.

169 A martingale is a horse collar with breastplate or strap that attaches to the bridle and keeps the horse from tossing his head back.

Johnny so insipid. Managed to have a fairly good time though, considering the circumstances. Climbed some box cars and ran along on top of them, jumping between cars with the black void between. Thrilling. No moon tonight so it was awfully dark.

Bought a card I'm sending to Dr. Scott wishing him good luck.

Friday, July 13

Went for a long horse back ride today—25 miles. Used Martin gale [*sic*] on Mac and it helped lots. Of course, he was moderately bad. Got in the middle of Grand Avenue. Cars coming N-S-E-W. He didn't know what to do so he just stood there and held up traffic. But then—it's all in a life time. Got home about 6:45—ate dinner and went swimming till ten. Some life!

Saturday, July 14

Down to the river today and swam—in Mother Nature's bathing suits. Fun. Mac's mean as ever—I'd like to trade him for a more sensible horse. He's so darned temperamental I'm at atension [*sic*] every minute. Tired.

Sunday, July 15

Went to the Mexican races today. Two beautiful race horses were there. Talked to Shorty Ward[170] about trading Mac for a more sensible horse. I'm going out and look at one he has tomorrow. Went swimming this evening. Tired but happy.

Monday, July 16

Shorty Ward's wife, Marjie and I went over to try out his horse. It was a long hot ride but I enjoyed every minute of it. Across a dried-up river bottom and along a hot dusty road. We stopped at a little store and bought

---

170 The likeliest horse-wrangler Shorty Ward and his wife Thelma are located in Arkansas by the 1930 census.

crackers, milk, balongny [*sic*] and etc. Ate it by the side of the road beneath the shade of a tree and talked horse-talk. Then home again on "Freckles." Got home about 4:30 (left at 9:30). I've decided not to keep the horse, however. He's too old and funny-looking and has a saddle sore.

We went to Mexico town this evening. Gee, but I'm crazy about them. They have such deep husky voices and they all seem to be musically inclined. Sit on their front steps and play guitars; all over you hear their deep, rich voices chanting love songs and [twanging?] at their ukes. They're such a romantic race. We talked to three or four little Mexican boys and they taught us some Mexican words. How to say "Hello. How are you? Smile at me, sweetheart. Yes, no, horse, goodby."

Tuesday, July 17
Went to the doctor's today—hate him. Rode this evening. Sometimes I think I like Freckles—'nother times not so good. Anyway, I'm taking him back tomorrow. Went to Mexico town tonight again and tried out our lingo. Funny thing—they nearly all laughed at us. Letter from Alyce.

Wednesday, July 18
Got up at 5:30 this morning to take Freckles back. Gee, but it was nice to get on go'old [good old] Mac again. He's the darned sweetest. The ride was fun. I enjoyed getting up at daybreak and starting out. The sunshine on the desert hills and the air was so cool and refreshing. Ate breakfast at a little country store and generally enjoyed ourselves. My side isn't behaving as it should. Damn.

Something has started me thinking about Micky again and I thought I'd forgotten him. 'Tis a trick of Fate, I guess. Marjie and Joe have gone swimming but I had a cold—and stayed home. I feel so virtuous. The water sounded so tempting and I wanted to go. But my better judgment won. Dr. Scott once said he admired me for my good common sense. So I had to see if I really had any. And I'm wondering if I have. When I stay home, all I can think of is hospital and sickness, etc. So—maybe it's better for me to be in action, and forget myself. Anyway, I'm going to stop and read poetry. Maybe I'll be inspired.

Thursday, July 19

Rode this morning before breakfast. Dear little Mac was so nice. Downtown this afternoon and another ride this evening. I'm glad I'm alive.

Friday, July 20

Rode this morning. Bummed around all day. This evening rode our horses up to the tank and went swimming. Lots of fun. Afterwards we went to the Holy Roller [meeting] and talked to those cute boys that were there last night. Met Ben and Don and they drove us home. Ate watermelon and acted silly. Then we went for a ride and ended at Cotton woods[171]. Marjie and I wanted to dance, but the boys wouldn't take us in because we had knickers on.[172] So they gave us the money and we went in alone. Danced once together 'nthat was all we needed. Danced with a cute brunette. Then home. Ben has a nice voice but he's dumn. Grand Canyon tomorrow.

A glimpse of the beautiful Grand Canyon.

---

171 Not the town of Cottonwood, but a country club called The Cottonwood, a mile from Camel Back, near Old Town Scottsdale.

172 Women in trousers (riding knickers) might not be served or allowed entrance, but they seem to have gotten away with it.

Saturday, July 21

Aha! The light dawned bright and clear (oh, yes! It did) and all laughing merrily as care free children should, we piled into the car and proceeded on the big adventure. Had a really wonderful ride through the desert and reached Prescott about 2 o'clock [p.m.]. Went to the Hassayampa Hotel[173] to freshen up and incidentally got a glimpse of Tommy. He looked awfully cute and I was sorry I didn't have time to talk to him. Then we rode some more and wonder of wonders, we hit some rain. Oh, good old rain. The first I've seen since April. We stuck our faces out the window and fairly drunk [*sic*] in the fresh, invigorating sweetness. That beloved old wet smell. But every rose has its thorn and the road was muddy. Oh, yes! Very! We were spinning along so merrily when—slip-slop-slush—and we were facing the other direction. Skidded clear around. Then proceeded to get stuck. After much swearing and wading around in the mud, we were once more on our way. Ate dinner about 6 and decided to try and make the Canyon by tonight. Oh, I wish I could describe the sunset. Beautiful beyond description. Billows and billows of rosy clouds. The desert, wet and damp, [then] gone dry.

Sunday, July 22

Oh! How can I describe today? It's been so perfect. So exactly what a day should be. We reached the Canyon last night and went straight to bed. This morning we walked over to see the Canyon. As I walked up to the edge and gazed down into that deep, deep chasm, I felt as if I had been suddenly whisked away to paradize [*sic*]. It would have been sacrilegious to speak. I felt as if I were looking at something I shouldn't see, as if God were giving me a glimpse of heaven, so that I might wish to do and be better the rest of my life. It is so big, so vast, so utterly beyond my comprehension. Even when I'm looking at it, I can't grasp the full significance of those great towering cliffs and ravines. The river so far below like a tiny ribbon. The

---

173 The Hassayampa Hotel opened in 1927 in Prescott on Courthouse Square, the pride of the town.

rocks like strange bits of Grecian and Egyptian architecture. We spent the day looking, looking!

Doris (left) and Marjie on the edge of the Grand Canyon, 1928.

This evening, at sunset, I took a walk—alone. Sat on a crag and watched the Canyon change from a wild flamboyant red to a soft dusky glow. A million shadows, a thousand mysteries—oh, that there should be such beauty as this.

After sundown we met some boys—naturally. Especially one tall, handsome, dark and adorable. He's a cowboy and takes parties down the trail on mules. We went for a walk—climbed trails and over rocks and finally landed on a small plateau. We sat on the edge—let our feet hang over into infinity and drank in the moonlight. Afterwards we walked some more and everything was so romantic. He kissed me thrillingly, master[ful]ly. Not cheaply. And said such wonderful things. I could fall in love with him so hard—if I could see more of him. But I'll probably never see him again—we're leaving tomorrow. Oh! The darling!

Monday, July 23

We left this morning—left paradise and my cowboy and came to Mormon Lake[174]. Really a beautiful spot and we're camping out. Fun! I feel so primitive and we're going for a long horse back ride tomorrow.

Tuesday, July 24

Gee, but it was cold last night! We went for our ride today. I had a peppy little horse—Mac's temperament. We went way up in the hills among the pine trees. Ate our lunch on a log. When we came home we left the trail and came straight down the mountain. Thrilling! Dead tired this evening.

Wednesday, July 25

Decided not to stay at Mormon Lake any longer. We left for White [Mountains][175] this morning but got on the wrong road and landed in the middle of the desert. We're going to roll up in a blanket and sleep on the ground. Barbaric—I call it!

Thursday, July 26

Came home today. Gee, but it's nice to get back to a bed and ice water. Letters from Fanny—Alyce—Elizabeth. Alyce is going around with Johnny. Nice old Johnny, up to his old tricks again. Gee, but it's going to be good to get back to Portland again. Much as I love Arizona—there's no place like Oregon.

Friday, July 27

Went riding this eve with Claradell and Leslie. Gee, but it was nice to get back on dear little Mac again. Bless his heart.

---

174 A shallow lake in northern Arizona, 27 miles southeast of Flagstaff.

175 The White Mountains are about 200 miles east of Phoenix, but Doris's party never made it there.

Saturday, July 28

Went riding this evening. Mac's a little darling. Hit an awful dust storm and ducked into a little eating cabin for shelter. The people were so nice and friendly. In fact, they rather over-did it—gave us a piece of Canalope [*sic*] and I detest the stuff. But I had to eat it. Do or die.

Sunday, July 29

Oh, gee, but it was hot today. The sun was scorching. We went for a ride and took some pictures of our horses. We started out bravely enough to see the races, but it was just too damn hot. We made a bee-line for home and ice water. Stayed undercover until after sundown. Then we dared to venture forth again. It was much cooler and we had a really nice ride. Came back by Holy Rollers. They had a sick girl a stretcher. Praying for her. Awfully weird. Jack was there but I don't think he's cute anymore. In fact, he's rather a sap. Leaving for Portland a week from this coming Friday. *Hot dog.*

Marjie (left) and Doris (white shirt) with their horses in Phoenix.

Monday, July 30

It rained this evening. Real honest rain—and it's still raining. Oh! How I love it. It's been so darned hot. All day long. Then along came the wind and down came the rain and maybe now it won't be so hot. Saw "Seventh Heaven." Really wonderful. Side hurts.

Tuesday, July 31

Went downtown and got two new dresses and new coolie coat—crazy about them. Went to see Mac. There wasn't anyone there. He had his head over the gate of the stall, looking so disconsolate. I led him out and gave him some water, then I went in his stall and he didn't have a bit of hay. I went over to get him some and when he saw me coming with it he whinnied so pitifully and fairly snatched at it, even before I put it in the manger. The poor little darling. I nearly cried. I'll move him to a pasture tomorrow. He's so sweet.

Wednesday, August 1

Didn't do a darned thing today. What more can I say?

Thursday, August 2

Downtown, bummed around. Dinner at Aunt Florence's. Marjie leaving tomorrow. Going to meet her in L.A. in a week. S'nice life.

Friday, August 3

Marjie left this morning. Everything seems so blank. Went riding this evening with Claradell, Leslie, Irvin, down by the river. There wasn't a moon and the night was so dark. We told ghost stories and boy! How Irvin can tell them. I think even the horses were scared—fun, tho.

Saturday, August 4

Washed and ironed and mended clothes all day. I'm beginning to get excited about going.

Sunday, August 5

Sundays are dumn.

Monday, August 6

Downtown from nine till five buying pajamas, underwear, purse, etc. Also shoes. Spent $30[176] but got some adorable things. Letter from Marjie, saying that she was staying two or three weeks more in L.A. She said she'd stick with me through thick and thin. This is an example of it, I guess. Anyway I'm going on alone and stay at Alyce's till she arrives. It'll be fun, anyway, but I am disappointed. Oh, well.

Tuesday, August 7

Fixed clothes nearly all day. Mother's white dress shrunk [*sic*] so she gave it to me—not bad. Irvin came up this afternoon about Mac. Gee! I hate to leave him (Mac—not Irvin). But I am excited about going. It's all I think about. I can't even sleep. Hope Alyce doesn't mind my staying with her. Think I'll buy her something in S.F. Like a compensation check. Gee! It's all going to be so much fun. I'll feel so independent and etc. I hope I won't have to go to the hospital. That's the only cloud in a blue, blue sky. I want to play around—before I start school. And an operation isn't my idea of playing.

But if I do go, oh, I hope Dr. Scott can be there. It's a funny thing—I think about him so much. I'm not in love with him, I'm sure. He's too old and besides he's married and has had a baby. Maybe more than one, for all I know. But just the same, I can't stop thinking about him. His engaging grin and gray eyes and the little boy way he has, and then his sympathy and

---

[176] That's a $397 shopping trip in 2012 dollars.

he thinks he's so hard. But he isn't. He has a wonderful character. That's why I can't understand this wife and baby business. But it hasn't spoiled him for me. I think there's more to this than meets the eye. I'll check up on him when I get there.

Wednesday, August 8
Leaving tomorrow.

Thursday, August 9
I'm on the train—in my berth. It's too wobbly to write but I'm having a scrumptious time. So happy. Hated to leave the folks and Mac and Patsy but I'm ready for the next adventure.

Union Station in Phoenix.

Oregon
(1928)

Friday, August 10

Had a wonderful sleep last night and awoke, ready for anything. It's lucky I was. The day was so full. Anyway—just as I was going into the diner [car] who should I meet but little Marjie. She had decided to come with me. Do or die. We changed trains at L.A. And it was so thrilling and exciting. Then we rode for miles along the ocean and gazed and gazed—lotsa fun. Rae met us [in San Francisco] and took us up to an apartment house. We went in a little room and Fritz (the owner of that apartment and bootlegger) made us a gin fizz. Good! That's not the half of it—then we went to a show. Saw Charles Farre in "Fazil."[177] Really a marvelous picture. And it was so good to get back to civilization. The theater was beautiful. So metropolitan. After the show Rae said he'd take us to Coffee Dan's[178]. We didn't know what that was but let him lead the way. We went down some funny stairs into a basement. Oh, it was sublime; everyone had little hammers. They pounded on the tables and talked and were so friendly. Then the entertainer sang some songs that were not nice but extremely funny and clever. All the women were smoking so we smoked, too, and ate hot tamales and banged on the table with our hammers. A boy with the most marvelous tenor voice sang. I could marry a man with a voice like that. Then we came home across the Ferry. That was a treat in itself. The cool sea breeze on our faces. Rae lives in the beautifullest house on top of the hill. And our room's so nice and cheery. Gee, but I'm happy.

Saturday, August 11

Today was so full. I know I'll forget something. First, we got up and took a cold shower. Then we had breakfast at a ritzy little place. Then Rae took

---

[177] Charles Farrell and Greta Nissen in *Fazil*

[178] Coffee Dan's was a "ham and egger," code for a speakeasy. Access was via a slide down to the basement level, which meant holding your skirt tight. Small wooden mallets were provided for applause, and the tables took a beating. The dishware was cheap and breaking dishes signaled high praise. The bar still exists as San Francisco's appropriately named Slide bar at 430 Mason Street.

us to the cannery[179] and introduced us to his friends. Then we went to the world's largest air port[180] and saw a German warplane. Then across the ferry to San Francisco. Saw beautiful hotels and apartment houses. Then to China Town. Oh! It was thrilling. So foreign. We spent money right and left but everything was so fascinating—"Get thee behind me, Satan." But he didn't. We met Marceline for lunch. A pretty, peppy little French girl. Perfectly adorable. Then we drove all over Golden Gate [Park]. Had our pictures taken there. Then we saw art museums and Japanese gardens and aquariums and Legion of Honor and, and, oh, so many things. We had dinner at an exotic little Italian place where they served white wine. I drank two glasses. Gee! It was good and made me feel so nice and warm and happy. Then we went to see Irene and Rēne[181], and then we came home. Tomorrow we're going to the beach and have a picnic. More damn fun.

Wednesday, August 15

Gee! I haven't written for a week nearly. I'm safely arrived in dear old Oregon. Staying at Alyce's. Had dinner at Fanny's tonight and drove around in her Packard but I can't hold it in any longer. I got a letter from my MD yesterday. Rather formal but it was a letter and he asked me to come and see him and oh, gee! I ought to wait about three months but I don't think I can. I want to go now, tonight. I don't have to have an operation but gee! I wish I had an excuse to go see him.

Thursday, August 16

Oh, Gee whiz! Gosh! What's the matter with me? I've never felt this way before. If this is love, it's hell. Yes! I went to see him. Like a fool—I haven't a darn bit of will power. Bought a new hat today and this evening Rae and another boy came out in a big Franklin. I had them drive by his office. I

---

179 The Del Monte Cannery No. 37 at Fruitvale Avenue and East Ninth Street in Oakland
180 Oakland Airport
181 Irene Van de Carr and her son Rēne are old family friends.

hadn't intended going in but the light was on. So I did. With thumping heart and a palpitating pulse, I climbed the stairs and went in. The door to his private office was closed and I didn't know whether to run or not. When I had just about lost my nerve (or regained my common sense), the door opened. He was with another doctor and had his hat on.

He sent the other doctor on downstairs and we went in his office. I sat on his desk and he sat across from me and we talked and talked. But I'll be darned if I know what about. All I could do was look at him. He looks much older but just as sweet, and was so worried about my side and said he was going to keep an eye on me this winter. But darn it, I want to keep an eye on him every day. He's so damned sweet and gee! I don't think I'm in love but I wish I knew what it was. I keep thinking of the way he combs his hair and his mouth and eyes and oh, Gee whiz. I'd go back right now if I could, but it's late and I can't and he's probably with his wife and damnation. I think I'm going crazy. He's *married*.

And I'm terribly afraid I love him. If I could only be in his arms and have him hold me, oh! So tightly and never, never, never let me go and oh, gosh! I wish I could snap out of it but I can't because I think I love him.

Friday, August 17

Came out to Marjie's today. It's nice to be back. Everything's so green and fresh and the river so blue. We've got the room fixed up so nice.[182] I have a lot of my accessories spread around so I feel that it is my room. I even have half of the closet and half of the dresser. S'great.

Saturday, August 18

Oh, damn it! I wish I could forget him. He's married but that doesn't seem to stop me. I didn't think any man on earth could make me feel this way. But he's always in my thoughts and it's lucky I'm way out in the country,

---

182 Doris will be living in Marjie's room and taking the train into Portland from Oak Grove for school every day. Marjie will soon be leaving for college but Doris still has more than a year of school to finish.

else I'd probably go back to see him. And I can't. I shouldn't. I'm going to try not to.

Sunday, August 19

Slept until 11 this morning. Felt so good all day. Went for a ride this evening. Stopped in at Alyce['s] and got some things I left. Letter from Rae and snap shots we took in S.F. Good! Happy!

Monday, August 20

Went downtown today. Met Fanny and we went to lunch at the Heathman. I like it there; a cute man flirted with us. Then we went to the Portland [Theatre, next door] to see if the gloves I left had been turned in. Had fun with the ushers. Rather, they had fun with us. Then to The Broadway [across the street]. Saw a marvelous show. Had loges and sat next to a cute boy. We acted like fools but Fanny and I always do. About the middle of the show we saw Marjie and had her come down and sit with us. George Stoll[183] asked for request numbers and we had him play "Dream House."[184] He's so damned sweet. After the show we went up to see Eddy Laccel. Then for a milk shake at that cute place. Spilt mine all over me—of course—and caused a lot of disturbance. Yes—I'm thoroughly disgusted with myself. Then we went to the Portland and I phoned [St. Helen's] Hall. Made an appointment for Wednesday. Talked to Sister Ellen Juliana. She was so nice. I'll be glad to see her.

Tuesday, August 21

Bummed around all day—washed my hair—went to a show this eve at the Hollywood. Jack Toslafason sat next to me. Fairly good show.

---

183 George Stoll was orchestra conductor at the Broadway; also apparently sometimes played the organ. See Appendix II for more details.
184 "My Dream House," by Adelaide Primrose, 1928.

Wednesday, August 22

Went up to school today and mapped out my course. I'm taking an awfully stiff one but it seems the only way out. Got a new sweater at Berg's for school. Met Fanny and we had lunch at the Heathman—good. They are beginning to know us in there. Went up to see Eddy. The fact of the matter is he's awfully cute. In fact I never realized before today just how cute he was. Went all over town looking for a desk. I went in all the dirty, dusty, smelly second hand stores on First Street. It was rather fun. Venturing into all the damp, musty, cluttered-up stores. I felt so adventurous. Wrote a letter to Daddy tonight.

Rae took this photo of his friend RuthMary Burroughs sitting with "gypsy children" in about 1924, outside of Portland.

Thursday, August 23

There is a band of gypsies in the auto-camp[185] tonight. We went down to see them. They were drunk, fighting and squabbling. It was exciting, and so picturesque. All those gypsies in their native garb, jabbering around the camp fire. And the fir trees and the big white moon for a setting. It was a scene I'll never forget.

Friday, August 24

Met Fanny downtown today. We bummed around generally enjoying ourselves. Bought a new pair of shoes. Saw lots of Hall girls and some old Grant boys. Had my picture taken for the paper.[186] Went to the doctor's and that's all. Oh, yes! Show this evening at The Broadway—dead tired.

Saturday, August 20

Marjie and I went downtown today. Bought a new blue silk blouse—pretty. Saw Hal Paddock and talked quite a while. He's cute. Also saw Marjie Painton and Chauncey. Went to a show, "Oh, Kay!" Awfully good. Saw Lorraine and she said she had a blind date for me last night but didn't know where I was. Some more of my luck. Bought a gray wicker desk for our room. Money's going fast. Only $11.27 left and I did have $53[187]. Letter from Daddy this evening. Jack's had Flu.

Sunday, August 26

Went for a picnic today at Champoeg[188]. Ate too much rich food and am now suffering the consequences. Such is life.

---

185 Campground with space for cars, still a novelty in 1928
186 Since Marshall Dana was the editor of *The Oregonian,* it was an easy matter to get Doris's photo taken and printed.
187 The $53 in 2012 would be about $700.
188 Champoeg is a town south-west of Portland, toward Salem.

Monday, August 27

Letter today from Mother, Joe, Rae, Elizabeth. Not so worse. Got my desk today. It looks so cute in the room.

Tuesday, August 28

Downtown today. Met Fanny. Had a marvelous time bumming around doing nothing. Saw a lot of people I know. Got my proofs. I don't know whether I like them or not. Saw Dr. Kiehle. Happy. Pen gone dry—

THE MORNING OREGONIAN,

WEDNESDAY,

SEPTEMBER 12, 1928

Miss Doris Bailey returned to Portland recently after spending the summer with her parents, Mr. and Mrs. L. R. Bailey, in Arizona. Mr. and Mrs. Bailey will remain in the south for the winter while Miss Bailey is a student at St. Helen's hall in Portland.

—Markham photo.
Miss Doris Bailey, daughter of Mr. and Mrs. L. R. Bailey, who will attend school in Portland this winter.

This is the photo and a brief on the society page that ran Sept. 12, 1928 in *The Morning Oregonian*.

Friday, August 31

Went downtown today. Saw Clara Boy and Georgie Stoll. Gee, but I'm crazy about him. Also, big thrill—saw Eugene Rossman himself. Slick and poised as usual, but the same old Gene. Fanny found [out] this afternoon

[that] Maryalene Martin[189] died this morning. Gee, but it made me feel awful. To have known her so well and then, to think that she's dead now. I can't bear to think about it. Death. It is so awful—and she was so pretty and popular.

Saturday, September 1

We went to the beach this afternoon. Arrived at Delake [*sic*][190] about 6:30 this evening. We were all famished and ate like pigs. Then Marjie and I wandered over to the dance hall. Had on our riding clothes but that didn't stop us. We danced about four dances with some ham[m]y looking soaks and left. We wandered back towards the house preparing to have a dull evening—but then—Fate didn't want us to have a dull evening. So it threw in our way two boys—they looked good to us so we decided to take a walk on the beach. They followed as we had hoped and eventually caught up with us. That sounds like a common case of pick-up. But it wasn't.

George Shade—his name is—is a Beta[191] at Oregon—Senior—lives in Irvington—studying medicine and knew all the Hall girls, Maryalene Martin included. We hit it off perfectly from the first, because we had so much in common. Walked along the beach with the waves lapping at our feet, arm in arm, talking, talking. And in 15 minutes we felt like old and tried friends. It was cold and we ran to keep warm, then sat down to wait for Marjie and Jimmy. I don't know how it happened, but there was a kiss—not a petting party—just the nicest kind of a kiss. I wanted to stay. Sit there all night with his arm around me. But the others had already passed so we got up to go. About that time Jimmy passed us at a running gait and then came Mr. Dana. They had looked all over for us and were naturally mad. I introduced George and he apologized for being so late and was so much the perfect gentleman. Then he said "Goodby, Doris," and was gone and I'll probably never see him again and damn! But he's cute.

---

189 Apparently a sister student at SHH
190 De Lake, resort town on the Oregon Coast
191 Beta Theta Pi

Sunday, September 2

We got up late this morning and the others had already gone for breakfast. So we built a fire, warmed our feet and read the funny papers. After they came back we had our breakfast and then went for a walk on the beach. I hoped, but didn't expect to see George. We did, tho. They were walking up towards us. George said they'd been down on the beach all morning hoping to see us. So we started out for another tramp. The air was so salty and cool, and we strode along, blissfully unaware of time and distance. Arm in arm as before. He has the prettiest eyes and every once in a while he'd say something funny and we'd look at each other and laugh and our faces would be so close together and his eyes twinkling into mine. Oh, sublime ecstasy.

We laughed over last night and he said I carried the situation off perfectly, with so much poise, and I said he did, too. Then we got tired and sat down in the sand and he told me all about himself and his work. He wants to be a good surgeon and I think he will. He's the type.

He has a lot of sense and also a sense of humor and is awfully well bred and I have an idea he has a lot of money—just from things he said. He likes to fish and hunt and swim and ride—"just a good outdoor boy," as he says—oh! He's sweet and begged me to stay another day so we could have a bonfire on the beach and roast marshmallows. But we couldn't and after we'd walked 10 or 15 miles we *had* to leave, and now he's gone and I made the mistake of leaving the impression that I didn't like him so very well. And so I'll probably never see him again but I *will* remember him. As a perfect gentleman, and absolutely the *nicest* boy I've ever met. Oh, yes! He said I shouldn't go to OAC. I wasn't the type. That only dumn bunnies that couldn't rate at Oregon went to OAC and I was the type for Oregon. Nice—

If we could have stayed tonight something definite would have happened and I probably would have seen him after I got back. But we didn't and he'll just remember me as a nice St. Helen's Hall girl he met at the beach and that will be all. One more evening would have cinched it. Oh, well! It's Fate, I guess.

Monday, Sept. 3 (Labor Day)

Letter from Johnny Leaverton today—washed hair—slept all afternoon.

Tuesday, Sept. 4

Met Fanny downtown today. We had the most atrocious lunch at the Hazelwood[192]. Then to the Columbia and saw 15 minutes worth of an abdominable [*sic*] show. That was all we could stand. We then went to The Broadway. I'd seen the show but was willing to see it over because of Georgie Stoll. As luck would have it, it was Georgie's day off and we had to sit through half hour of Herman Kevin. By that time our bad luck was becoming a joke. We left, and later discovered the loss of Fanny's gloves and a letter I had addressed but not stamped to Mother.

We went to the Columbia and found her gloves on the floor, then back to the box office at The Broadway and the girl had found, stamped and mailed my letter. After all that excitement, I met Marjie and we went out to Meeds'[193] to dinner. Thurlow's rather nice but awfully dumn. Made us look at his college year book all evening and read a story he had written. I'd have had a better time if I hadn't been so hungry.

Wednesday, September 5

School started today. It was good to see all the kids again. Bishop Sumner[194] gave the most marvelous talk in chapel. Fanny had her car and we drove all over, raising hell. Met a new girl that knows Jack Pillar. She said his brother was here from the East and they stole a car and forged some checks and skipped the country and the police caught his brother but hadn't caught him yet.

Also, Thelma, who knows Moody, said he became a fond father this summer. Feature it? Moody a father. Going to have a gang out Friday

---

[192] The Hazelwood was at 240 E. Broadway, according to the 1928 Portland City Directory. A postcard from some years before shows it on Washington Avenue.

[193] Family friend Myra Meeds, 40, was divorced and living with her uncle, with her son Irving, about Doris's age. Thurlow was perhaps a friend of Irving's.

[194] Bishop Walter T. Sumner, Episcopal bishop of Oregon from 1915 through 1935, was a frequent visitor at St. Helen's Hall.

night. Wish I had the nerve to ask George Shade. Had the most wonderful dream about Dr. Scott last night. Oh—la la. It was *hot*.

Thursday, September 6

I liked school today. I like the atmosphere. Judy had her car and we bummed around. Everybody's happy.

Friday, September 7

Fanny came out to dinner tonight and we had a gang out this evening. All the old bunch! Jimmy Morgan, Ed Miller, Al Pearson, Bob C., Alyce and, Lorraine, even Gene honored us with his presence. I paired off with Rex—an adorable boy from [University of] Oregon. Tall and dark and terribly good-looking. Alyce, as usual, determined to get him and, as usual, made a fool of herself. Bob's as silly as ever and the life of the party. There were a lot of petty squabbles and quarrels. Bob left his girl for Fanny and Al his for Ruth. But it was fun, and I think everyone had a good time. Rex and I hit it off perfectly. He's a good dancer and a good talker and not *slow*. We went for a ride and it was cold and he kisses nicely. We took Fanny in [back to town] and that was another nice long ride. Had a nice long talk with Gene and his girl. She was awfully sweet and refined and asked me to her house. Gene's nice, too. He's growing up. Bob has a new Ford Roadster. It's now 2 o'clock [a.m.] and I'm tired and happy.

Saturday, September 8

I slept nearly all day, but feel great. Letter from Mother today and Joe.

Sunday, September 9

Went to church this morning. Visited a poor family this afternoon. It was awfully pathetic and I'm awfully lucky not to be poor and I'm awfully glad to be alive. Had chicken for dinner. Good.

Monday, September 10
School today. Saw Fred Yarnell downtown. Also had a long talk with Maxine. She said she saw Jack H. last week and he looked hard.

Wednesday, September 12
Had another wild dream about Dr. Scott last night. I can't understand it. He seemed to need me terribly and I went to him and of all the hot kisses. It was all so real and the third one I've had about him lately. The last exactly a week ago.

Thursday, September 13
Worked hard at school. Feel rotten tonight. Side hurts and etc. If Dr. Scott were here, he'd make me feel better. S' funny thing. Whenever I feel awful, I wish and long and sigh for him. Exactly three months ago today his baby died.

Friday, September 14
School today. After school I came up to Fanny's. Had dinner and bummed around. Staying all night. S'nice world.

Saturday, September 15
Saw "Wings" today. A perfectly marvelous show. I cried all the way through. This eve. Gene and Dick Manning and Ruth came out. We had a good time, just bumming around. I like Gene. He's just the same and we hit it off fine. Bless his heart. Marjie fell for Dick—and *how*.

Sunday, September 16
Went to church this morning at Trinity [Episcopal Church]. Good service. This afternoon Alyce phoned and wanted me to come out, so I did. She's going to college Thursday. And has some of the most marvelous new

clothes. This eve Bob and Dana McCroskey came out. We played Bridge, went for a ride, came home and cooked waffles. Nice time. Nice boy. Nice world.

Monday, September 17

Didn't go to school today. Bummed around the house until noon. Then downtown where I contracted the wild, foolish impulse to go see Dr. Scott. So before I had time to reason with myself I got on a Monte Villa [*sic*] [street]car[195]. When I was almost there I changed my mind and decided to look up his house instead, and see what his wife looks like. So I walked and I walked and I walked, miles and miles looking for the damn thing, and at last I found it. The most adorable little yellow and green bungalow, with a nice green lawn and window boxes and shrubbery. Just the type of house I'd like to live in with him. I finally gathered nerve enough to ring the doorbell. Then I waited, with palpitating heart, but no one came. So I peeked in the windows and feasted my eyes on the dining room table that he ate at.

Then I started to leave. I looked back and saw that the washing was on the line in the backyard, and a long gangly suit of men's under-wear was there. I had a sudden terrible impulse to kiss his under-wear, so started back. Then I realized that the lady next door was in her back yard and I had to give an excuse for wandering around people's lawns. So I asked if Marjorie Smith lived there and if not, why not. She said no, the doctor and his wife lived there and they weren't at home. Then she went on to tell me of all the Smiths in the neighborhood. But I didn't listen because I was staring at a little pair of bloomers and a little girl's dress and a little girl's under skirt that were hanging on the line.

Somehow or other I escaped and fairly ran down the street. I cried then, cried like a baby, and didn't care who saw me. It was too awful. That he should have a little girl about six. It put him so far away. Made him seem so hopelessly alien. Oh, it isn't fair! Why does it have to be. I love

195 The Montavilla neighborhood is northeast of Mt. Tabor. Shortened from "Mount Tabor Village"

him so. I'm sure now that I do, and she's probably little and curly-headed and calls him Daddy and he's been married for just ages probably and oh! Gee whiz—my feet ache and my head aches and my heart aches and I'm in love with a married man and am a perfect fool. But hell! Can I help it? I didn't know he was married when I fell in love with him. Why, oh, why didn't he tell me? And there I go trying to blame it on to him when it's all my fault for making something out of nothing.

Tuesday, September 18
Didn't do anything but study and think of Dr. Scott.

Wednesday, September 19
The folks went to a show this evening and I stayed home and studied. But I finished about eight and so phoned Rex, and asked him down. "Nothing venture, nothing earn [sic]." He was all excited and said he'd be right down. I barely had time to change my dress before he arrived. All wrapped up in a big overcoat. We built a fire and played Poker. Then we popped some pop-corn and sat on the floor in front of the fire and ate it and talked and were happy.

He's awfully intelligent and we discussed everything. Religion. Love. Prohibition. Politics. Morals. Will power. The Bible and Benjamin Franklin. It's fun to argue with him. He's going to be a lawyer so had an unfair advantage. But I kept up my end of the conversation all right. He said he likes the way I stuck to my point, whether it was right or not, and I said I stuck to it because it *was* right. Anyway, pretty soon the folks came and went upstairs and we realized it was 12:30. Then he got sentimental and oh la la. He's so big and strong and when he kisses me I feel all wobbly inside. I'd hate to be absolutely alone with him. I'm afraid I couldn't control myself. He's too domineering. Oh, gee whiz! And he whispers such nice sentimental things in my ear, and says, "Gee! Doris but you're sweet," and I melt absolutely. I've always had a reputation for being cold, but with him, never! He awakes [sic] all the hidden fire in my being. I don't know why his kisses should affect me that way. Because I'm not in love with him. But the fact remains that of all the boys that have ever kissed me, he is the first and only to really make me enjoy it, and want more and more and more. And then he put on his coat and I stood on the porch and leaned against the door and he strode over and kissed me so passionately and fiercely and then he was gone and here I am, living over the memory of that last kiss, and wondering, wondering—when the next one will be.

And I think I'm being something of a fool. This sounds like a silly little schoolgirl and I wish I hadn't written it. But it *is* the way I feel. Gee! You'd think I'd never been kissed before but, I haven't, not like *that* anyway.

Saturday, September 23
Went downtown. Got hair curled. Bummed around. Letter from Marjie and Daddy. Daddy says I can buy new rain coat if I wish. Nice.

Sunday, September 24
Fanny and Mrs. Taylor came out and took me home with them. (Large scrawling script) I'm sick of this paper. The lines are too small and it's hard to read and I'm not going to write on the lines anymore—

Monday, September 25
School and plenty of it.

Tuesday, September 26
A marvelous rainy day and I'm glad to be alive.

Friday, September 28[196]
Another week gone in the passage of life. And I'm still thinking and dreaming wild dreams of my doctor. Something has to happen. I'll either

---

196 Doris has misnumbered the dates of the past week.

suddenly hate him or suddenly be able to have him. This can't go on forever. I dreamed last night that he kissed me—and awoke full of the ecstasy and thrill of his lips against mine. I felt all day as if I had seen him and he had taken me in his arms and held me close.

Wednesday, October 3

Hell, I'm too damn lazy to write—having fun doing little bit of everything—write when I get new paper.

Thursday, October 4

At last! Some more paper—now I can write coherently and talk about my doctor. Oh, yes! He still occupies all of my thoughts, doggone it! *Something* ought to be done. I read his letters over last night and then proceeded to cry. It's really awful the way he affects me. And I couldn't help noticing the way he stressed the point of "if I couldn't be good, to be careful" and to "beware of inebriated lovers" and that "he admired me" and "that he wasn't especially happy"—all of which makes me believe more and more that he married because of the result of the aftermath of a drunken college party and he didn't love her—and maybe he likes me. But can't admit it. Damn! Of course that isn't it. I'm just a plain fool. And he doesn't know I exist.

Friday, October 5

On the Deficiency for French—worse luck. Had fun at school today. There's a cute new boarder, Coie Bernard. I like her. Show this evening. More or less bored tonight but glad to be alive. Wish I had a horse to ride.

Saturday, October 6

Fanny took an exam this morning and I was to meet her at 12 after the exam and go to a show with her. She flunked the exam, though, and had to take it over so she couldn't go to a show. I was mad, of course, so went alone. I was blue and down on the world when I got out, and of course my thoughts turned to Dr. Scott. It was only 3:30 so I decided to go see him. Yes! Really.

It was nearly 4:30 when I got there. No one was in the outer office and I didn't know what to do. Then a girl came out of Dr. Hunkel's office and I told her I wanted to see Dr. Scott and she told me to knock on his door. So I did! And then he was standing before me. "Well, well! Doris, how *are* you? I thought you'd left town or something. I haven't seen you for so long." Of course, that was just what I needed. So I sat down. As usual I unburdened my heart to him. Told him how discouraged I was with life in general and everything. He was so sympathetic and sweet and said so many nice things—how he admired me, and what a good sport I was and oh! I can't remember half of it.

Then I took a big breath and asked him how Mrs. Scott was. He looked kind of funny and said she was all right. Then he said, "You heard about our trouble last summer," and then I was all sympathy. And he told me all about it. I said, "You didn't tell me you were married" and he said, "Oh, yes! I did," and I said, "Oh, no! You didn't," and he looked kind of sheepish and said, "All right, then, I didn't."

And then *he* did some unburdening. Said he married his second year in college and that it had been a long stiff, grind to make both ends meet—and then, somehow or other, I manufactured a romance of my own and said I was tempted to get married and end all this boresomeness [*sic*]. Just to see what the effect would be. Then he *did* talk and said *not* to marry in haste and *especially* if he wasn't making his own money and I'd always regret it and etc. He said, "If I didn't think so much of you I wouldn't tell you this, Doris. But I'd hate to see you ruin your life, and etc." for just ages. And I said, "Well, if I don't marry now, I may never get another chance." And he looked at me and he said, "Doris! Let me tell you something—that's one thing *you'll* never have to hunt for—a husband. I'm not saying that to flatter you. I'm saying it because I mean it."

Besides, he said, "You don't love this boy, and someday you will meet the man you love and then you'll be in an awful fix. Take my advice and don't marry before you know your own mind. You're in a romantic mood now like I was, and marriage is a business proposition and etc." That married life wasn't any fun, and then I looked at my watch and it was 10 till six. And I was supposed to take a 5:30 train. He asked me when the next one left and I said six and he said I couldn't make that one and he said he'd take me down in his car. Oh, la! La!

I couldn't help thinking, while we were dashing along in the rain, what a scandal there would be if we had an accident. I said how I appreciated his taking me clear down there (to Oak Grove). And he said, "I'd be a fine friend if I couldn't do that for you." And I said, "I do feel as if you were a real friend, as if I can talk to you," and he said, "That's the way I want you to feel. I want you to come and see me often. You will, won't you?" And then we talked some more. We reached the station just in time and he patted my back and said goodby and "Come and see me," and then I was gone! And I feel so differently about him now. Before I've always felt so guilty about him, even thinking about him, but now—there isn't anything wrong. I feel as though I've gained a real, honest, trustworthy friend.

I think there's something beautiful about it. To have a man think as much of me as I'm sure he does, and to be able to talk to him about *everything* and not be self-conscious. To feel that if I ever am in any real serious trouble I can go to him. Oh, he's wonderful. I still love him, but not as I did—in a different way.

But he made me feel so awful about marriage. I never want to get married now. It sounds so drab and dreary. He said marriage was a contract between two people and after the first thrill wore off it was just a plain commonplace existence and to make it at all bearable you have to be madly in love with your wife or husband. Be willing to work for them and go through anything. And knowing myself as I do, I know I'll never love *any* man that much. Enough to give up everything and live with him the rest of my life. To feel that I was bound to him and had to cater to him all the time.

Men only want you for what they can get anyway. And after that is gone they can play around with other women and yet—you're always there, waiting for him to come back to. Damn it! I say it isn't fair. I wish I never had to get married. Life is becoming so darned complicated. There aren't any illusions left. It's all plain hard facts. Marriage—a *business* proposition. Instead of the uniting of two souls. Oh, it's awful. Isn't there anything left in life? That is pure and beautiful. Even religion is suffering. People all around are saying that there isn't a God, and now they say there isn't love. Oh, hell!

Sunday, October 7
Marjie came home today. Gee! It was wonderful to see her. I love her so darned much. It's wonderful to have a friend like her. In fact, it's a wonderful world. I've been so happy all day today—every time I think of Dr. Scott I have the nicest contented feeling way deep down in. I'm the luckiest girl in the world, to have a friend like him. Someone who I know I can turn to. I'd rather have him as a friend than all the hot-headed lovers in Portland. Than all the handsome, rushing, romantic, passionate lovers in the universe. I really mean that. No one will ever know how I value him now. I never felt that way about him before. But yesterday changed everything. I lost a fantastic idealized dream and gain something which money can never buy—a friend.

Monday, October 8
School today and that's about all.

Tuesday, October 9
Work, work and more work. But I'm happy just the same. Went to see Dr. Kiehle about my eyes. Then down to see Eddy about new glasses. He's cute and collegiate and I had fun.

Wednesday, October 10
Rather a long, drawn out day. Had coat fitted. Looks funny. Letter from Marjie. She's dashing around being made love to. Wish I were at college where I belong.

Thursday, October 11
Old Girl-New Girl party tonight. Wore cowboy outfit. Liked it. Had a good time but tired.

Friday, October 12
Bought a new hat today—$10—terribly good-looking[197]. Bought tie at Mathis' for Joe and Mr. Otis waited on us. He's cute and has a mustache and we had fun—what I mean. Miss Cooper put me on the Deficiency for Botany because I ~~didn't~~ forgot to hand part of my experiment in. I told Sister and she took me off. S'nice to be a privileged character. Helen came out tonight. Rather like her.

Saturday, October 13
Went downtown to take Rae's girl[198] to lunch and show. Wore my new hat and coat and felt like a million dollars. Crazy about my coat. It's so sophisticated and rich-looking. Bought new gloves. The girl was sweet and nice and we saw a good show. Then up to see Eddy. He was waiting for me and was so nice. Said he got so lonesome all alone and wished we'd come in oftener. Walked to the front door with me—Ah ha!

---

[197] Her $10 hat would cost $132 in 2012 dollars.
[198] Editor's note: The first appearance of my future grandmother, Ruth Crum. She and Rae married in October 1930.

This is Ruth Darlyn Crum from Montana in a photo she sent to Rae in 1928.

Sunday, October 14[199]

~~Went in to Alyce's for dinner today. She came home for the weekend. Then went to see the Paintons. I'm unbearably *home*sick tonight for the first time. I don't like the way things are. Alyce going away, and making new friends. Marjie going away and making new friends. Mother and family in Arizona. Rae in SF. Me here, adrift, bored, cursing all appendix that disrupt people's lives. I don't like it. I want to hang on to old associates. I don't want to grow up and drift away from all that I once held dear. Oh, for the good old days on Westover. Having the maid call me. Gulping down breakfast. Saying hello to Gene. Running for the street car. School. Gym. Happiness. Home at night, to dinner with Mother and Daddy and the boys. Studying and phoning to Alyce at intervals in the evening. Just happy=go=lucky. But now! Oh, hell! I didn't know how happy I was. Oh, to grasp that intangible something called time. That speeds on and on heedless of laughter and~~

---

199 Sometimes Doris changed her mind about her diary entries and crossed them out. They are still worth including, however.

~~tears. I can't stop it. I must be swept onward, whether I wish it or not. I can't stand still and drink in the wine of youth. Day by day I'm becoming older, more serious. Life is becoming more complicated. Before I realize it I'll marry and have children and won't be a schoolgirl, but a matron and then sometime I'll die, and others will take my place and there you are. That's life and I don't want to grow up. I want the folks to come back and live in my own house and go to school and be happy.~~

Later—I take it all back. I'm so darned glad to be alive and well! I'm lucky not to be dead and I'm sublimely happy and I'm going to spend my life doing good—being friends to people and being happy.

Monday, October 15
School naturally. Went to see Eddy and had fun. Wonderful letter from Marjie.

Tuesday, October 16
Same old thing. Got hair curled. Mr. Leon died last night.

Wednesday, October 17
S'funny life. Went to see Eddy and crawled out on the roof (Fanny and I), [and] had a gay old time. Then we wanted to get back into Eddy's office but the room was full of men. And so we crawled into another man's office and walked down the hall and back into Eddy's. Guess he thought we were magicians. Fanny has a case on him. More power to her. Life's fun.

Thursday, October 18
Mr. Dana gave a lecture at school today. *Très bien*—everyone liked it and him. He said that a man on the street car asked him who I was. He (M.A.S.C.) [*sic:* man on street car] said he couldn't keep his eyes off of me because I was so unconsciously pretty. Darn it. Sounds conceited to repeat

it. Just consider it unsaid. I'm all alone tonight and scared. Everything's creaking. I'm sure there's someone downstairs. I'd like to undress and go to bed but I'm scared to go to the bathroom. Silly. I know, but it's the truth. My imagination's too active for comfort. Creak! Crack! Knock! I'll go goofy pretty soon. Darn it! I'm a fool! It's getting late. Well, here goes—

Friday, October 19
On the Deficiency for French. But handed Sis a big line and she let me off. Fanny and I walked downtown and acted silly. A funny old Turk with turban and beard was wandering around. We followed him. Then he realized we were and tried to ditch us, but we wouldn't be ditched. Finally he dodged into a stage terminal and we to drink a Coca-Cola; while we were watching a cute man, he gave us the slip. Also went around and made a lot of beauty parlor appointments. Silly? Well, so is life. Marjie came home tonight. Love her so darned much.

Saturday, October 20
Went to the big game today. Oregon versus Washington. It was so thrilling downtown. The streets just packed and everyone so full of pep. We stood in three different lines before we got our tickets. But we finally got in. Oh! What a mob. The Stadium was simply packed. It was a perfect day. Blue skies and a mild sun with just enough coolness in the atmosphere to make you feel peppy. O played as they've never played before, 27-0. The first big game [Oregon has] won in three years. Gee, but it was a happy, hilarious crowd that left the stadium and stampeded down Washington Street. Oh, youth! Saw bunch of kids we knew.

This evening went to The Broadway—Gee, but we hated to come home. There was something electric in the air, and me, I felt ready for anything. But luckily (I guess) we were sped swiftly home away from temptation. But tonight was one time I regretted not living in town, where there is youth and fun and excitement. Especially with all the college kids in town.

Sunday, October 21

Felt rotten today. A year ago tonight my appendix broke. Cheerful thought! My whole life was changed. This time last year I crawled in my bed on Westover—I couldn't sleep because of a sharp gnawing pain in my side. The hours crept slowly on and the pain became worse. Finally at 4 o'clock I half stumbled into Mother's room and fainted. I woke and the pain was unbearable. From that time on I didn't eat or sleep. Those few weeks are still a horrible nightmare of misery and suffering. Finally the ambulance came and I was whisked up to a green-tiled surgery. A mask was placed over my face and I passed into oblivion. Four days I hovered between life and death. And through it all by my side remained a tall handsome intern, young, sympathetic and comforting. Then I got better and went to sunny Cal. And from there to Arizona, where the joy and thrill of life were once more in my possession. I rode and lived with the best of them in good old Arizona. For the first time I realized the joy of being able to live, and laugh, and love. The intense thrilling merely being alive. I love the heat, the desert, the moonlight and the plain, common people. But even in my joy, in the back of my mind, was always the gratitude, the thankfulness to the young intern. Come to me in my hour of need, and by his smiles and youth had lifted me from the black walls of death and made possible the hours of sunshine I was enjoying. And then—I came back to my Oregon. The green trees and blue rivers. I reveled in coolness and Oregon's autumn beauty. I went to see my young intern who in the intervening time had become a serious, hard-working doctor—and realized that he still was a friend. That he wasn't just a fantastic dream, but a realistic man who helped me when I was on my bed and was willing to help me now when I was on my feet. And thus, a whole year has passed. I am much older in wisdom and experience. I have lived in unbearable pain and unbearable joy in one short year. But I am glad it was so. I have emerged from it with an increased joy of life, with a deeper gratitude for the small favors in the world. I think differently than I did. Things have a different value and at the end of the year, that has been the crisis in my life. I wish to thank God or whoever was responsible for it, for bringing me through a hard mixed-up year of pain and pleasure, safely, surely and with only a few scars and many happy memories. Never again will I say, "Damn all appendix." Instead, "Bless Fate that it was made possible for me to see the finer deeper side of life and human nature. And for giving me a true and honest friend." It took a year to shake away the superfluous, egotistical fool I was becoming, and a year with many hard knocks. But I have emerged "a bigger, better man" and I can truthfully say, "I am glad my appendix broke."

Monday, October 22
Studied hard. (C.S.[200]) S'nice day.

Tuesday, October 23
Been a rotten day. Got bawled out in English to start it off, and it's been ruined ever since. Even though I did get five letters—Mother, Daddy, Joe, Jack, Alyce.

Friday, October 26
Fanny was coming home with me after school tonight. I was on the Deficiency and she was to meet me afterwards. But when I got out she wasn't to be found. Then commenced the grand rush, phoning everyplace she might be. Then running all over. I was to meet her at 3:30 but didn't find her until six. Then she had to come out on the train alone. We had evidently played tag all over town. School, O.W.[201], school [St. Helen's Hall], Journal Building[202], First and Alder, Journal Building, and finally Oak Grove. 'S'funny world.

We all went to a show this evening. I'm terribly, unutterably bored. But what's to be done?

---

[200] This is the first reference to C.S., which seems to be private notation about her period.
[201] OW: possibly Olds, Wortman and King department store.
[202] The Journal Building is at SW Broadway and Yamhill, now known as the Jackson Tower.

Saturday, October 27

Got up late and went downtown. Bought new stockings at Berg's where we encountered Mrs. Taylor hunting for a coat for Fanny. Fanny was snippy to her mother because she couldn't have a certain $200 coat she wanted[203]. She'll probably get it—that's the way with life! While I wear Mother's last-year's coat and consider myself lucky. Then we had a rotten lunch at the Heathman and saw a rotten show at The Broadway. Then up to see Eddy. He was nice and said the superintendent complained about our crawling on the roof. Fanny raved about Mel Smith all the time to him. Trying to sound hot. I don't think he fell for it. It got on my nerves so I came right out and said what a sick undernourished individual he was. Then we had a nice little row right there, and Eddy took my side. Then home. Everyone went out and I stayed home and studied. So far this has been a very unsuccessful weekend.

And I'm going to do something desperate if something doesn't happen. Marjie just came home with Bob. Of course, I just got undressed so I'm marooned to my room, which all tallies with the way things have been going lately. I try not to complain and keep reminding myself how lucky I am to even be here. But I can't be a little ray of sunshine all the time; damned if I can. Ha! ha! ha! downstairs. Am I the type to sit here and listen while they laugh and talk and eat? Damn it! Something's got to be done. This is a darned funny world and if it weren't for Dr. Scott I'd say I got a rotten deal.

Sunday, October 28

Marjie and I slept till 11—then bummed around. About 4:30 Bob came to take her home. He's a terrible sap, and I'm not the least bit jealous. Also, if they're all like that, I'm not sorry I'm not at college. And she seemed to think he was the best, just about, and I'd rather stay home and be slightly bored and have to go to college and be made love to by his type. So it isn't such a bad world after all. In fact, I'm rather happy tonight. Fanny called. She got her $200 coat. I knew she would. She's just a spoilt baby enough to.

---

203 That $200 coat wasn't cheap. In 2012 dollars, it's a $2649.28 coat.

But I shouldn't worry. I'm me and I'm proud of it. I'd rather be me and not have $200 coats then be Fanny and have $1,000 coats. The fact is I like me better than I do Fanny. So that's that.

Monday, October 29

Happy today. Why? I'm alive. Fanny brought some butter scotch candy to school and we passed it around in Botany. Everyone got their teeth stuck together. I, of course, was sent out of the room until I could get my teeth unstuck. After school Fanny and I wandered downtown. Saw Billy Bader. He looked cute. Went to the Hazelwood and had the soda jerker fixed up two strong Coca-Colas[204]. Then we had a race to see who could drink it the fastest. It burned all the way down, of course. Then we got another. 'N then some more candy. Consequently, we felt woozy. But I managed to eat dinner. Tha's all. Guess I'll turn in. Nice rainy day. My poor tummy!

The Hazelwood Cream Store

---

[204] When one ordered a Coca-Cola at the soda fountain, the soda jerk (clerk) would pump a few pumps of cola syrup into a glass and then add soda water. The drink could be made stronger or weaker to taste, and other flavors added (like cherry, lemon or chocolate).

Tuesday, October 30

Nice day—flirted on the street car with a cute man. S'nice life. Saw a man today who I know I could fall in love with. He was evidently just in off of a ranch. He had on a big sombrero and his face was bronzed by the sun. It had that same tint that all the cowboys I've ever seen have. Clear, healthful, and vibrating with life. His eyes were a clear, steady gray. He held his head so erect and he was tall, and broad-shouldered and strong-looking. Of course he didn't even *glance* at me. But I'd like to know him. I could go to the ends of the world for that kind of a man. I've been wondering just what my type is—and now I know. One of these big outdoor he-men—with tan face and piercing eyes.

Wednesday, October 31

Halloween Day. Cider and pumpkin pie for dinner. Feel like hell tonight. Head ache.

Thursday, November 1

Going to Monmouth[205] for the weekend. It's home-coming. Big football game and dance.

Friday, November 2

One grand rush getting off today. Skipped school and got a 3 o'clock bus and rode for three hours in Oregon's autumn twilight. Alyce met me and we dashed over to her dorm and went to a pep rally. Then to bed.

Saturday, November 3

Got up early this morning and ran hither and thither meeting people. Met one girl I liked especially well. Also met a gang of men. The football game was perfect. Then this evening a date with See Barnum (Barnum

---

205 The college Alyce attended, Oregon Normal School in Monmouth, is now Western Oregon State University. The "Normal School" was the teachers' college.

and Bailey's Circus)[206]. Terribly good-looking. We went for a long, wet ride in the rain. Then stopped and the usual thing happened. He was rather hard to control—but could have been worse. I liked the boy Alyce was with, and I think he liked me. He knew Joe and had heard of me. Went to Grant [High School]. The seats were so close together that we could hold each other's hands in the darkness without See or Alyce knowing it. And every time See would kiss me he'd squeeze my hand and I'd get a bigger thrill out of that than See's kisses. Then we came home and sat in front of the fire and talked. S'nice life.

Sunday, November 4

A perfectly beautiful day. Alyce and I donned old clothes and went for a hike. Tramped down a muddy road and through the damp fragrant woods. Happy and carefree. Then we emerged (damn! this pen) from the woods onto the most gorgeous sight imaginable. Oh, this blessed Oregon of ours. There will never be another like it. There were fields and fields of gently rolling hills, all colored in a rich autumnal brown. And here and there a farmhouse nestled among the maple trees. Never before have I seen the trees with such dazzling bursts of color—red and gold and orange. All shrieking defiance to each other. We tramped across the farmer's freshly plowed fields, jumped ditches, climbed fences, and chased cows. We came upon an old barn perched on a hilltop and filled with hay. We wanted to play in it but it stuck in our clothes. So we undressed. Took off every doggone thing and jumped and rolled and turned somersaults and laughed till we were sick. The hay scratched our backs and legs. But did we care? We did not! We were young once more and still willing to do and get a kick out of the unconventional thing. Oh, it's great to be alive.

After dinner we met the boys (Kenny and Eddie), went over in the Gym and monkeyed around. Then went to get something to eat. Then all decided to drive to Salem. It's against [college] rules to go driving in a car with a boy, so we sneaked around. Met them on a side street and sat on the floor of the car until we were out of town. Went to a show in Salem and

---

206 Possibly C. Barnum or Seeley Barnum; see Appendix II.

missed my bus. The boys had to dig up money for another ticket which broke them. We all got terribly well acquainted and I like Kenny. He's so darned much like Micky a pang goes through me every time I look at him.

I finally reached Rupert[207] at midnight. Penniless, alone and scared to death of that long black road (a good pen at last!) but I gripped my suitcase. Thought of Dr. Scott and went—n' here I am. Sleepy. Tired as hell but happy.

Monday, November 5

I could hardly drag myself around today. I was so doggone sleepy. Going to bed now.

Tuesday, November 6

Went to Dr. Baird's today and he tried his best to kill me. Then to see Eddy. We talked and talked, about golf courses and people. I like him.

Wednesday, November 7

Fanny and I bummed around after school. Had fun.

Thursday, November 8

I went flooey today at school and nearly fainted. Got a lot of sympathy. Everybody's nice to me. Letter from Joe and Marjie. Daddy deposited $40[208] for me. Hot dawg. The wind's howling outside and I love Dr. Scott.

---

207 Rupert Drive, where the bus let her off, is about a mile distant from the Danas' house on River Forest Road (now SE Dana Avenue).
208 That's $529 for her allowance in 2012 dollars.

Friday, November 9

Marvelous rainy day. Went to see Eddy and he was *oh,* so nice. Marjie came home. Love her so darned much.

Saturday, November 10

Went downtown this morning. Marjie and I bummed around. Went to the Bohemian[209] for lunch and then met Mrs. Dana and went to the horse show[210]. Oh! How I love horses. I could hardly stand it when those beautiful creatures pranced around the ring. Marvelous specimens of horseflesh with gracefully curved necks, slenderly tapering legs and lean narrow faces. Aristocracy from the tips of their ears to the tips of their hooves. About half way through we went "back stage," that is, back of the gate where the horses come in off of the track and we were close enough to touch. Back where they were in their stalls, one beautiful creature was being curried and combed when a lot of yelling commenced in the ring.

In an instant he changed from a gentle domestic animal munching hay to an animal of the wild. All his instincts were aroused. He quivered in every muscle. His eyes dilated and he pranced and stamped and snorted like a demon. He was so beautiful, I could have cried. Oh, for a horse like that! A blue blood. A king of kings. Then we had dinner and went to a show. Really a wonderful show.

Sunday, November 11

Bill Hanley[211] came out for dinner. He has a wonderful character and is a true philosopher.

---

209 The Bohemian Restaurant was at 384 Washington Street (now SW Washington).
210 A large horse show took place in November 1928 at the Pacific International Livestock Exposition center in north Portland. This is probably the one to which she went.
211 William D. Hanley, an Oregon rancher who owned the O-O ranch where Marjie and Doris stayed in summer 1926, was good friends with Marshall Dana.

Monday, November 12 Armistice Day

Got up late. Went over to Alyce's for dinner. She says that See's been asking about me and that Eddie just raved about me. Says he wished he'd met me long years ago. Bob and Dana came over. Went to see Lorraine who is sick. Came home. Folks went out. Dreamed in front of the fire all evening. Am bored and lonesome for Dr. Scott. Wish I could see him. He's so hellishly sweet. Gee whiz! But he means a lot to me.

Tuesday, November 13

Found my pen at last. Got our report cards today. I was disappointed. I expected too much I guess. All Bs. I'm terribly dumn. Been thinking of Micky. Wish I wouldn't.

Wednesday, November 14

Nothing s'much happened.

Thursday, November 15

Had a tea at school today and I had to serve coffee. Changed my clothes after school in Coie's room. I like Coie awfully well. She's sweet and, if I board, I'd like to room with her. It was fun—[to run] around being polite to be-furred and be-jeweled women. Afterward I came home with Fanny to stay all night. Bummed around. Popped pop-corn. Listened to the radio and talked. Glad I'm alive.

Friday, November 16

On the Deficiency. But Sis let me off. Ahem! I rate! Saw Darrel downtown. Oh, yes! Rode downtown with Dr. Palmer this morning. He's fast as hell. Letter from Alyce. Happy!

Saturday, November 17
Went to Corvallis to see the game today. OSC versus U of O. A marvelous game. Oregon won 13 to 0. Every time I get near a college it makes me mad that I'm not there. Damn it! Sat in the box with the president of the college. Marjie took some dumn girl along. Stopped on the way back and ate at McMinnville[212]. Good dinner. Love Marjie desperately.

Sunday, November 18
Bummed around the house. Love Marjie.

Monday, November 19
Dumn day.

Tuesday, November 20
Nothing ever happens. I'm blue and down on the world tonight. I hate to get that kind of mood. But they come anyway. Whether or no. I think it's about time I went to see Dr. Scott again.

Tuesday, November 20
Bored and sleepy.

Wednesday, November 21
Mediocre day, but I'm glad I'm alive. Letter from Marjie. Gee, got a scrumptious letter from Ned. Gee, but I'd be happy if they finally decided on each other and settle down in a "Bungalow Built for Two."[213] They are so perfectly suited for each other.

---

212 About 30 miles from Oak Grove
213 From the camp song, "Let's Build a Bungalow Big Enough for Two."

Thursday, November 22

Oh, hum! I'm sleepy. Fritze walked down from the [street]car line with me tonight. A whole mile, through the fog. I hadn't seen him for ages 'n he was nice. He's coming down and bring Marvin tomorrow night. Fanny's coming out.

Friday, November 23

Gee, what a night! The folks went out and we got all dressed and waited and waited. About 8:30 Fritze phoned and said he couldn't get Marvin. But I told him to come anyway. So he did. Looked adorable, by the way. He was nice to me so Fanny went upstairs to write a letter and we had a nice little party by ourselves in front of the fire. He got more than I could handle, though, so I called Fanny back. Then we popped pop-corn and sat in front of the fire, and drank grape juice and ate cake and told stories. N' I was all cuddled up in his arms, which was also nice. Pretty soon the folks came home. They gabbed for a while and then went to bed. Then the fun began! We were all three sitting on the couch and Fritze insisted on kissing me [in front of] Fanny. Of course, that made Fanny feel like a third number so I said, "Kiss Fanny, too. Fritze, I'll let you." And he did! But that's not the half of it. He had me in his arms and Fanny was on my lap. First he'd kissed her and then me and then her. He didn't make any bones about it. He was frankly enjoying himself. Talk about fun! It was so dumn it was funny. We all laughed and laughed. Then they began to maul me around and we had a good rip-roaring fight. All of us tangled up like a bunch of kids. I really enjoyed myself immensely. We got along so well and I had the last kiss so everything was hunky dory. But damn it. Every time I think of old Fritze going from me and then Fanny it strikes me funny. He was right in his element all right. And tomorrow we're going to Eugene to the game. Hot Damn! S'darn nice life.

Saturday, November 24

It's even a nicer life than I thought. We got all dressed and ready to go to the game this morning. Then we waited and waited and waited about 9:15 Phil called and said it was too foggy. We weren't going. Mad! Oh, boy!

So we decided to go to luncheon and a show downtown. We did. Had a rotten lunch and a rotten show and went to see Eddy. We talked to him about a half an hour and Gee whiz! But he's getting nice. Fanny has a terrible case on him and the line she hands him is enough to sink a battle ship. Then we went to the Hazelwood. Then Fanny went home and then I boarded a Montavilla car and went to see Dr. Scott. Doggone it! But that man means a lot to me. More than I like to admit. At the last minute when I get up to his door I always have cold feet and begin to think, "Oh, he doesn't want to see me." But the minute I see him, the look on his face always changes that thought.

Oh, gee whiz, golly, gosh but I'm lucky. He said he was getting ready to write me a letter and find out what was wrong. He hadn't heard from me for so long, and he'd thought of me so *much.* (Oh, my *heart.*) Then we had a nice long talk and I told him what a friend he'd been and that I wanted him to count me as one of his friends. And he said he would and did. And he said he was awfully particular about choosing his friends, that there weren't many people he really cared to have as a friend and he, for some reason, liked me the first time he ever saw me. He said, "You know, it's a funny thing, when someone is awfully sick their real nature comes to light, and you could see what they are really like." And he said he got a glimpse of the real me that first day and have liked me ever since. Oh, *gosh!* And pretty soon I simply had to go and he got up and said he'd take me downtown. He said I came to see him so seldom that he could at least take me downtown.

On the way down I politely inquired about Mrs. Scott. He never brings her up himself. I always have to. Anyway he said she had an operation for appendicitis about two weeks ago and by an odd coincidence had the same room I had, number 520. I asked him if he told her I had it and he said, "No, she might have been jealous. But I thought of you every time I went in. She doesn't know about you." And he looked right at me and oh!

I didn't think I could stand it. I wanted to cuddle up to him and have him kiss me again and again and again. But of course I didn't. I merely folded my collar up and said, "I'd like to meet her some time. What is she like?" And he told me: very dark and short. That's all he would say. He has an annoying habit of avoiding discussing her. Just before I left he said, "Now I don't want you to go this long again without letting me hear from you. If you can't come over, why, write or phoned me. Because I really want to keep track of you. And whenever you want anything, no matter how small or how big it is, remember I always want to help you and will." Oh, he's *such* a darling.

Sunday, November 25
We went to the country today. Had a regular old-fashion[ed] dinner in a big farmhouse. Then went hunting with a little wart[214] about 13 years and he killed two birds. It was fun. Climbing over logs and getting knee deep in mud. Then they gave us a big live turkey for Thanksgiving and we brought it home in the car. So glad I'm alive.

Monday, November 26
School—more or less dumn. Nice rainy day. Feel hellish. Love my doctor desperately. Letter from Mother and Daddy. Thass all.

Tuesday, November 27
Gave a debate at school. Rather good, I think. Everyone said so. The hell of it was it was the first time I'd ever debated and I didn't have a rebuttal. So had to forfeit the debate. Oh, well! S'all in a life time.

Dr. Scott—Dr. Scott—Dr. Scott. That's all I can think of. I tried to study. I think I am studying and I find myself writing his name all over the blotter. Gee whiz! But it's awful. If he were only here. Maybe it's lucky he isn't. Oh, how I'd like to be in his arms. Oh, gosh! But it's misery to even

---

214 brat

think about. What's the matter with me anyway? Oh, damn! This time last year I could see him every day. I can see him now. The way he opened the door. The way he sat on the bed. The way he'd hold my hand. I saw him *every day* and didn't even get a thrill out of it. Now I see him once every two months and only for a short while, and can't even touch him. Have to sit primly in a chair while he sits at his desk. And oh, gosh, I almost wish this were last time last year and I were in the hospital. I could stand the pain and horror of death—if only because I could be able to see him every day and talk to him and have him hold my hand. Oh—

I don't think I'll go to see him anymore. It leaves me too restless. The last time I came away feeling contented. But this time his friendship apparently wasn't enough. I want *him*. Him and only him. I mean *he*. It seems as though there was something lacking in this last visit. Maybe he feels the same way I do. But how do I feel? I don't know. Three weeks ago I was happy in the thought of a newfound friend. Now—well, what is wrong now? That's what I'd like to know. I don't know my own mind. Yes, I do, too. I want him here, by my side, close, closer, closest—and he's married, and is probably kissing his wife now. Oh, damn.

Wednesday, November 28
School—naturally. Marjie appeared seventh period. Gee, but I was glad to see her. And proud of her, too! Then we walked downtown and then came home. Fritze was on the street car. Marjie thought he looked cute!

Thursday, November 29 "Thanks Giving Day"
The end of a perfect Thanksgiving! I had such a lot to be thankful for today. It couldn't be anything but happy. My life! My health. My friends and my Oregon. Marjie and I took a walk in the woods this morning, and I couldn't help contrasting this Thanksgiving with last. Then I was on a narrow, high bed in a drab room, absolutely helpless. Couldn't turn over on my side without being lifted. Death all around me. Death in my heart. I tried to choke down the turkey Mother had sent me, but I couldn't

even do that. And now, now I was trudging down a fern-covered path. Climbing over logs. Hatless, strong, alive. I came back to a big dinner. A typical ~~dinner~~ Thanksgiving dinner with all the trimmings. We had a big crowd—16—little, big, old, and young. I ate and ate and ate and kept repeating a silent prayer: "Oh, I'm glad, glad, glad to be alive."

The New Heathman Hotel, next door to the Portland Theatre and across from the Broadway, was convenient for afternoon and evening outings.

Friday, November 30

Marjie and I went downtown today. Had lunch at the Heathman and then went to the Portland. Then bummed around. I ordered my Christmas cards. Cost five dollars, but they are worth it[215]. Gee, it costs a lot to live.

---

[215] They must have been specially printed or engraved; the cost today would be $65.

Marjie and I were going to a dance tonight. But Marjie decided she didn't want to go so we canceled our dates. Then I wanted to stay downtown and have dinner but she didn't want to do that. Then I phoned Alyce but she wasn't home. So I accepted the inevitable and came home. I thought perhaps Marjie and I could have some fun just being together. I phoned Alyce again when I got home and she was mad that I had[n't] come over. Said she could have gotten Kenny and Bob and had some fun. Well! The long and short of it is that See phoned and wanted Marjie to go out with him and she did. And here I sit. If I were a few years younger I would cry. Why should I have to sit at home? Damn it—next time I'll follow my own impulse. Whether someone else likes it or not. Oh, I want excitement. I crave it. And I—who crave it—never get it. Oh, gosh damn it!

I wonder if life does hold anything in store for me. Anything wonderful and breath-taking. Other girls get it. Why shouldn't I? Am I so drab, and plain, and ugly? Isn't there anything about me that anyone likes? Nothing. Oh, surely there must be someone in this world who will love me for myself? There must be, some place. And still, there may not be. I may go through my life without meeting anyone who loves me. It wouldn't be so unusual. After all—what is there about me that would attract anyone? I'm not so much for looks. I'm not so very clever. I haven't much money. I've got a funny side. I'm not in perfect physical condition. I'm rather egotistical and I hate myself. And if I hate myself, is it so unusual that people aren't in love with me? No! Of course not—so I guess I'll just have to make the best of a bad bargain and go wipe the dishes for Mrs. Dana.

Saturday, December 1

Met Alyce down[town]. We were going to go to a show but decided not to. We met Bob and Stewart and they wanted us to go to the OAC dance at Multnomah Club[216]. I didn't have a dress with me so Alyce and I boarded a street car and went clear home. When we got there every doggoned door was locked. I didn't know *what* to do. I didn't want to go back without it after having come clear out. I got a ladder, took off my coat and dress,

---

216 An exclusive, private social and athletic club in Portland, founded in 1891

and tried to climb up to my window. But I couldn't quite make it. I was desperate by that time and so I took a rock and broke the window pane in the kitchen door, reached my hand through, turned the key and came in. Alyce swept up the glass while I threw my clothes into my grip.[217] I left a note telling why I broke it and I'd pay for it, and we dashed away. Got a lift from a funny old man in a 1912 Ford. After many giggles we arrived at Alyce's house. Ate dinner, dressed, and the boys came. I wore my hair behind my ears and wore earrings. It looked sophisticated and I liked it. Had a marvelous time at the dance. Jack Freidel was there. Also a whole bunch of others. We left the dance about 12 [midnight] and went to the "Cottage"[218] to eat. A bunch of cute people there. Some girls from S. H. H. included. Two perfectly adorable six-foot[-tall] football men were drunk. They managed to keep the crowd amused by sitting down in the middle of the floor and taking off their shoes, then loosing [*sic*] their garters, and dumping lump sugar into their pockets. Then we went for a ride. Stewart was one of those heavy neckers and I had a rather hard time. In fact, before the ride was over, I was thoroughly disgusted with him. I *hate* to be pawed over. It's absolutely nauseating. We reached home at 2:30 and a good time was had by all. It was worth a broken window pane but I'm beginning to be leery of going home tomorrow. I'll probably get hell personified.

Sunday, December 2

Did I get *Hell!* And then some. I'm not going to write it down because I'll never forget it anyway. I'll merely say it was *awful* and I want my mama! I feel so lost and alone. I'm lonesome and homesick and I'm a damn fool and everybody hates me and nobody loves me and I've bawled and bawled and the more I write the more I cry—so I better quit.

---

217 overnight bag

218 "The Cottage" was likely the Gray Cottage Tea Room on the third floor at 362 ½ Alder.

Monday, December 3

I can't stand this. Things will never be the same again. Oh, why! Oh, why! Did I break that window? I wonder if anyone in the world really likes me. I'm an alien—an out-cast. An impulsive fool. I hate myself and the things I do.

Tuesday, December 4

Oh, what a wonderful world! What a wonderful life! What a wonderful thing is friendship. Yes! I went to see him. I always do when I'm in the dumps. And he puts new life into me. He gives me a different perspective on everything. He's divine. There will never be another like him. Today began worse than yesterday, and I was ready to jump in the river. I couldn't figure life out and I knew I couldn't go on staying here feeling as I did. And then I thought perhaps Dr. Scott could help me. So I went to him and told him everything. Oh! What a relief to get it off of my chest and be able to talk to someone about it. And he was his usual sympathetic self and talked to me and I wanted to cry in his arms. But of course I didn't. He told me wonderful things about soldiers who had been reprimanded by a superior officer and the way they reacted. I really can't put into words just what he did say. All I know is that when I left him my problem wasn't a problem at all, and everything was all right. And the sun shone once more and people looked friendly and life was a song. He took me to the [street] car line as per usual and just as we were leaving his office we were both standing by the door and he turned out his lights and we were shoulder to shoulder and I said something about going back to Arizona and he said, "You're just blue now, Doris. And a sweet little girl like you shouldn't be blue. You'll get over it." And he looked right into my eyes and that simple little phrase, said the way he said it, made my heart [thud thud thud?] All over the place. Then as we were going down the steps he took my elbow and we walked down arms touching, faces barely an inch apart, and the contact was almost more than I could stand. Oh, damn his wife.

Wednesday, December 5

Went to Dr. Baird's today. He darn near killed me and every time it would hurt especially much[219], I'd close my eyes and think of what Dr. Scott said about soldiers. And I'd pretend he was beside me. And I have a good imagination. Dr. Baird seemed to divine my thoughts because he said, "All the young doctors that were there when you were have left the hospital. Have you seen any of them?" And I said, "Yes, I saw one the other day. He has an office in Montavilla." And he said, "Which one was that?" And I said, "Dr. Scott." And he said, "Ah ha! So he's keeping an eye on you, is he?" And just that slight mention of his name was enough to make my pulse quicken—Oh, life!

Thursday, December 6

School—a cold, icy day and oh! I'm glad I'm alive.

Friday, December 7

Rather dumn day.

Saturday, December 8

Was going to have my pictures taken today, but Mrs. Dana wanted me to serve at a luncheon. So I did. Mrs. Hoge said she didn't recognize me. I had grown so much better looking. Considering the way I looked, that's not much of a compliment for the way I used to look.

Sunday, December 9

Feel—like—hell.

---

219 Dr. Baird is most likely palpitating Doris's abdomen where she had her surgery; she has "lumps" under her skin which could be scar tissue or pockets of infection. Probably terribly painful.

Monday, December 10
Got the Flu.

Tuesday, December 11
Sick—

Wednesday, December 12
Still sick.

Thursday, December 13
I'm wasting a whole week in bed.

Friday, December 14
Got up today and bummed around the house. Addressed my Christmas cards, 36 of them. They're good-looking. Daddy sent me only $20[220]. I wrote for more. Letter from Johnny.

Saturday, December 15
Went Christmas shopping today. Also had pictures taken. There was such a Christmasy spirit in the air and the streets simply packed. Saw Dr. Kiehle. He's an old darling.

Sunday, December 16
Felt blue all day today. Took a long walk in the woods to see if that would help me. I guess it's just because Christmas is coming and I'm not at home.

---

[220] That's $265 for spending money in 2012 dollars.

Monday, December 17

School and more work. Rae came today and I met him at the Seward Hotel[221]. It was so darned nice to see him. We got my picture proofs and I ordered the pictures.

Doris Louise Bailey, circa 1928.

Tuesday, December 18

Met Rae after school and bought some Christmas presents. Then home.

Wednesday, December 19

Fun at school. Walked downtown with Fanny and two other girls. Saw Fritze after I left them and we talked a long time. He said he could get a car towards the end of the week and we'd go for a ride—umm. Then I met Alyce. Dear little Alyce. And we did some Christmas shopping. Then

---

221 Now known as the Governor Hotel, at 611 SW 10th Avenue.

I went home and changed my clothes and we went to the Mathis[es]' for dinner. Then I went to Alyce's and stayed all night. Alyce is *all right*.

Thursday, December 20

Alyce and I did some Christmas shopping. Then we met Rae and went to a show. Saw Herb Perry in the lobby. He's so cynical and thrilling-looking. Talked to him a long time. He said he was going to come and see me. Hope he does—it would be exciting.

Then Rae drove me home. This evening Fritze phoned and wanted to come down. So I said he could. The folks stayed downstairs so we played Poker a while. Then they dispersed. We sat on the couch and talked. It was so cozy and nice for the fire. But every once in a while Mrs. Dana would appear, which wasn't so good. She finally came down to stay, and Fritze left in desperation. I really didn't mind her coming because he doesn't mean anything to me. In fact, it was funny, the way he acted, and she, too. As if we had been doing something we shouldn't. I felt as if I were away from myself and watching a comedy of three very foolish people. Everything in this world is so very foolish. Anyway, the next time I have a date with Fritze, we are not staying home! Poor boy! He looked so puzzled.

Friday, December 21

Went to the Crums' for dinner[222]. They have a perfectly gorgeous house. Winding stair case and marvelous chest[s?] all over. Oh, it's thrilling. Then Rae and Ruth and I went to Marjorie Cram's[223] for a while. Then home. Marjie came home today.

---

[222] Luther R. Bailey's business partner was Portland attorney Virgil Crum. The Crums' niece, Ruth Crum, from Montana, came to stay with Virgil and his wife, Beulah, in 1928. The Baileys and Crums had lived on the same street, The Alameda, until the Baileys moved up to Westover; the Crum house at 1252 The Alameda (4438 NE Alameda) is where Rae and Ruth were married in 1930.

[223] The Crams lived near the Crums. Marjorie Cram was Ruth Crum's best friend.

**Ruth Crum and Rae Bailey, at the Crums' house on
The Alameda. This is probably their engagement photo.**

Saturday, December 22

Shopped nearly all day. Met Alyce and we shopped together. Saw a lot of people we knew. Went in to Mathis'[s] to buy Alyce's brother a tie. A funny girl started to wait on us, and I asked Mr. Mathis to get us a nice man—and he did! Alyce wanted me to go home with her, so I did. It looks as though nothing was going to happen, so we went to a show. We were bored so took one of the Christmas decorations off of the tree in the lobby when no one was looking and stuck it under my coat. It was all very foolish and plenty of fun. Adventure is where you find it. Dr. Scott got my Christmas greeting today. Wonder what he thought.

Sunday, December 23

Got up at daybreak, dashed home, changed my clothes and went to Uncle Herman's[224] for dinner. Plenty of good food. Then Marjie and that cute little boy and I went hunting. And shot a robin. And I wanted to cry over it.

Monday, December 24

Downtown all day. Doing last minute Christmas shopping. Met Fritze on the way home and he took one of my pictures. Card from Johnny. Going to meet him downtown Thursday. Christmas Eve and excitement reigns supreme.

Tuesday, December 25 Christmas Day

My first Christmas away from home has come and gone. We got up at daybreak and filed downstairs. The lights were lit on the tree and a fire in the fireplace. Mr. Dana played Santa Claus and called out the presents. Lotsa nice things. Bracelets, earrings, turquoise ring, pajamas, stationery, Shriner pin[225] and crystals. Rae and I went to the Davidsons'[226] for dinner. Then we went calling here, there and everywhere. Marjie says Fritze called while I was gone.

Wednesday, December 26

Bummed around the house.

Thursday, December 27

Met Johnny downtown. We had lunch at the Heathman and discussed his love affairs. I patched up a quarrel between Alyce and he. We had it all arranged that he and Ed were to come out and get me in Ed's Packard

---

224 Friend or relative of the Danas
225 Luther Bailey was a member of the Shriners.
226 Family friends

and then go to Alyce's and supposedly surprise her and go someplace. I left him and went to Lorraine's for a Bridge luncheon. Alyce was there and I told her, and she said she had a date that she couldn't break. Which left me with two men. So I came home and asked Marjie to fill in. She refused point blank. So I had to call Johnny and tell him everything was all off. He was so disappointed and downhearted. I felt mean and I was blue, too. Johnny's adorable and sweet. I like him. And the other boy might have been cute. Damn, I feel like bawling. I also lost one of my new earrings which doesn't help matters in the least. And I'm mad at Marjie. To think that she couldn't do that for me. She says she loves me and etc. but when it comes right down to doing something not because she wants to but because it will make me happy—does she? No.

Dr. Scott is the only one for me. He's interested in the things I do and [in] me. He wants to help me. He's the most unselfish, self-sacrificing and sympathetic man I know. He's a friend in the true sense of the word and I'm glad, glad, glad I know him. I'm glad people like him exist. It strengthens my faith in humanity. But I am disappointed in Marjie. It's a hell of a life.

Friday, December 28

Met Rae for luncheon. Then we met Alyce and looked at dresses and shoes. Found an adorable dress and bought it. Then it seems there was some mix-up with Daddy's account[227]. I went up and talked to the credit man, who was, by the way, the lowest, vilest, most insulting specimen of humanity that I have ever met. I lost my temper and he lost his, and we had words. If I ever meet him in a dark corner, I'll kill him. I know I will. I stalked out and got Rae. Rae went up alone and said the man said I came up with "fire in my eyes, ready to fight." Anyway I won't know until tomorrow whether I get the dress or not. But I do know that I hate credit men. Rae took Alyce and me to dinner. Then gave us money and sent us to a show. Alyce was blue because she hadn't heard from Johnny. And I

---

227 Another indication about the Baileys' finances

was blue on general principles. So we had a fine time. I met the Danas afterward and we went home, and that's that.

Oh, I forgot! Had a divine dream about A. D. Scott last night.

Saturday, December 29

Didn't get my dress! Damn, double damn. Went to a luncheon at Fanny's and was guest of honor. Really had a marvelous time and plenty of good food. Then she took us all to the Duffy players[228], which was marvelous, then home. Dreamed about Dr. Scott again last night.

Sunday, December 30

Bummed around house. Went for a walk in the woods.

Monday, December 31, 1928 New Year's Eve

Downtown and show with Fanny. Luncheon with Rae. Plenty of fun. I'm so full of thoughts tonight. To me, the beginning of a new year and the passing of an old is a sad and yet happy time. My mind is so full. I don't even wish to write. So I'll think and plan and hope and resolve to do and be better things. But I simply can't put it into words; it cheapens it somehow. For once, words actually fail me. My thoughts go beyond material things. Perhaps tomorrow I won't be in such an uplifted state and will be able to write. But until then—

---

228 Best guess is the comedy team of Duffy and Sweeney, performing in vaudeville shows around the country

Oregon
(1929)

A chapter of my life in which I absolutely refuse to be the least bit interested in any man. No matter what his recommendations are. Rich or poor, fat or thin, handsome or otherwise. Their [*sic*] all alike and I'm going to leave them alone.

The world looks like a multiplication table or a mathematical equation, which, turn it how you will, balances itself. Take what figure you will—its exact value, nor more nor less, still returns to you. —Emerson[229]

---

229 Ralph Waldo Emerson's *Essay on Manners, Self-Reliance, Compensation, Nature & Friendship*, 1923.

Tuesday, January 1, 1929

Another year in the passage of time. I always feel as if I am on the brink of something new and wonderful. The year stretches forth for hope and adventure. As I look back, this time last year, and think of all that has happened during the year that I never dreamed could happen to me and realize that just as many new things are bound to happen this year. Well! There's some cause for excitement. Last New Year's day—California, Arizona, Mexican race tracks, desert, Grand Canyon, Mac, Jimmy, Irvin, Claradell—just *weren't*. They didn't even exist. If someone had told me that during the following year I would own a race horse or be bucked off a bronc or sit on the edge of Grand Canyon and be kissed in the moonlight by an Arizona cowboy, I would've said, "That sort of thing doesn't happen to me." And yet—it did happen. Why, then, shouldn't this year be just as full of romance and surprises? It could and it will! Mrs. Dana gave a dinner party tonight. Marjie and I served, between giggles. Plenty of fun.

Wednesday, January 2

Bummed around house and studied. Bored.

Thursday, January 3

Met Fanny downtown. We wrote a letter in the Heathman and the place was simply mobbed with good-looking men. And flirt! Oh, boy. Two of them followed us out. But we ditched them. Went to the Portland, then Dr. Baird. Then up to see Eddy. But he wasn't there. Fanny gave me a beautiful mesh bag that she didn't want. And I found my pearl earring. Everything considered, it's a rather nice world.

Friday, January 4

Bummed around the house all day.

Saturday, January 5

Marjie and I went downtown. Saw Eddy. Went to show. Ate lunch and looked for dress and shoes for myself. If Daddy would send me some cash I might do something besides look. Found an adorable pair of shoes, only $7.50[230]. Been thinking of Dr. Scott all day. If I had some new clothes, I'd go see him. Such is life!

Letter from home and Elizabeth Painton and Alyce and Joe. I rate—like [heck?].

Sunday, January 6

Took Marjie back to school. We stopped at a gas station in Milwaukie and Rex was there, talking to a boy. He didn't see us but I saw him! And my heart did some foolish flip-flops. He always affects me strangely. I know I'm not or ever could be in love with him, and yet, he's so big and handsome. The kind you'd like to have a tempestuous affair with. Fritze phoned tonight. Wanted to know why I never stayed home. Said whenever he had a car and phoned I "wasn't in." S' Fate. We talked for about 30 minutes. Nice kid but I'd rather have Rex.

Monday, January 7

Felt like H— all day. Studied and cleaned out my desk.

Tuesday, January 8

School today. It was hard getting back into the old grind. Nice to see everyone again, though. Fanny and I bummed around after school. We had fun. We usually do. S' nice life.

Funny man to dinner tonight. Everything he would say would strike me funny—I had an awful time to keep from laughing in his face. A sense of humor isn't always the best thing in the world.

---

[230] This is comparable to $99 in 2012 dollars.

Wednesday, January 9

Life becomes more complicated every day. I had intended boarding at St. Helen's Hall after the first of February and now I wonder if I'm doing the right thing. It cost[s] a heck of a lot. And I don't know whether I'll even like it or not. I won't have any freedom. I'll probably be bored. Perhaps I should go back to Arizona and help Daddy. Quit being a drag to him and be of some use[231]. Oh, I wish I knew what to do. I want to do the best thing. In the meantime, I wish I'd get some money. I have 60 cents[232] to my name!

Thursday, January 10

By careful manipulation, I still have my 60 cents. Rode out on the street car with Fritze. He was all for a date but for some reason he bores me. I'm lonesome for my doctor. Yet I won't go to see him until the 26th, [or until] the 2nd of February if I can wait that long. Here's to see how much will power I have.

Friday, January 11

I'm so darned tired tonight. I'm ready to drop. Studied like hell all day. Letter from Daddy. Still have only 30 cents. Daddy says he may have to have [an] operation for appendicitis. That would be awful.

Saturday, January 12

Daddy sent me $60. Whoopee! Spent $10 of it for new shoes already. Went to a show with Fanny. Also luncheon. Then met Mrs. Dana, had dinner at the Heathman and went to The Broadway. Good show. Then home. Happy tonight. Why shouldn't I be?

---

[231] She is starting to pay attention to economics.
[232] Her pocket change would buy $7.95 of streetcar rides in 2012.

Sunday, January 13
Studied like Heqq [*sic*] all day.

Monday, January 14
Studied.

Tuesday, January 15
Took my shoes to Zinke's[233] and the cutest dog and boy waited on me.

Wednesday, January 16
To Zinke's again and my same boy. What's the matter with me anyway?
Just a school girl's fancy, I guess.

Later—Guess what? and who? and why? Oh, gosh, Gee whiz. Jack
Hibbard just phoned me. Say it again and again and yet again—Whoopee!
I just looked back in my diary and it's been exactly three years and a month
and four days that I last saw him. And we have a date for Friday night.
And if he still anything like he was—HOT DAMN.

Thursday, January 17
Got my shoes at Zinke's, and my same boy again, and he was nicer than
before. And I love his eyes. And when I left, he said, "Come again, Doris."
But I'm disillusioned. He said, "it don't" three different times. If I can find
a man that 1) knows how to wear his clothes, 2) is athletic, 3) has a sense
of humor, and 4) speaks correct English, I'm going to grab him quickly.
But the hell of it is, those four virtues never appear in the same man.

---

233 Zinke's Shoe Corp., at 354 Washington Street at Park.

Friday, January 18

Well! I went over to Alyce's after school and ate dinner and got all dressed up. Jack and the rest were to arrive at 8:30. About 8:15 it started to snow, and a regular blizzard held sway. Consequently they didn't get there until 10. We were going to go to "Berg's Patio."[234] But it was snowing and blowing so that we couldn't drive. So after riding around aimlessly for two hours we came home. I made some vile coffee that no one could drink. Then Evaline played [piano] and Jack and I danced. Everything had been so muddled and confused that I hadn't time to realize I was actually with him, *until we danced.*

Then all the old fire returned. There's something about him. Perhaps it comes under as common a heading as sex appeal[235]! But whatever it is, it's there. And I don't want to talk or even tried to be intelligent. I just want to be in his arms and feel them tighten around me, and dance, cheek to cheek. Vulgar? Well, maybe. Perhaps he learned it in the Navy. He's so damned good-looking and tall and slender and has just loads of "it." And 12:30 [a.m.]—1:00—and 1:30 came and still he hadn't kissed me. And about 2 [a. m.] They started to leave. And I was getting desperate. And then they went out, and he stayed back, and the door closed.

And THEN we were alone for the first time that evening. And he took me in his arms and pressed his lips against mine, and I simply melted. After all the agony of waiting, it was worth it. He's so big and he['s so] mannish. And oh, that kiss. It's lucky the kids were in the car and the folks upstairs. I might not still be what I am today[236]. It seemed hours that we stood there, wrapped in each other's arms. Unconscious of reality. And then honk! honk! honk! outside—and one last glorious moment—and then he was gone! And I won't see him again for a whole year. Three years ago I said goodby to him the same way. Now tonight and I suppose next year it will be the same. Just a glimpse of him, a few words, a kiss, and he'll be

---

234 Berg's Patio was presumably a small café on the premises of Berg's Department Store.

235 "Sex appeal" came into popular usage in the early 1920s from advertising.

236 A virgin

gone again. Oh, if he could only be here in Portland always. But perhaps it's just as well he isn't, considering the way he affects me.

Saturday, January 19

Met Fanny downtown. We had luncheon and went to a show. The streets were covered with ice and snow. And it was fun. A couple of weeks ago we wrote Roy Reigles, the football captain [who] made a goal for the opposite team[237] a letter of sympathy. We wrote it on Heathman Hotel stationery and signed fictitious names. Today we got the nicest answer from him. Saw Billy Bader downtown.

Sunday, January 20

Studied all day.

Monday, January 21

School! Fanny and I bummed around afterwards. I've decided that— (phone rang and I forgot what I started to say.)

Tuesday, January 22

Nothing much. Saw Fritze on street car. Wanted a date. Tired.

Wednesday, January 23

Dreamed that Dr. Scott died last night. Oh! But it was an awful dream. Lots of studying to do tonight. They've been trying to get me to board at school. Sister got me in a corner and did her damnedest. It's a wonderful feeling, to know that they like me. I hope I can keep their respect.

---

[237] See Doris's Jan. 1, 1929 entry. Roy "Wrong Way" Riegels played football for the University of California, Berkeley; his wrong-way run to a touchdown in the 1929 Rose Bowl is cited as "the worst blunder in the history of college football."

Thursday, January 24

The world was enshrouded in a blanket of snow this morning. Car wouldn't start and I was an hour late to school. We had half-day vacation and I met Fanny downtown about 12:30. We ate lunch and went to a rotten show. Then, not having anything better to do, we went to see Eddy. In the course of the conversation, it developed that he had a gallon of pure gin behind his screen[238], and he gave us some. And boy! Was it good! Then a man came in and we wanted some more but couldn't take it while he was there. Fanny hit upon the bright idea of asking for "water." So we trotted back and drank "water," like heck. Then we felt devilish and went to a second-class hotel and the vilest man stood outside of his door and flirted. Oh! We had fun! Fanny's a real sport. Frankie Davenport rode out on the street car with me. I don't like him. He's low.

Friday, January 25

Went to the Consecration of Bishop Jenkins this morning. A beautiful, awe-inspiring service. Then to school, where I studied like hell for a few hours. Then up to Fanny's for dinner. We talked till doomsday. Fun.

Saturday, January 26

Went to see Eddy and he was all cuteness. Then to Zinke's. That boy is so damned cute. His name is Mr. Olson. He was nice today, to—and I was all het up. Then some darn woman appeared and said, "I'll see you tonight," and he said, "All right, little girl!" So that's that! I don't rate! Gee, I wish he'd say, "All right, little girl" to me. I'd fall in his arms. He was rather brusque with her and said, "Why don't you comb your hair?" But that just shows how intimate they are. Yes, I'm frankly jealous. 'S what I get for falling in love like a 15-year-old schoolgirl. I'm never going there again.

The Danas went to Salem and I expected them back by dinnertime. It is now 10:45. I'm terribly worried. Sleepy, too, and yet I hate to go to bed

---

238 In his examination room

before they come. What to do! Walls [Wallace?] phoned and wanted me to raise Whoopee with him tonight, but I declined. He's too old.

Sunday, January 27
Studied and slept. Just like most Sundays. Also ate. Final English exam tomorrow. Not so good.

Monday, January 28, and final exam today.
The thermometer was down to 16 degrees and the snow [is] inches deep. I was darn near frozen by the time I reached school. I left a package at Zinke's, and went to call for it today. There was the usual amount of banter and then the other boy stepped up and said, "If it was silk stockings, he probably kept one for *his wife*!" Go ahead and laugh! It has ceased to even be funny. You think I'd get a break sometime. But no. It's funny. There are so few men that I really do ever like. And yet, if I even should happen to find one to my liking, he's either married or going to be, or has been. It's no better than I deserve. But why! Oh, why! Doesn't the man that destiny meant for me appear? I'm tired of waiting and watching and hoping and wondering. But then—life is like that!

Tuesday, January 29
French exam this morning. I think I barely made it, by the sweat of my brow. Went to Fanny's for luncheon. We studied Botany and then took a walk. Started to walk down the hill then Freddy, our old grocery boy, appeared, and he said he'd ride us down. So we clambered in and went rattling all over Westover in a Ford delivery wagon. He stayed too long in one place, so I slid over into the driver's seat and we drove up and down and all around. Everyone we passed stared and stared and stared some more. When we thought we had punished him enough we went back. Nice kid. Then home to cram for Botany exam tomorrow. Snow a foot deep. Cold—brrr.

Wednesday, January 30

I think I flunked my exam this morning. Zowie. But it was stiff! After the exam, Fanny and I went to The Broadway. Sat in the front row and flirted with Georgie Stoll and had fun. Then we went up to Mardy's[239] to play some records. A bunch of cute boys in the booth next to ours. Finally the cutest one came into our room and brazenly asked our names and etc. We tried to high-hat[240] him but he refused to be high-hatted. As it turned out, he knew Joe and everyone else I knew. Boy, but he had nerve. We acted blasé and bored and disgusted, and finally walked out on him. But just the same, it was fun and I'm glad it happened. If I were a boy I'd be like that—and get a kick out of life.

As it is, I'm merely bored and can do nothing about it. Doggone it! But I wish something exciting would happen. Really thrilling and different, I mean. Not just rides with grocery boys and flirtations with brazen men. And tiny drinks of synthetic gin. But something big and stupendous. A love affair with a wild, dynamic man. Overpowering. A man of the world who has seen lots and knows lots, or a wild, wild party with liquor galore, a real honest to goodness brawl. The fact is, I'd like to misbehave. Give the old town something to talk about. I'd like to get absolutely pie-eyed. But—hell! Fat chance of ever doing it!

Thursday, January 31

Fanny came home with me after school, and after dinner, we put on our pants and riding boots, took our sled and went up to Oak Grove Hill. No one there but Oscar so we decided to walk to Milwaukie. We parked our sled. Put our hands in our pockets and walked 5 miles with the snow and sleet in our faces. It was cold and blowing and thrilling. When we got there, there were icicles on our hats and our jackets were like sheets of

---

239 A shop called Marty Music Store at 332 12th Street, run by Mrs. Fanny Marty, is listed under "Music Dealers" in the Portland City Directory in 1928. Presumably this was an early-era record store. Mr. Carl Marty was a music teacher at the same address.

240 See Glossary, Appendix I

ice. We went into a barbecue place, took off our boots, sat on the counter and stuck our feet towards the fire (there was no one there). Then we went out and danced our way homeward. Met Jack Waldron and he wanted us to go to a marshmallow roast at Concord. But it was 12 o'clock, and we were proud; a riffraff bunch was going. So we came home. And that's all. A good time was had by all.

Friday, February 1
Downtown. Bought records[241]. Long talk with Eddy.

Saturday, February 2
Damn it! I'm bored to death and I'm not going to write again until something worth writing about happens.

Saturday, February 17[242]
Well, enough has happened. My whole plan of life has been changed, and all because of the two people I love most in the world. Marjie and Dr. Scott. Oh! What a lot I owe to them. To go back, last week, I went to McMinnville to see Marjie. Saturday night we went out with Bob and Charlie. I don't know what was wrong with me that night. But I talked awful. Wild and etc. It was only natural that they should take the wrong impression, and when Charlie and I were alone, on the footbridge, in the moonlight, and he overstepped his bounds, I let him get away with more than he should. It was the way of least resistance. Then after I came home I got a letter from Marjie. The most wonderful letter of love. But also the

---

241 This is the first time she mentions buying records. Previously she has mentioned buying sheet music or singing popular songs.
242 Should be Sunday; she misnames the dates for a week here.

most terrible letter of cruel, hard facts. Charlie had told Bob and Bob had told Marjie, and said I wasn't the kind of girl for her.[243]

Imagine it! Oh! How that hurt, and especially since it was true. Of course, I didn't really do anything. But I had given the impression that I would, which was just as bad. Oh! I hated myself. And the most marvelous part was that Marjie still believed in me and loved me and stuck by me, and told them it wasn't true. Oh! I didn't deserve it! Of course, the outcome was to make me resolve to live up to her and be good clear through. Always and always. No more cheap necking or drinking. Then Thursday she came home and we talked it all over and she was so wonderful. All that was enough to make any girl a saint. But then to top it all I went to see Dr. Scott today—that man of mans [*sic*]. King of kings.[244] Oh, was there ever a man so fine and straight, so clear thinking and intelligent and downright divine? He's perfect. I got there at four. He was cool at first, said it had been so long since I'd come and that maybe I didn't want to come. But I assured him that I did. And we were on the old friendly basis again. I told him all I'd been doing and he, all he'd been doing.

Then somehow we got on the subject of life and marriage and morals. And I poured out my soul as I usually do. And then he gave me the most marvelous talk. I can't reproduce it now. We didn't seem to talk in words; it was our souls that talked. All I can remember is sitting there, looking into his eyes, which his self shines through [*sic*] and losing myself in paradise. I've never seen such eyes as his—great amber pools that contain multitudes of goodness. They are so frank and clear and full of the wonderful light of pureness. Oh, how can I explain it? His eyes seem to be his personality, that he turns on at will. I've seen him before when his eyes are like anyone else's. But today, when he was trying to convince me of the necessity of self-respect and etc., he didn't do it by mere words. He put his very being into his eyes. He let me see into his soul and thereby did more than a dictionary of words. He was so earnest, so engrossed in his topic, that I

---

243 An interesting glimpse of dating in the 1920s: The boy pushes Doris further than she intended to go, and then blames her for allowing it, as well as shaming her to their friends. She accepts all the blame and responsibility for this interaction.

244 Doris is literally comparing Dr. Scott to Jesus here.

became lost, too. He carried me on. He made me see things in a different light. And the one thing that I do remember is his faith in me. He seems to think he knows me through and through. ~~And he said that he knew, he *knew* that I would never do anything risqué.~~

He said if I looked at him and told him that I never had erred that he would believe me as he would himself. And for a minute we stared into each other's eyes and I said I hadn't (because I haven't) and he looked into my eyes and believe me, and said he would always believe me. That no one could ever shake his faith in me and that he knew I would never do anything risqué, that I was too fine fundamentally. And the way he said it! Why, now the devil and all his followers couldn't tempt me. To have the faith of a man like he is, to have someone believe in you as he does me. I wouldn't anymore think of being cheap and searching for a thrill then I would of murdering a man. It's become unheard of. I've always been between two fires. But now I'm on the safe, sunny side and away from the tawdry murkiness of evil. He told me startling things of people, especially women, that did go the wrong way. But it wasn't the disgusting, vile facts but his beautiful faith in me that helped.

He took me downtown at 5:30. We got there at quarter of six and he had a quarter of six appointment, so I started to get out, saying as I did that I hated to. He reached over and slammed the door and said to heck with his appointment. I was more important, and talked 'til my [street] car came. And in those 15 minutes my Fate was cinched. And I'll never, never, never be anything but a lady again. I couldn't if I tried. And even if I never see him again, his eyes and the faith in them will always be before me, and help me lead a straight, clean life. Oh! But I'm lucky. To have two friends as staunch and true and unfaltering. I don't deserve them but I'm going to do all in my power to be worthy of them.

Sunday, February 18 [*sic*]

Alyce appeared out of nowhere this morning and got me out of bed and we drove in to her house. [Brother] Joe was to arrive from Arizona and we had a big yummy dinner for him. But he didn't arrive. So we bummed around, went over to Lorraine's, met her man, and finally Herb and Blackie got us. Brought me home and went back to Monmouth. Blackie is a dear, and I told him about Marjie and me being married.[245] Anyway, here I am, and in spite of all the Alyces and Lorraines and Joes and Blackies, all I can think of is two gray-brown-flecked amber pools with all of the wisdom of life and love and sincerity looking out of them.

Monday, February 19 [*sic*]
School seemed unbearable today. Everyone got on my nerves, including Fanny S. We had a big row—whoops. Also I went in to get my shoes at Zinke's, and just because I didn't have my slip he said I couldn't have my shoes, and I got mad and told him it was crazy to drag a silly little slip around with me and I could go someplace else after this. Then he got all gooey and squishy and when I didn't thaw out, he said, "What's happened to that big smile you always carry around with you?" And I said, "I haven't seen any occasion to use it," and grabbed my slip and stalked out. Tomorrow I'm going to march in, bang my 40-cent[246] damn slip on the counter and march out and he'll never have any business from me again. Damn. But I hate that man!

Tuesday, February 20 [*sic*]
Joe came out to dinner tonight. It was so nice to see him and hear all about the family and etc. Fritze phoned tonight, and we had a nice long talk. He said that Blackie wanted a date with me—interesting if true. He also said other things. I won't repeat them, but it made me feel nice. He wanted to raise Whoopee but I had to study. Life is like that.

---

245 As in "best friends forever"
246 That's a $5.30 shoe repair job, quite comparable to 2012.

Wednesday, February 20 [date correct here]
Worked like hell. Saw Rex today but he didn't see me, and my heart beat like [in] a movie. I wonder why he affects me that way?

Thursday, February 21
I've studied steadily since morning. Yes, I'm tired. Bishop Sumner came to school. Talked to him. He's nice. Fritze phoned again tonight. I liked the way he talked. As if he were endowed with a little sense. Ms. Hawk read my essay in class, and gave me A plus. 'S nice.

Friday, February 22
I was never so doggone tired in all my life. Too much burning of the midnight oil. I'm going to bed. Fritze called again tonight. It's becoming interesting.

Saturday, February 23
Met Ruth Crum downtown. Ate at "The Sign of the Rose"[247] and saw a good show at Broadway. Fritze phoned but we were eating so had to cut him off short. Hope he isn't mad. Like him better than I did.

Sunday, February 24
Studied from morn till night.

---

[247] A tea shop in Portland on the eighth floor of the Woodlark Building, at 813 SW Alder St.

Monday, February 25

Spring is here! In all its glory—warm, caressing Spring. I'm happy to be alive. Joe is sailing for Germany tomorrow[248]. Some people have all the luck. But I guess he deserves it. Life hasn't been so nice to him as it might have been.

Tuesday, February 26

Saw Rex from across the street again today. I love the way he slouches along. But that's all the good it does me. Damn!

Wednesday, February 27

My Chem[istry] essay gets sent to Salem[249]. Nice! I've decided on my life's career. I'm going to *write*. Fritze phoned tonight. The folks had gone to a show. I had a peck of work to do but he wanted to come down. Begged and begged. Said he'd only stay 45 minutes but had to see me. So I let him. He started his usual stuff as soon as he got here. But I stopped it pronto. Let him know I didn't go in for that anymore. That made him all the worse. He couldn't let me alone. Kept pawing me. Disgusting. I'd hoped he might be different if I was. But he wasn't. No more of him! He really likes me, I think. Just my luck to get the ones I don't want. I kept thinking, now if he were Rex, my will power wouldn't be nearly as strong. I wonder if I affect him the way Rex does me. Oh, why can't I have the ones I want??

Thursday, February 28

Bought a new hat. Tired and feel like heck personified.

---

248 Joe Bailey, who was partially deaf from birth and struggled in school with his hearing as a child, nevertheless became a journalist and English teacher and traveled the world; he was an ambulance driver in World War 2. However, he did not go on this scheduled trip. Some kind of health problem kept him in Portland.
249 Her essay was sent to the state capital to compete for honors.

Friday, March 1

Came home from school with Flu. Raging headache. Saw Rex again. Wish I wouldn't. But was glad I had on new hat.

Saturday, March 2

Played the invalid all day today. Letter from home.

Sunday, March 3

Earl Wells and Evaline and Bud Perkins came out and we went for a drive in the country. The way Evaline acted with Bud made me wish even more to be a lady. It was disgusting and I showed her up. Marjie and Dr. Scott would have been proud of me. It was a beautiful spring day and we found the prettiest little stream and got our shoes all muddy.

Saturday, March 9

I haven't written for a week. Been busy studying. Marjie came home. We went downtown and had a perfect time. I bought a new spring coat, tailored and good-looking. Mother sent me five dollars for my birthday, so we rambled on First Street in pawnshops and bought some weird-looking second-hand rings. It was fun. Then we ate dinner at the Heathman and met the folks and then to a show. Life is fun and I'm broke.

Sunday, March 10

Had my birthday dinner today. Fried chicken and a delectable angel food cake. Marjie gave me some new earrings; Joe, a book, and Mrs. Dana had framed for me a perfect picture of Arizona desert. Life is a game and I'm going to play it. I've decided to be a bachelor lady and follow roads to romance, over the hills and far away. Beautiful spring day.

Doris on her way to a party, circa 1929.

Monday, March 11—C.S. [Doris's birthday]
Today I am nineteen years old. Nineteen and such a short time ago I was 16. I'm grown up—presumably. Fanny gave me a little bottle of violet toilet water[250], and Mother sent me some more doodads.

Tuesday, March 12
Joe had an operation on his nose this morning. I went up to see Dr. Kiehle after school to see how he came out. I don't like the way he acts. He's too,

---

[250] Perfume

well, personal in both actions and speech. And I can't say anything. He's worse than Fritze ever was. Old men are funny.[251]

Wednesday, March 13

Went up to see Joe after school. Cute intern and, of course, it brought back a combination of pleasant and painful memories. Oh! My Dr. Scott! Day by day he becomes more real and more a priceless treasure. He's beyond this earth. Oh, gosh.

Thursday, March 14

Took my coat down to be lengthened but it couldn't be. So now I'm without a new coat. Fanny and I had fun downtown. Saw Fritze on street car. He blushed and stammered and tried to high-hat me. It was all so silly. He thinks he's teaching me a lesson and that I won't rebuff him next time. That's where little Fritze gets fooled. If he only knew how glad I was to be rid of him.

Friday, March 15

Met Fanny. We went to luncheon at the Heathman. Had George Olsen play some request numbers on the pipe organ. Nice. Then to The Broadway to see Colleen Moore,[252] after which we looked at shoes and had fun with the shoe clerk who, in turn, had fun with us. Then home. Marjie and Leita were here. Mrs. Dana went out and we played with the radio and were happy. It's been a perfect day. In other words, I've enjoyed myself.

---

[251] Doris experiences the flipside of her infatuation with a doctor in Dr. Kiehle's unwanted advances. She feels unable to speak up or protest, and rationalizes his actions to herself.

[252] Colleen Moore was a prolific silent film star; they could have seen any of half a dozen of her films in 1929.

Saturday, March 16

We got up at six and drove Leita to the station, wearing our coats over pajamas. Then we came back, piled into bed and slept till 10. Spent the day bumming around the house. I do love Marjie. We decided that since only one life has been given us, we're going to live. We're going to Wallowa Lake this summer if possible, and after we finish college we're going to roam. Oh, it's going to be divine. Obstacles simply don't exist for us. We want to do it—therefore we're *going* to do it. And we're not going to marry until we've filled our fill with adventure.

Sunday, March 17

Marjie and I took the car and went for a long drive. Wrote letters to Crater Lake and Wallowa concerning jobs for this summer. Oh! I hope we get one.

Monday, March 18

Marjie and I saw "The Iron Mask"[253] this afternoon. Tha's all.

Tuesday, March 19

I feel like philosophizing tonight—but have too much studying. 'S Fate!

Wednesday, March 20

Fritze phoned tonight. I think he was pie-eyed. Oh! He's vile. Also Jack Waldron. They are both scums and, compared to my doctor, are mere worms.

---

[253] This was Douglas Fairbanks' final silent film.

Thursday, March 21

Rainy day. I love it. I love the whole darn world, in fact. I love life and youth and humanity. But most of all, I love Marjie. I forgot my car-fare this morning and when the conductor appeared—lo! No money. I said, "What do you do in a case like that?" And he smiled (he's a nice old man) and offered to loan me money to return on at night. Who says the whole world hasn't a heart of gold? I don't!

Friday, March 22

Met Alyce downtown after school. She bores me lately. Don't know why. Almost had a fight with Fanny but she averted it. These girls! It makes me appreciate Marjie thrice doubly. What would I do without her?

Saturday, March 23

Met Ruth downtown. She also bores me. I wonder what's wrong with me? I'll be bored with myself before long. And that would never do. Because I could never leave myself. Saw a good show.

Sunday, March 24

Just a nice, lazy day. Marjie went back to school. Gee, but I'm going to miss her. It'll be just plain hell after having her.

Monday, March 25

A nice stormy day. $40 from home—bought shoes[254]. Tired. Sleepy but happy.

---

[254] Nice shoes: Doris received the equivalent of $530.

Tuesday, March 26

This morning while I was waiting for the [street]car at Milwaukie[255], I saw Rex from across the street. He went into the Service Station[256] (not glancing my way) and I proudly turned my back and gazed out over the river. Then the train hove into sight just as he walked out of the station to get in a waiting automobile. And our eyes met—and held—but neither of us smiled. I turned my head first, but Fate turned it back just as he was driving off. And he had his head turned clear around—and our eyes locked again. That was all. But it was enough to turn my insides into a foolish turmoil. I wonder what the morrow will bring forth?

Wednesday, March 27

Drove to school in car. Didn't see Rex. Damn.

Thursday, March 28

Drove again. Damn! That's all off.

Friday, March 29 (Good Friday)

Met Fanny downtown. Joe took us to luncheon at the Heathman. Then I bought a new coat and Joe bought me an exquisite scarf. Nice! The coat isn't all paid for so I haven't gotten it yet. Saw a good show at The Broadway.

Saturday, March 30

Wired my mother a corsage for Easter. Went to see Dr. Baird and the following conversation ensued:

He—"Ah, that young doctor that was at the hospital, what was his name?"

---

255 About three miles from the Dana home in Oak Grove
256 The gas station across the street from the train station

Me—(with palpitating heart) "Oh, you mean Dr. Scott."

He—"Yes—he's a nice young fellow. He was asking about you the other day."

Me—"He was?"

He—"Yes—he wanted to know if I ever saw you. I said, I did, occasionally, and he said, he did, occasionally!"

A pause—and I, in an effort to continue the conversation, "Do you think he's a good doctor, Dr. Baird?"

"I think he's going to be a good doctor. He's intelligent and he has a good education."

But the point is, he's asking about me, and thinking about me already again. And I was just there.—Oh, he's divine.

March 31 Easter Sunday

Went to church this morning. The altar was beautiful. The church always bores me. I like Stewart McGuire[257], the baritone [who] sings in the choir. He's sad and melancholy and thrilling looking. The type that women sell their souls for. Deep set eyes, narrow face, and a grim mouth. His wife committed suicide because he was untrue to her. I wonder if he is as sad as he looks. I wonder if he loved her. It wouldn't be hard to love him. I'm going to church oftener.

Joe came out to dinner and we went for a walk in the woods this afternoon. Beautiful day. But I'm bored as hell.

-THE CLOSE OF MARCH-

---

[257] Stewart McGuire, much sought-after baritone, appears in Oregon newspaper items as early as 1905, singing at Pioneer Day events, churches, college graduations, and more. He was the grandson of an 1857 pioneer, and a dentist by trade. His wife, Corinne, appears in both the 1920 and 1930 censuses, so it's unlikely that she had killed herself, as Doris speculates.

Monday, April 1
Same old grind. I just looked back to see what I did last April 1 and I had looked back then to see what I did the year before. I wonder why. Last year I was in Cali. The year before I had a party on Westover, and Micky was there. Wonder where I will be next year. I'm going to notice. Micky, Micky, Micky, and still I haven't forgotten him. I've lived on less than no hopes, and yet—there shall always be a "maybe." He will always be "a might have been." I wonder if I'll still feel this way next year. Time will tell.

Saturday, April 6
Went up to school. Got Coie. Met Fanny and we three had lunch. A good lunch at the Heathman. Then to a good show. Then bummed around. Coie came home with me for dinner. She's a darling! I'm simply crazy about her. So sweet and pretty and we have so much in common. I feel as though I've really added a new friend to my list. I'm happy.

Sunday, April 7
Studied. Tired.

Monday, April 8
I'm so damned sick of the same old grind.

Tuesday, April 9
Same. I like Coie, and Dr. Scott is all-important today. I can't stop thinking about him.

    C.S. yest[erday].

Saturday, April 13
Fanny and I had a big row over the phone. It seems she thinks that I got her in bad at school because Sister asked [her] a question and I answered. Now

she thinks it's my place to lie her out of it. I'll be damned if I will. I went to school this evening 5:30. Met [illegible] at Oak Grove and he took me to Milwaukie in a nice new Ford. Wore my new coat. Julia was going to orate at Oregon City for the district championship. So I went with the boarders to hear it. We all piled in a big bus and rode through the night. Sang and had fun. Julia won, bless her heart. The only girl competing against five boys for the Honor of the school. The girls simply went wild with joy. Then we came back and I slept with Julia and Coie. Only we didn't sleep.

Sunday, April 14
Stayed at school until 11. Then home. Leonard and Mildred came by. Leonard is good-looking but Mildred's SOL[258]. I have a feeling that they won't be happy.

Wednesday, April 17
Had a heck of a sore throat so went to see Dr. Kiehle. He acted terrible, but I can't do anything about it. I suppose it is just a fatherly attitude—and yet—the fact remains that if any boy ever acted like he does I'd tell him where to head in. But I can't tell him. I just can't.

Thursday, April 18
Same old grind.

Friday, April 19
Bought material for new dress.

---

[258] While the vulgar expression "shit out of luck" was around in the 1920s, Doris's middle-class version was more likely "sure out of luck."

Saturday, April 20

Oh! My gosh! Another red letter day in my life. And I love him. I know I do. I took an exam this morning, then to a show with Ruth, and then—to see my darling, oh, so darling Dr. Scott. I went in and he smiled and took my hands and looked down at me and said, "How's my little girl?" And then we sat down and he looks so damned sweet and glad to see me. And I told him I'd been good since I'd been there. And he said he was glad. He said he'd worried because I hadn't come. Afraid that I didn't like him because of the lecture he gave me last time. He also said that he received a call late one night and chased all over in the country in the rain, frantic, afraid that I was in trouble. I told him about Dr. Kiehle, too, and he got mad and his eyes snapped and he said for me not to go and see him anymore; that some doctors were that way but that it was awful.

And I said, "You wouldn't act like that, would you?" And he blushed and looked embarrassed and looked into my eyes and said, "You wouldn't like it, would you?" And I wanted to scream, "Yes, yes, yes, I'd love it." But instead I said no, I wouldn't come anymore. Damn fool me. And he said, "That settles it. I won't."

Then we talked about various things and before I realized it, it was 10 minutes of six. And he said he'd drive me home, clear home. And I said no, he couldn't do that. And he said, "Why not?" I allowed these other doctors privileges. I could give him this little one. And what could I say? So we went downstairs and he had the prettiest new blue Essex and was so boyishly proud of it. Bless his heart.

And he saying what a privilege it was for me to let him drive me home. We were talking about my coming over so seldom and I said, "You know you wouldn't like it if I came every week. Be truthful." And he looked at me and said, "Yes, I would like it." And I said, "But you'd be bored, and it wouldn't be half so interesting." And he said, "Oh, so that's why you come—for a variety. I'm a break in the monotony." And I said, "No, I come because I like you." And then we were talking about my never having flirted with him, or tried to "get him" and I said, "I wonder what would happen if I did."

And he said, "You'd better not try. There is no telling where it would end." And then he said, "Why haven't you ever tried? Is it because you don't want to break up a happy home, or don't I thrill you like another boy would? Is it just that I seem like an old man to you?" (Now why should he say that if he didn't want me to encourage him? He did, I know now. But at the time I didn't. If I had only said, you are married and so I couldn't let myself take that attitude and then he would have said "Pretend I'm not married.") But I was a fool. And merely said, "No, it's just that you haven't had the chance to be thrilling." And he said, "You'd better not give it to me; you might discover that I'm dynamite under control." And again if I had only said, "All right, I don't believe it, and I'll give you a chance." Then he would have kissed me. I could kick myself, to let a chance like that slip by. Oh! I'm a fool.

Then I asked him what he really thought of me and he said, "I think you're a good sport and I think if I had met you before I was married and we had gone out together, we would've had a good time, and it would have been an out and out love affair." We kept it up, that kind of banter all the way home. The first time we've ever talked that way. And I might have had my heart's desire—his arms and his kiss—if I hadn't been so damned slow-witted and dumn. I'll never have the same opportunity again. Never!

And I love him. Gee whiz, how I love him. I paced the floor when I got back. I couldn't hold myself in. I still want to scream and shriek. I want him. Oh, God. How I want him, and I might have had him. Except for my dumnness. Oh, damn, damn, damn. He thinks now that I think he's just a man and that I'm not interested and etc. and I love him—oh, my gosh, how I love him.

Sunday, April 21

All I did today was stand around and stare out on to the river and into the fire and think and think and think about my darling. And the more I think, the worse it becomes. Oh, how I love him, and oh, that glorious ride. I kept looking at his mouth and jaw and wanted so to run my fingers over his lips. He had on the prettiest tie and suit, and his smile is incomparable. Oh! To be in his arms, to have those great strong arms tighten around my waist and to be held against him. My head on his shoulder, or to be able to look up and run my hand through his hair and to caress his cheek. I'd sell my soul for it—almost. Just to be enclosed in his arms, to be his, his, his, and let the rest of the world go hang.

He said once, if I wanted a man, to go get him. But I can't do anything when he's married. I shouldn't even dream of his kisses, much less wish for them. And yet I do, and somehow, for some reason, I think he almost wishes for mine. And he could have had them, if I hadn't been such a damned fool. I wonder if he's thinking about me now. I wonder if he had the same sensations I had, when I left him. I wonder, even that would be some consolation. To know that he was in a turmoil, too. Oh, damn his wife. No. I don't mean that. Perhaps he loves her—but I love him and—that is life.

This isn't a schoolgirl fantasy. It is real. I know it. I almost wish I were sick, and desperately, so I'd have to call him.

Monday, April 22

I can't eat. I can't study. I can't breathe. He haunts my every thought. He keeps coming before me. I'll die, pretty soon.

Tuesday, April 23

I'm thoroughly disgusted with myself. Behaving like a lovesick fool—and yet I can't help it. I tried to study. I try not to think about him. But what's the use? I love him. And he's all I can think about.

Wednesday, April 24

A wonderful letter from Marjie today. About Dr. Scott. She sorta thinks I'm letting my imagination run away with me about him. I wonder—am I? But no, no, no.

Thursday, April 25
Life goes on—and on—and on.

Friday, April 26
Still life goes on, and I love my doctor, oh, terribly. The new medical building is finished, and Fanny and I wandered in. We poked into a circular room and found a big blackboard with a list of doctors on it. And halfway down Dr. Abel D. Scott's name shone out at me. I asked a workman what it meant, and he said it was a list of men to be voted on to enter a medical society[259]. Oh! I hope he gets in. I love him.

Saturday, April 27
Met Fanny downtown. We went to the dentist, then up to her house where we indulged in a delicious luncheon. Then took the Packard and hunted for Botany specimens. It's a nice life.

Sunday, April 28
Went fishin'. And I fell in the creek and got my pants wet. And it rained, and the cake got wet, and I'm happy, and I love my doctor.

Monday, April 29
On the way home, Fanny and I stopped at said medical building and wrote A. D. Scott's name all over the blackboard. Oh! The satisfaction it gave me. Marjie appeared out of a clear sky. She has the itch!

Tuesday, April 30
Fun today, just being alive. Fanny and I had fun downtown. S' all.

---

[259] Perhaps the Multnomah County Medical Society

[manila cardboard separator]

Important

Punishment is a fruit—that unsuspected,
ripens within the flower of the pleasure which concealed it.
(Emerson)

The conflict is infinitely greater than the victory or the defeat. [260]

Wednesday, May 1
Today is the first of May. This time last year, Arizona, horses, life. Now: school, work, stagnant existence, lonesomeness. But what's to be done? Not at damned thing. Life simply revolves in a circle. Sometimes nice, sometimes not so nice. I feel now as if Arizona had been a dream. Oh! I wish I were back. I do. I do. I'd give anything tonight to be there in the soft dusk, happy. And the hell of it is I might have stayed. This was all my own choosing. I begged to come back. Oh, damn, damn, damn. I was a fool.

Thursday, May 2
Had a good time today, being happy, and alive.

Friday, May 3
Saw the best show tonight. It made me feel that when I love, it's to be on a South Sea Island, the palm trees and ocean; my only god—nature, and my only law—love. And I want my man to take me. To say the hell with conventions and be united by love, not ceremony.

---

260 Emerson's *Essay on Compensation,* 1906; other source unknown

Saturday, May 4

Marjie and I went downtown. Saw Eddy and he acted cute. Rae sent me five dollars. Mother, a skirt and sweater.

Sunday, May 5

Just a nice lazy day during which I cleaned out desk, dresser drawers and studied.

Friday, May 10

I'm unutterably blue and lonesome, and down-hearted tonight. So guess I'd better not record my thoughts.

Saturday, May 11

Dr. Harrison's married[261]! So now there is another broken heart added to the world. Meaning Fanny. Eddy broke the news to us. It was brutal—the way he did it. I was afraid Fanny was going to faint. Instead, she laughed hysterically until we got outside, then in the theater broke down and cried. Poor girl.

But then life is like that. We all have our little tragedies. They go to make up life; it's the price we pay to be allowed to partake of the blue skies and cool night breezes. Ah, life—what a strange mixture of sorrow and sweetness, tears and laughter, riches, and poverty. And some people go along in their narrow paths seeing only their troubles enjoys, never visioning beyond the scope of their own meager horizon. Drudgery, sordid, squalid, little. Never realizing what lies beyond themselves. And others lift up their heads, get a whiff of desert air or the tang of mountain pines and absorb the blue skies, and thrill to the early robin's call at daybreak.

Life is not people, and trouble and money and make-believe talk and laughter that grate on the ears. "Life" is the mountain stream that tumbles and rushes to reach the sea. Life is the moonlight through the

---

261 The optician, not Dr. Keihle's partner.

lacy trees. Life is the roar of the wind up a deserted canyon, behaving in fiendish delight. Life is barren hills, sage brush, cactus, clear untainted air, wild horses with quivering nostrils and flying mane. Life is a lone coyote, sending forth its death cry on a snow-laden hillside. But how many people see that? How many people realize that it is there? And if they did see it with the two orbs given them and known as eyes, how many would see it through their souls? Not only see, but feel and live it. Few, very few, but that is because of the smallness of humanity, and not because of the bigness of life.

Sunday, May 12
Marjie brought her Rus home to dinner today. He's a sweet, shy and wholly lovable blond Adonis. I liked him. He's deep. Though not, I think, very domineering. I'm tired tonight—of what? I'm afraid.

Tuesday, May 14
I want to go to Arizona. Damn it but I do, I do, I do!

Thursday, May 16
Had a party at school today. Danced and ate, and danced some more. Had fun, but I'm tired as the very devil tonight. Daddy sent me some money—nice! I have a pain in my heart. Whether from exertion or love, I know not.

Friday, May 17 C.S.
Stayed home from school and studied and studied and studied some more. Final exams are only a week away, and I must get by.

Saturday, May 18

Got my hair curled. Met Fanny and went to a show and bought a hat and necklace and ate and came home.

Sunday, May 19

Beautiful day. Just sat on the porch swing and read and loafed and slept all day. Fritze said he was coming down. He didn't and I'm glad. The day was too perfect to be spoiled. I love my comfort!

Monday, May 20

No one shall hold the key to my heart. I am myself. I shall control my destiny. My mind is going to be a storehouse of knowledge, and I won't have to depend on others for my happiness. I shall find happiness within myself. I am a being that belongs to me and no one can take me away from me. Ungrammatically phrased, perhaps, but that's exactly what I mean. I'll be independent. I'll never be unhappy, because I'll never be mean to myself.

And I'll never be lonesome. Because I'm going to enrich my mind and will always have a room full of interesting thoughts. The results of all this is that from now on I'm going to be happy. It's utterly ridiculous and silly because no one chooses to fall in love with me. Micky chooses to ignore me, or circumstances placed in a position I'm not particularly fond of, that I should become depressed and blue and downhearted. In doing so, I am merely admitting my own weakness. I'm admitting that I, myself, am such an uninteresting person that I require foreign elements to make me happy.

But that is no more, and oh! What a nice feeling to know that no matter what happens—if I flunk 50 exams or never have a date again or am reduced to dire poverty—it shall not affect my state of mind.

Wednesday, May 22

Junior-Senior Luncheon today. I wore my new ensemble and like it. Fanny and I rode in the rumble seat of Evaline's Roadster. Fun! The luncheon was at the University Club. Beautiful table. Exquisite flowers. Soft music and delectable food. Yes, I enjoyed myself. I have a weakness for just that sort of thing. Formality and pleasant society. Afterwards we danced, then Fanny and I bummed around town. Went to see Dr. Kiehle. He was better [behaved]. Saw more darn good-looking men, also. Whoopee!

Friday, May 24

Worked like heck, trying to finish all my work up. Exams start Monday. Gee whiz! But I hope I get by. I'm really worried. It all seems so hopeless. I'm going to study all weekend, though—*I will get by. I must.*

Saw Dr. Baird today. Also got a lift from an illiterate boy [which] made me realize more than ever the value of an education. Daddy sent me 20 more dollars[262]. Nice.

Saturday, May 25

Studied all day long! Believe it or not.

Sunday, May 26

Marjie bounced in at dawn this morning, before I was out of bed. We took a long walk in the woods and then lay down on the grass on our backs, looked up at the blue sky and talked and basked in the sunlight. Oh, gee whiz, but I love her. She's so damned sweet. And she's in love with Rus and he's in love with her and he took her to a "Cottage Small by a Water Fall,"[263] a cottage built of rustic logs nestled in amidst the trees. Someday he'll come along—the man I love, but when and how and who?

---

[262] Luther sent her the equivalent of $264.
[263] "Just a Cottage Small by a Waterfall," words by Buddy G. De Sylva; music by James. F. Hanley, 1925

Monday, May 27
English Exams today. Bought new hat, good looking. Tired, but I will get through these exams. See if I don't!

Tuesday, [May] 28
French and Shorthand exams. Terribly afraid I flunked French. Zowie! But it was hard.

Wednesday, May 29
Well! Lots of little interesting things have happened today. First I had a mild but nice little flirtation on the street car. Then I took a perfectly impossible Botany exam. It was simply preposterous. Then I bought a new white dress and some white Deauville sandals[264]. Then I came home and dressed to go and meet Rae. The Danas let me out on the east side and I walked across the bridge. It was dusk, and the skyline was enclosed in a soft mystical haze. Oh, beautiful. I loitered along, enjoying my Portland.

But I had forgotten the terrible neighborhood just the other side of the bridge[265]. And instead of taking a street car, I decided to walk through it, to the station. Never shall I forget that walk. Men, men, everywhere—dirty, one-eyed, loiterers. And not a woman in sight. The way they looked at me made me feel as if I had already indulged in a life of sin. I'd pass a man and have the most awful sensation that he was following me but didn't dare to look behind for fear he'd take it as encouragement. There were black, gaping doors everywhere that I forced myself to pass with sheer willpower. I rather enjoyed being scared and being stared at—at first. It was an adventure. But then, I passed an especially grotesque looking man and he made a dive at my leg, making the most horrible noise in his throat. He

---

264 Deauville sandals were hand-woven sandals, with flat or low heel, "made in Czeko-Slovakia" and were "cool and comfortable and smart for summer wear." Authentic ones had the name stamped in the heel. Still extant today.
265 Doris has crossed either the Steel Bridge or the Broadway Bridge, and is passing through then-unsavory Chinatown (Skid Row) on her way to Union Station.

was goofy, I guess. But, oh! My heart. He followed me for about a quarter of the block. And then some men took him away.

I ran then—yes, ran! until I reached the station. Then I met Rae. We went up to his hotel while he changed his clothes, then he went to see Ruth and I came home. There's more, but I'm too tired to write it. I'll remember.

The train station to which Doris ran when meeting Rae.

Thursday, May 30 —Armistice Day[266] [*sic*]
Just a nice lazy holiday incarnated with life.

Friday, May 31
Met Fanny at 10 bells.[267] We hoofed around town, tried on costumes for her, looked at shoes, ate lunch in. Oh, I forgot—went to the bank.

---

[266] Doris is incorrect. Armistice Day was Nov. 11; it morphed into Veterans Day in the U.S. and Remembrance Day, aka Poppy Day, in the United Kingdom. Memorial Day, also widely called "Decoration Day" until the end of World War II, was on May 30.

[267] She means 10 a.m.; she is misusing the Navy's bell-count, which doesn't go above 8 bells.

Cute pay teller. And then went up to school. It's a dear old school. Fanny practiced for the play while I wandered around the garden. Then we had tea at O.W.K.[268] then I met Rae and we went to Ruth's house[269] for dinner. A delicious dinner and I like the Crums. Then, eventually, home.

Saturday, June 1

Went to a luncheon at Alexander Court[270] with a lot of piladery[271] [*sic*] females. Good food. But the overdone cordiality got on my nerves. I detest insincerity. Afterwards Coie and I went to Fanny's house and had our pictures taken in the garden. Then we took Coie home and Fanny and I had dinner at a good-looking place filled with good-looking people. Then again, homeward-bound and to bed!

Sunday, June 2

Met the Hall girls and went to church. Bishop Sumner preached a beautiful sermon on friendship, and Coie and I sat and squeezed each other's hands. Bishop Sumner asked me why I wasn't at the dance last night. Said he missed me. Well, why wasn't I? Then we went to school and had some good food, compliments of the school. Then we went in, unveiled the senior picture, sang school songs and everyone wept. Wept and wept, including yours truly. Then the *Delphies*[272] were given out and everyone signed everyone else['s]. Then Rae came to get me and I came home. That's all, except my story was printed in the *Delphie*.

---

268 The Paris Tea Room at Olds, Wortman and King, at Morrison, Alder, 10th and Park; the building occupies a full city block. It has housed the Galleria and Brooks Brothers, and currently, a Target store.

269 The Crums' house on The Alameda

270 Alexander Court was a residential hotel for high society, appearing frequently in the newspaper as a site for luncheons, teas and events in its dining room. It is located at 125 NW 20th Place.

271 Doris's attitude is clear, even if her word choice isn't.

272 Annual magazine and yearbook

Monday, June 3
Home all day.

Tuesday, June 4
Practice for commencement all morning. Fanny and I went to a show in afternoon, and had some food. Then this evening excitement reigned. Commencement!

White dresses and sweet girl graduates. Fanny was excited and scared to death. I was even a little shaky myself. Everything went off beautifully. The ceremony was marvelous. I wish I had been graduating. Fanny got a lot of gorgeous flowers. I gave her some pearl-colored satin step-ins[273].

Wednesday, June 5
Said goodby to Coie [for summer]. Went to Fanny's for luncheon. Then to school where I was struck with the staggering blow that I flunked my French. Damn, damn, double damn. I'm too discouraged to even write. Hell.

Thursday, June 6
Went to school to see about taking a re-examination. Then met Fanny and went to the Portland Theatre. Good show rather. Then killed time until four. Fanny came home with me. We went for a walk in the great outdoors. Went to see Mrs. Tailor who lives in a rustic stone house and has a room filled with antique furniture. Then we ate dinner. Mr. and Mrs. Dana went out. We built a fire and talked. Fritze dropped by but we didn't let him stay. He tried to kiss me but I didn't let him. He looked adorable, for him, and it was a temptation. We went for a tiny drive and I drove. After that we turned out the light (Fanny and I) and sat on the floor and listened to Georgie Stoll over the radio.[274]

---

273 Underpants; tap pants
274 Georgie Stoll played with his jazz trio, quintet and orchestra on the radio.

Friday, June 7

Had a nice time just being home and loafing.

Saturday, June 8

Well! At last I have had his arms and his kisses—and now, I almost wish I hadn't. To begin at the beginning, I took a French lesson is morning. Then, being bored, I went to The Broadway, and saw a good show. Then to see Eddy—and suddenly, on impulse—a M.V. [Montavilla] car and my doctor. He was all smiles and we hit it off perfectly from the first. My feet were wet so he lighted his heater and I held my feet out and he drew his chair up and held my feet. And we talked and laughed and were happy.

He asked me if I had been good—and I said I had—but that I was getting fed up and was ready to be bad. And instead of lecturing me as I expected him to, he sort of agreed with me, and said he felt like letting loose himself—that life was the bunk and business was rotten and he was tired. Then we talked about this, that, and the other thing, until it developed that I had a cut finger and a sore throat. He proceeded to show his worth. He put iodine in my finger, holding my hand in the process, while I perched on the table.

Naturally that contact sent shivers here, there, and everywhere. Then he felt the outside of my throat and I felt I would scream. His strong hands on my neck. He painted it and it hurt like hell[275] but I said nary a word. Then a patient arrived and I started to go, but he gave me the keys and told me to wait in his car. I did, and finally he came all bundled in a big overcoat. Then something possessed me. I felt desperate. I had to have him.

So I exerted all my wiles in an effort to "get" him. I curled up on the seat beside him, laid my head on the back of the seat in a position so that I could see him, and he me, in the mirror and talked. And teased and fought. It was much the same as last time, only when we reached dangerous ground I didn't hedge away from it. The gas was low and he said I might

---

275 The doctor likely painted the inside of her throat with a 5 percent iodine solution, a then-common treatment for sore throat, tonsillitis and coughs.

have to walk home and I said if I did it would be because the gas was low and for no other reason.

"Oh, is that so?" He said, "You don't even think I'm human, do you?" And I said, "No, you're one of these noble men that never do anything wrong." And he said, "Listen here—if a man wouldn't have the natural reaction and desire towards you, there would be something wrong with him." And I said, "Well—there's something wrong with you." And he said, "You think so? And if I proved differently, would you still like me as well?" And I said, "I'd probably like you better. But I'll never have the chance to know because you'd never let me."

We kept that up all the way home of course my declaration of his "goodness" was all he needed to spur him on. He drove, oh, so slowly, and I'll always remember that ride as a battle of our eyes in the mirror, each remark becoming more daring. The way I was seated, my knees just touched his coat, and he laid his hand on them, just sort of caressingly tender. And again, my heart did various flip-flops. By the time we reached Oak Grove, he was holding both my hands in one of his, and life had reached the peak of ecstasy.

Then instead of turning into Dana Road, we drove below the bluff, through the woods and to the end of the road. There we stopped—and then, some way or other I was in his arms and his lips were pressed against mine. Oh, that mouth that I had longed to run my fingers over was at last pressed against mine. Not once or twice but again, again and yet again. And I ran my fingers through his hair, as I had dreamed of doing. And he kissed my neck and cheek and lips and the world was at my feet.

But after the first thrill was over, the most terrible all-gone feeling possessed me. My dream had been realized. But it left a vacantness. And I lay with my head on his chest and his arms around me and wanted to cry. Then sat up and looked at him and he must've seen how I felt and he said, "I'm a fine doctor." His voice full of disgust at himself. And he said, "Well, anyway, you can't say I'm not human. You see—I'm as bad as the rest." Then he began to apologize. And I hated myself for making him kiss me and I told him so and he said I didn't make him—that he wanted to. But I know better. And I said, "I can't come to see you anymore now." And he said, "Yes, you can. I'll always be your friend, Doris, and we'll just pretend that this never happened."

And then, by mutual consent, we sealed it with a real kiss and I said, "Hold me tight." And his big arms held me against him and his mouth and mine were one for just an instant. Then it was over and we were on our way home and all the way up to the hill he held my hand and said he was sorry. I don't know yet why he was sorry, unless he felt as I did—that our wonderful friendship had been blasted. Perhaps he did, and no matter what he says, it can never be the same again. I knew it would be this way, if it ever happened—and yet, I'm a fool, and when I want something I want it, regardless of the consequences.

And now! What have I? The memory of two gray eyes and a wonderful kiss. But friendship? Oh, I wonder? He said he would see that it never happened again. But I'm not so sure that I don't want it to happen again, and yet—I don't think I love him. Oh, well! I'll just have to list it as one of life's experiences, and forget him, I guess. He shall always be a distant chapter in my life and he shall always have a very special corner of my memory.

Oh, damn! I don't want to not have him. It leaves such a void, and yet—now I've had my kiss, I guess it is the only thing to do.

Sunday, June 9

"It's over—all over." That's all I can think of, over, over, it is no more. I wanted it with every fiber of my being, longed for just what I got, and it was wonderful, wonderful while it lasted. His eyes, his amber-flecked eyes and his firm mouth and his strong arms—they were mine, mine, and I reveled in it. But now that I've had them, it's just as I knew it would be. No more dreams. No more wonderful declaration of friendship. No more banter and jumpy pulses. No more lectures. He said he wanted me to still come and see him, but I wonder, can I?

Oh, he's sweet. I like the way he reacted. Not violent apologies, not dramatic words, it wasn't cheap or low or sordid, because he wouldn't know how to be cheap. It was just a silent understanding of the way I felt.

He's a man in a million. But I guess I don't love him. Else I wouldn't have that terrible unutterable all-gone ache in my heart. Instead I would feel hilarious.

It's dreams that I love—beautiful golden dreams and not material kisses. The dreams themselves are so much more wonderful than the fulfillment of them, than reality. In fact, I feel worse at the realization of my last dream than I do happy that I got what I went after.

I was wearing a rose on my coat, and it got crushed when he held me against him. I'm going to press it and keep it always. He does kiss nicely.

Monday, June 10
Monkeyed around home.

Tuesday, June 11
Had French lesson. Then met Fanny. Had lunch and went to the parade[276]. Good. Home.

Wednesday, June 12
Marjie and Bill Adams and Ralph somebody and I went out this evening. It was fun. First we went to the circus at the Stadium[277]. Then we went to the Grill[278] about 10:30, and danced, and talked to the strains of music.

---

[276] The first broadcast of the Rose Festival Grand Floral Parade was Monday, June 10, 1929, on radio KGW. On June 11 were the Coronation and the Merrykana Parade, according to Rose Parade historians.

[277] Multnomah Stadium was built by the Multnomah Athletic Club in 1926, though Multnomah Field (sports fields with various grandstands) had stood on the site since 1893. The Multnomah Athletic Club in downtown Portland stands next door. The site also hosted the Portland Rose Festival coronation.

[278] There are half a dozen restaurants in the city directory of 1928 with "Grill" as part of their name, but most likely place is the Seward Grill at the Hotel Seward, at 10th and Alder, where there would have been dancing, as she indicates.

Ralph is unutterably conceited and Bill rather dumn, but I enjoyed myself nevertheless, because my Marjie was there.

Thursday, June 13
Took French lesson. Then home.

Friday, June 14
French exams today. I'll be waiting in suspense till I hear the verdict.

Saturday, June 15
Marjie and I went out with two of the dumnest boys tonight. Just the last word in impossibility. They were so awful, it was funny. We saw a good show, though. Rod La Roque in "Captain Swagger."

Sunday, June 16
Today has been just what a day should be. I wish all Sundays were like this. It was a windy blowing morning and I conceived the idea of a horseback ride. Marjie didn't want to go. So I struck out alone in the wind and rain. A funny man at Oak Grove offered to row me across the river. He said he couldn't refuse a nice blue-eyed girl like me anything. Of course that started me off on the right foot. I reach the corral and asked for my horse.

The nicest fatherly man ran the stable. He gave me a peppy little brown horse and I trotted away. We rode over the most entrancing paths through the woods and around the mountain. He was well reined and stepped right along. The only difficulty was the English saddle. I had never ridden one before. I made the mistake of giving him his head. He turned a corner sharply and I landed in the brush, and the fool horse ran up the road. Mad—oh, boy! I felt so hopelessly foolish and inadequate. Some men picked me up and drove me to Oswego. I told the nice man and we sat down on a pile of hay to await said horse's return. Oh, I loved it—the informality and that fresh hay odor and the smell of horses. Arizona came back with a rush.

**This photo, which is captioned "Doris at Mt. Hood Lodge,"
shows a younger Doris (right), about 14 years old, and either
Joe or Rae to the left. The Baileys loved to ride horses.**

Finally I and the nicest blond boy in white pants and tan riding boots started out to get him. The second horse was even better than the first and we cantered down the path and talked horse talk and I lived once more. Finally it was all over and I started home. Walked across the trestle[279]. The wind blew down the river and I threw out my hands and yelled for the sheer joy of living. The blue river so far below, the green trees, and me way up on a narrow rail—living. A gust of wind nearly blew me off and left such a pleasurable thrill of adventure inside of me. Then I sat down in the field of daisies and rested and sang. Then home to a delectable chicken dinner and strawberry pie. Oh, life is good to me, and I'm going to ride more. I do like that man. I'd like to buy a horse and board it there. Well, perhaps I shall. It's been done before.

---

[279] There is no bridge near the Danas' neighborhood, so Doris crossed the river on the railroad trestle where Rivervilla Park is now.

Monday, June 17

Started summer school today[280]. Funny looking people. Met Alyce afterwards and we ate at Caroline's[281]—an exquisite little artist hovel beneath the street. More good-looking men! Then we went to a show. Afterwards I spent money.

Tuesday, June 18

Today was my unlucky day from start to finish. I'm supposed to be at school by eight, but I missed my train, got downtown at 8:30. Got splashed with mud from head to foot from a passing auto. Came home and stayed home. Tired. Blah.

Wednesday, June 19

Somebody forged [a] check on my account. I haven't any money in the bank and a bunch of phony checks all over town. They gave me a nice opportunity to talk to my cute bank man, though.

Thursday, June 20

I fixed things up at the bank. Archie Fries[282] is his name. He's not so hot but rather nice.

Friday, June 21

Nothing much.

---

280 Night and summer school classes in the late 1920s took place at Benson, Girls' Polytechnic, Commerce, Jefferson, Ladd and Lincoln high schools. Doris most likely went to Benson or Jefferson, based on her auto routes and meeting places.
281 Caroline's was at 350 Taylor Street.
282 Archie C. Fries, Jr., was the (married) bookkeeper at the West Coast National Bank.

Saturday, June 22

Marjie and I went downtown this afternoon. This evening we went to the Oasis [283] with our two "Betas" [284]. My boy was a slick dancer and we didn't waste any time in not dancing. I love the Oasis. I'd like to go there with the man I love. It would be thrilling to say the least. I lost my glasses.

Sunday, June 23

Went to Alyce's for dinner. Good food and plenty of fun. She's a good egg.

Monday, June 24

Got new glasses from Eddy—and we talked and had fun. Geometry is hard. I'm simply lost. Went to the Oaks [285] tonight. Marshall's birthday [286]. I liked it. Brought back so many childhood memories. I also like Archie.

The Oaks amusement park, from The Chutes, Portland.

---

283 The Crystal Springs Oasis, on Sandy Boulevard at Barker Road, was a reputed speakeasy/drinking spot.
284 Members of Beta Theta Pi
285 The Oaks, a beloved Portland recreational destination, had a swimming pool, carnival rides and more.
286 Marshall Dana was Marjie's younger brother. He was turning 11.

Tuesday, June 25

There's a passably cute boy at school. Looks like Jack Hibbard, but that's probably all he will ever amount to. I'm mad at Marjie tonight. She's losing her good disposition, or else I'm homesick.

Wednesday, June 26

Met Fanny after school. We went to the "Cottage" for luncheon. Then a long drive all over. I like Fanny. We get along great together. Going to play golf Saturday[287]. Saw Herb Perry downtown. Looks dumn. Oh, yes. Went to see the Paintons. Like them all.

Thursday, June 27

Show with Fanny this afternoon. Feel like Hell personified. Got an invitation to Kappa Kappa Gamma[288] tea.

Friday, June 28 —C.S.

Dinner party this evening. Marjie and I served. Fun.

Saturday, June 29

I met Fanny at 10 and we drove out to the Columbia Country Club[289]. We played golf until noon. More darn fun. I love it. Then we had luncheon at the clubhouse overlooking Oregon's river. Afterwards we sat on the terrace and Mel Smith came over and hung around for an hour or so. He is absolutely the personification of "sophisticated." His conversation is subtle, witty and get[s] real friendly. He's a bachelor, about 35, and English as hell. I didn't feel like myself when I was talking to him. Then I changed my

---

287 Luther Bailey was a very good golfer and won tournaments and at least one silver cup. Doris may have learned from him.

288 A sorority to which Marjie will pledge at the University of Oregon.

289 The Columbia Country Club, now the Columbia Edgewater, was built in 1924, and located on the Columbia River's bank.

now and then. And, oh, yes, I made what might be called a little progress with Bob. But it's nothing to build dreams on.

Tuesday, July 9
I'm still in love with my sophisticate. Hot damn! I wonder, is this really me?

Wednesday, July 10
I like Bob and he never even sees me. He's a Secret Sorrow in the true sense of the word. I sit behind him and feast my eyes on the wiggles in his sweater and the way his hair grows at the back. I know every little wrinkle and scratch in his neck. Gee, I am a damn fool. Had luncheon at the Portland Hotel with Mother and Mrs. Davidson and Helen. Fanny and Alyce came up this afternoon and we had tea in my apartment. More damn fun.

Thursday, July 11
Today—as days go—hasn't been so hot. But I'm happy just the same.

Friday, July 12
Daddy let me take the car to school today, and everyone was properly impressed. There's the cutest fireman next door. Blue eyes and an Irish smile, and he helped me unpack the car. Bob was rather nice, but still alarmingly indifferent. I had luncheon with Bill Adams. He wanted to know why Marjie was so cold, and I had to tell him she was in love with somebody else. Poor boy. I was afraid he was going to cry. Life is a frightfully mixed-up affair. The trouble with most people is they take it too seriously. After I'd finished with Bill, Mother and Daddy and I went to a show. Then home, and a drive this evening out to Danas.

Saturday, July 13

Mother and I went shopping "cet matin"[*sic*][293]. Then I had the car for a while and Fanny and I played around. Then we went out to [the] Portland Golf Club to get Daddy. Fanny and I fixed dinner all by ourselves in our little apartment. It was a darned good dinner, too. Then we didn't know what to do with ourselves. About 9 o'clock we decided to go to a show, so dressed and went downtown and discovered the bank wasn't open to cash a check so had to hoof it home again. Talked to the fireman. But not my Irishman. I didn't like the others. They were sorta cheap.

About 11:30 we undressed for bed, and then decided some ginger ale and pretzels would taste good. So we put our coats on over our pajamas and our shoes without any stockings and went to the drugstore. My pajama legs kept falling and we had an awful time. But that's not all. There was a snazzy night clerk. And he grinned when we came in as if he knew something was up. And then Fanny forgot and put her hands above her head and revealed her maidenly charms exposed under a silken nightgown. The poor boy's eyes nearly popped out. "Hey—I'm trying to work," he said. We grabbed our ginger ale and ran and didn't stop until we reached the apartment. Then we sat on the bed and ate and drank and giggled foolishly.

Sunday, July 14

The nicest day—just "being."

Monday, July 15

Took car to school again today. Alyce came over for lunch and we had the best time. We took off everything but our brassieres and bloomers and cleaned the apartment from top to bottom. Rearranged furniture 'n everything. Between gasps we drank tea. This evening she and Gordon came over and we had fun. Nice kid.

---

[293] "This morning," but her French is incorrect. She means *ce matin*.

Tuesday, July 16

Fireman called. Rather embarrassing, that. S'what I get for flirting with every good-looking man I see.

Wednesday, July 17

Ahem. I was sitting out in front before school and Bob walked by and I asked him if he had his Geometry and he grinned (as if he knew I was making an excuse to talk to him) and came over. Hung on the side of the car and talked. Brown eyes and white teeth and a flashing smile. He asked about the car and where I lived and where I went to school and the like. He doesn't say much, rather gives the impression of laughing at you. Sort of cynical, fascinating. But I'm being a fool. Had the car all afternoon, and Alyce and I went places.

Thursday, July 18

Just a "hello" in Geometry class. Then I studied from 10 to 11 and talked to his pal, who incidentally helped me with my Geometry and seemed rather interested. But his nose is sunburned and he isn't Bob. Bob came in about 10 [minutes] till 11. Sat down a minute, then went out. Hell. Damn. Fireman phoned. I was cold.

Friday, July 19

Well—I was late to class, and he had my assignment written out for me. Afterwards he said, "Somebody else overslept this morning," (He's usually late), and then we decided that since I didn't have my history assignment we'd go for a ride instead, and did. Way out to the highway. He said I was a good driver, so I returned the compliment by letting him drive. It was fun, and nice.

But I'll have to admit I'm sorta disappointed. Some way I thought he'd be different. Silly—of course. No one ever is. But I'm always hoping so. He smokes a cigarette (I wanted it to be a pipe), and he isn't particularly thrilled about horseback riding, and he'd rather ride [in a car] than walk. And there you have it. Just little things that mean so much to me. I wonder if I'll ever find someone that really understands me, that actually has the same desires and taste and wants. That certain something inside of me craves for companionship of the soul as well as the mind. Marjie comes as near fulfilling it as anyone.

But even she sometimes can't quite qualify. Oh, if someone could only understand how I love that moon out there. Peeping between the branches [of] the trees, the sky, the wind, all of it. But they obviously can't—so why should I hope for it? Maybe, maybe there is still a part of Bob that I didn't reach. Maybe; at least, I'm *not* going to try and find out. I'd rather *think* there might be than *know* there isn't! He tried once to get exciting, and I said it was rushing the issue. At least I won't take a chance just yet of that dreamily kissable mouth reverting into realism. Letter from Bill Cedars.

Saturday, July 20

I picked him up on the way to school. He was cute. And he has a nice smile. I didn't talk to him between classes or anything though. Technique. This afternoon I—and Alyce—went on a boat trip down the Willamette and up the Columbia with the University of Oregon Extension. There was a mob of college graduates and one interesting-looking sailor. We kept up a mild flirtation of glances until after dinner. Then they danced and he asked me to. I was disappointed. He was cheap and not even sophisticated. So after I had danced a while I sneaked away by myself on the deserted upper deck.

There was a moon, a glorious big orb, and the water was silver and black. The wind blew my hair away from my face and I felt free and alive. I stayed there for ages, reveling in the beauty of the elements. That's one thing I can depend upon never to be disillusioned about. Men—they're always interesting until you have them, then blah, it's all gone. Dream kisses are divine. Material kisses—nothing. Perhaps the trouble with me is I expect too much of mortal man. I'm always hoping, looking for

Edited by Julia Park Tracey

something stupendously big and wonderful and when it happens along, the jolt is too much.

But the moon and the stars and the water and wind and sky are stupendously wonderful and breath-taking. And they always will be. So I'm glad. They'll be my refuge. While I was sitting on the rail some damn middle-aged man appeared and talked and stood too close, and took it upon himself to hold me and prevent me from falling off, until I thought I should scream. I finally had to leave my moon and dance—in self-defense.

Sunday, July 21

Went to church this morning. Then dinner and a show, though that's a state secret[294]. Then home to study. And think. I'm too damned big of a rover. I philosophize and kick life too much. I'm the bunk. Alyce and Gordon came up and we talked and drank ginger ale and ate pretzels. As I said before, he's a sweet kid.

Monday, July 22

Talked to Bob after Geometry class. That is, he wandered out to the car with me. He said he wandered all over town Saturday night looking for Montgomery Street[295], believe it or not! I don't like his nose. But considering mine, I guess I shouldn't say anything! Just as I was leaving to go home, I met him and Johnny and he asked for my telephone number. So that's that! Looked for fall coats all afternoon. Found a scrumptious one but it cost too damn much.

Tuesday, July 23

Blue skies and sunshine this morning, and he's not a Secret Sorrow anymore. I met him on the way to school, just after I'd had a narrow

---

294 She went to a show on a Sunday and doesn't want to get caught.
295 Where her apartment building is presumably located.

escape with a Hudson Roadster, and drove him to school. We decided it was silly to waste the morning digesting Geometry. So he bought a gallon of gas and we struck out on the open road on the Washington side. He drove—miles—and we stopped at a pretty stream and climbed over the rocks, and I fell and tore my stocking. And he picked me up. Then we drove some more, and found a shady spot 'n stopped. And he took me in his big, brown arms, and I wasn't disillusioned in that mouth. It was divine! And he kissed my hair, and said, "You have pretty hair." So boyish. Finally we had to leave, and drove like hell to get back on time. I would light his cigarettes for him, and he said he couldn't get along without me. Oh, yes! He's Catholic[296], and has had one big love affair—that lasted. That's why he was so indifferent at first—he's skeptical. This afternoon Fanny and I went to a show—good! And afterwards to see Eddy. Stayed a long time, and had fun. He's cute and I like him. Fanny's all thrilled about going east to school[297]!

Later—Bob phoned to give me my Geometry assignment and to tell me that everything was KO[298] with Mr. Harrigan[299]. He's sweet!

Wednesday, July 24

Oh, Gee whiz! I guess I'm goofy. I met him at Williams Avenue. And we drove to school together, and sat out in front till eight. After school I bade a hurried adieu. This afternoon Mother went to a luncheon and I took her, then started to school to take a Geometry lesson. Met Bob and Johnny. Didn't take a Geometry lesson. Drove them to Johnny's house, all three sitting in the front seat. Bob next to me, so close, held my hand. He'll soon hold my heart if I don't check myself. It was all so nice and intimate and

---

[296] Doris won't mention this fact to her parents, who, as pillars of Westminster Presbyterian Church (Willie Doris was Baptist), wouldn't approve.

[297] Now that Fanny has graduated high school, she, too, is leaving for college. Doris will again be left behind.

[298] OK

[299] The Geometry teacher.

jolly. Johnny's sorta sweet, too. But Bob—my gosh! His sister has a horse. I'll have to look into this!

Later—He phoned, just to talk. What can I say but that I'm happy?

Thursday, July 25

And I thought I was over this silly unsophisticated stage. Apparently I'm not. Met [Bob] this morning, and it was early so we drove around and I got kissed. My gosh! I'm ashamed of myself, but it's fun. Alyce came up for lunch and I washed and curled my hair. She's all right. I hoped he'd phoned tonight but no luck. Fireman did. Lost my glasses.

Friday, July 26

Took [Bob] to school again today. Then skipped history and we drove and drove. Went out to Columbia [County]. Stopped at a barbecue and had breakfast. More damn fun! Course, I got kissed again. I can't resist him. Be better policy if I could, perhaps. I don't know whether he likes me or is just having a good time being carted around. One minute he doesn't interest me a bit. The next I think I'll die if he doesn't eat me up with his kisses. So there you are! He had an exam at one and I was to take him to it. But when I got there he'd already gone. So I went to Washington and met him and we talked. He was worried about his exam. He seemed glad enough to see me. Well, anyway, he's coming up tonight and bring[ing] Johnny, and Alyce is coming. So tonight shall tell whether I really like him and he, me, an' everything. Till tonight.

Tonight—late—two bells[300]

Well… I don't know much more than I did before except that I'm pretty damned happy. They came about nine. Alyce acted up and we sorta fought. But Bob and I didn't. We sat on the floor and played Black Jack and put the Victrola down beside us. Bob was all that could be desired, except he wanted to drink. That was easily averted, however. Later we ate and then the folks came and then about 12 o'clock, just Bob and I went

---

[300] She means 2 a.m.

for a walk. It was beautiful out. Sort of exotic and pungent with life. And we crept around and got in to the grounds of [St. Helen's Hall] and sat in the summer house with the roses and the moon. But it was near an arc light so we found the most exquisite spot all secluded by the shrubbery and a weeping willow tree. We sat on the grass and the moonlight filtered through the branches and there was a breeze and the night was soothing and warm and vibrant. Oh, my gosh!

"Deep night—deep in the arms of love."[301]

I didn't think I could stand it when he'd take me in his arms and kissed my forehead and neck and mouth. I didn't want it to ever end. I didn't try to think or reason. I just gave myself up to the joy of the moment and allowed myself to be bathed in kisses and love. And during it all there was nothing low about it. I'm so glad he didn't spoil it with vulgarity. He said he loved me. I don't think he meant it but I pretended he did for the moment. I'll never forget tonight—never. It was too wonderfully perfect to even be.

Saturday, July 27

Got up at 5 [a.m.] to study. Three hours sleep last night. Bob sat in front of me during math exam. It didn't seem right after last night. Too damned realistic. "Was it a dream, was it a dream, I was in your arms last night?"[302] I'm afraid my exam wasn't all it should have been. Then I took my history and went out to the car, and he had waited for me to see how I came out. We went up to Mount Tabor and stopped and I wish I hadn't. It was broad daylight and hot as hell. But what's a mere woman to do when a man has a mouth like that? I can't refuse. I haven't any will. I'm weak. Shameless. Palatable. And pliable. But hell! He shouldn't have that mouth. It isn't right. It gives him an unfair advantage.

At 12 [noon] I came home and Fanny came down and we guzzled some food. Now it's 8:30. Going to Seattle at five tomorrow. Getting back

---

301 "Deep in the Arms of Love," Nat Shilkret And The Victor Orchestra; Gloria Geer also recorded this, 1929

302 Source unknown

Tuesday. He said he'd phone me Tuesday night. How can he like me? I haven't any force. I'm easily led. Well! It won't happen again. I'll show him and myself how purposeful and strong I can be. Just see.

Sunday, July 28
Arrived in Seattle [by train] about 10:30 [a.m.]. Ate and talked and went canoeing in the most divine lake with Lucy and a nice boy. It was so cool and lazy and drifty. Then saw the most perfect show. The kind that leave you all throaty and weepy.

Monday, July 29
Slept till noon. Then called Royal Oliver. He was surprised and rather glad to hear from me, I think. He took us downtown and I bought some stockings. This evening about 20 of us went on a [illegible] up a lake. The boys were just so-so. But I managed to have a good time. Millard's not so hot but there was a nice boy named Howard. Well, anyway, I had fun. But kept thinking how Bob and I would have taken advantage of the water, and the moon.

Tuesday, July 30 (C. S.)
Came back this morning. Bob phoned this evening. I liked the way he sounded. He was working and had to cut it short because the boss came in. He said he might come up about nine if he could. But it's 10:15 now, so I guess he couldn't.

Later—2 o'clock. I'd just got undressed when Bob and Johnny came. So I hid and dressed and they came up. They were sweet—both of them. I was strong and filled with stamina for a long time. He couldn't understand it. Then Johnny went to get a drink and I weakened. Course I'm a fool but hell! We live but once. He was terribly tired and looked it. Johnny kept playing "Blue Heaven,"[303] and Bob said this was his blue heaven. About

---

[303] "My Blue Heaven," recorded by Gene Austin in 1927.

11:30 [p.m.] we went for a drive up Terwilliger[304]. And there were one million stars and one million city lights and I was so darned happy. We stopped at a barbecue on the way back. Then came up to the apartment again and stayed till one [a.m.]. Oh, yes. My legs ached and Bob rubbed them. There's something so very nice about him. I'm happy when he's around. Just merely because he's there.

Wednesday, July 31
Saw Marjie today. Stayed home this evening. Sorta bored. Bob didn't phone. Wonder why? Damn!

Thursday, August 1
Gene came up this afternoon. He's a dear—looked so nice. But! He said Micky was in town and not only that, but his picture was in an art gallery downtown. So I hunted up said gallery, and saw it! My gosh! I guess I'll just keep on loving him the rest of my life. His picture was a perfect likeness and made me ache all over. I felt as if I'd suddenly come face-to-face with him again. His eyes smiled into mine and I felt all shaky! I'd sell my soul for that picture. I think I could always be happy just having it around. Oh, why can't I have him? You'd think I'd outgrow wanting him. But I'm afraid I never shall. And that picture brought back all the old fire. Oh, damn!

Friday, August 2
Bought $40[305] worth of material for new dresses today. Nice! Then Fanny and I spizzed around. A cute boy in a Chrysler Roadster followed us and fed us cookies. Good! Wanted a date but we spizzed away. Bob phoned this evening. Said his car broke down Tuesday night and he and Johnny had to walk home. Made a date to go canoeing Sunday. But he wants another

---

304 Terwilliger Boulevard winds up through the hills in Southwest Portland and ends up at Lake Oswego.
305 They purchased $530 worth of materials, by 2012 values.

couple. I don't like that—I'm mad! Why go? Why live? Why bother? I want Micky. He makes Bob seem—I want Micky—yes, I want Micky. But hell! Will I get him? No! Damn! Life is like that.

Saturday, August 3

Dressmaker this morning. Show with Fanny this afternoon. Bob can't get his car so maybe we can't go canoeing tomorrow. Damn! I'm mad! I could cry. I wanta go canoeing!

Very much later — I was sitting on the couch reading poetry and eating crackers when Bob and Jimmy arrived. Bob said I sounded so blue over the phone that he had to come. We ate and drank and bummed around for a while. I didn't like Jimmy. Second-class and conceited. But Bob was sweet and loving. It worries him when I won't let him kiss me but when I once give in I don't want to ever quit.

Sunday, August 4

Alyce and Gordy and Bob and I went canoeing. It was a perfect night and there were a million stars. He sort of irritated me tonight though, for some reason. All evening I didn't let him kiss me. We just talked and drifted and first he'd get mad and then he'd coax and then he'd try force and nearly tip us over. The poor boy couldn't figure it out. It was really fun. Then he said "Why, why, why?" and finally I said because it didn't mean anything and I was tired of kisses given just for the sexual thrill, and that was the signal for him to tell me just how much I did mean. And he did. Punctuated it with "sweethearts" and it was—nice…. But still I didn't weaken till we were nearly ready to come home. Then I did. And boy! He got hot! To put it bluntly. And I wasn't exactly cool. But he overdid it—nearly ate me up. Guess it doesn't pay to keep him waiting. Finally we came home.

But I don't "like" him anymore, I'm afraid. He seemed so young. I'm out for new worlds to conquer now. The whole trouble is, he doesn't quite register. He doesn't get a thrill out of the stars and the moonlit waters. His soul isn't filled with romance and he hasn't any ambition. Gosh. I wonder, is there a man that would actually fulfill my ideal—is there?

Monday, August 5
Alyce and I slept till noon. Then ate and went downtown. I looked at Micky's picture again. I shouldn't. It's only self-torture, but I can't help it. This evening we went to Jantzen Beach[306] with the family. Alyce and I went canoeing and nearly got tipped over into the cold, conceited Columbia. Got in bad with the folks because we ran away from them and slept all the way home. Tha's all.

Tuesday, August 6
Dressmaker all morning. Luncheon at Mrs. Mackie's. Then home. This evening Ed Gerlinger and Dick Jones came up. Dick was tall and good-looking and rather nice. We danced and played cards and finally went for a ride, ended up in the woods and Dick and I talked philosophy and religion. After Bob, it was a relief to be with someone [who] could talk. He was really interesting and had some rather unusual views. He believes in God, something which so few of the boys do. We were all alone sitting on the ground in the woods on a hill. After we had exhausted life we did other things, which, though I shouldn't have, was nice. I'll probably never see him again. I don't know that I want to. But I'm glad I met him. Because he's a type. Forgot to say he was a Sigma Chi at Oregon and majored in journalism. Bob phoned.

---

306 Jantzen Beach is located on Hayden Island at the Oregon-Washington border, in the middle of the Columbia River. It opened as "The Coney Island of the West," in 1928. It was named for one of the park's investors, Carl Jantzen of Jantzen Swimsuits.

Wednesday, August 7

Slept till noon. This afternoon Fanny and a man came up (he's married and she thinks she's in love with him). Then this evening Alyce and I were laying around [*sic*] and Dick arrived. Alyce (being third party) set out to get him. And there was a merry fight on between us. Later two of his friends came up to get him, and I asked them up. How shall I describe them?

The door opened and there stood the biggest, tallest, most overpowering piece of flesh existing. I say stood, not entered. Stood and stared at me without even the semblance of a smile. Then he strode in and sat down. He had a mustache and was frightfully good-looking. But his eyes—they seemed to hypnotize me. I almost expected him to call me mademoiselle and kiss my hand. He chose his words carefully, as if he were either foreign or drunk, and talked about Death Valley and [illegible] and complexes. While I just sat and stared. If he had made one move towards me, I should have run. Frankly, I was scared to death.

In fact, I was so petrified that I didn't watch Alyce and before I realized it she had Dick. Then I wanted him. But no chance. Then I was mad and want to throw things. Finally they left and my heart went down. Then on impulse, I dashed after them, called Dick back just as he was getting in the car.

He came in and we stood by the banister in the hall and I said, "I just wanted to tell you I like you. I'm rather particular and don't like many people. I don't know whether you appreciate that or not. But I do like you and any time you want to come over, why, come." It was sort of dark, and my voice sorta trembled and he took my hand and looked into my eyes and said, "I'll remember, Doris" and went. It was all dreadfully dramatic and tense.

Now I don't know why I did it because he doesn't mean so much. And yet I'm glad I did it because it was fun. So everything considered, today has been eventful. Fanny's man and that weird handsome devil of a freshman and Dick's kiss and eyes.

Thursday, August 8
Show with Fanny. Car all morning. Eddy's this afternoon. He's the sweetest thing and we had more darn fun. Mother said Bob came over three times today. Somehow he doesn't interest me as he did. He hasn't any technique nor any finesse. Show this evening with the folks—very good. I've decided to be like Norma Shearer—less silly and more charming and elusive[307].

Friday, August 9
Downtown with Fanny till four. Then home and Bob and Jimmy came over. We lay around but it was so damned hot and they both got on my nerves. Jimmy needed to shave and Bob kept pawing me. Disgusting. Finally they left. Then about 9:30 the two of them plus a new boy named Mickey McGrath came over. Fanny had gone home so there was I with three men. Mickey and I danced. He was a perfect dancer and Jimmy and I played cards while Bob just sat.

Eventually we went for a drive. I was in the back seat with Bob and the other two were in front. Poor Bob kept trying to be interesting and succeeded in merely boring me to death. So I got in front with the other two. But that was crowded so we three climbed in back and let Bob drive in front alone. I felt mean and horrid and low. But I couldn't help it. Jimmy and Mickey were amusing and big and new. Bob will get over it. He's not nearly as much in love as he thinks he is, and I had to let him know how I felt sometime.

When we got home Mickey came up with me to say goodby and say he'd look me up when he got back in town. I don't think I want him to. The truth is I'm rather ashamed of myself.

Saturday, August 10
Had the car all afternoon. Fanny and I went to see Dr. Scott but he wasn't there. Fate! We had the bestest time, though. Just breezin' around to see people who were not at home. This evening a show with the folks. Letter

---

[307] See Appendix II: Popular Culture.

from Bill. He's in love again and yet such a short time ago his heart was—I wish mine healed that quickly.

Sunday, August 11
Went for a picnic today at Gordon Creek[308]. Alyce went with us. It was a perfect day and we ate and went swimmin' and hiked and had the most scrumptious time. I felt so outdoorish and alive. Now I'm all scratched and bruised but happy as heck. It's a pretty nice world, to my way of thinking.

Monday, August 12
I want companionship of the soul—there's something lacking some place. Dick might give it. In fact, I think we are kindred spirits. He likes to hike in the rain and he loves a windswept cliff. He said so. Also he knows how to neck. He has finesse and he can dance. But unfortunately I apparently mean zero to him. Oh, it's Fate. But I suppose if I did get to know him as I do Bob, he'd turn out to be just as much of a flop. It's life!

Tuesday, August 13
Forgot??

Wednesday, August 14
Alyce came over and we couldn't get any men, so decided to get drunk all by ourselves. We tried. But it tasted so awful that we merely got dizzy. Then we tried smoking Bob's pipe. That didn't work, either. Finally we went to bed and [lounged].

---

308 Hiking area about five miles east of Gresham.

Thursday, August 15
Fanny and Alyce and I went to a show this afternoon. This evening we three went to a picnic with family. Afterwards we came back to the apartment and Mother and Daddy went to the Parkers' and left the car with us. We went places. Drove all through town and sang and cut up unconventionally and had the best doggone time. Really! We ate at the cute drug store with the good-looking man and everything.

Friday, August 16
Played golf with Daddy and Fanny. This afternoon I went to a sort of tea at Helen's. She's getting married and I had to inspect her wedding gifts and trousseau and fairly die with envy. Oh! That such gorgeous things should even *be*. The lucky devil! I want money! Still, perhaps she's not so lucky, because I don't think she loves the man she's marrying. Forgot to say Bob and Johnny came up this afternoon.

Saturday, August 17
I had the car all afternoon and Fanny and I went to see Dr. Scott. I was surprised at my calmness. He said he was afraid he'd lost me because I hadn't come. And he looked nice and was nice. Still, it wasn't anything to what it used to be. All the glamour is gone and I'm sorry. I'm beginning to wonder if I'm capable of loving a man at all.

This evening Bob and Johnny and Fanny came up. Also Ed Gerlinger and Al Baker surprised us, and only stayed a short time. There was something funny going on. Cars stopping, bells ringing, cats fighting and dogs howling. Fanny and I were simply on edge. Then when, out of a silence, three knocks—knocked above. We both simply screeched. We climbed up on the roof and looked, and found less than nothing. Bob was very dramatic this evening. He really thinks he loves me, and the more he thinks so, the less I like him. If only he wouldn't say *these kind* and *they was* and would quit *pawing* me. It would be nice as 'tis.

Sunday, August 18

Went for a drive around the Loop today. Plenty pleasant. This evening Gene Rossman and a nice boy named Bob Gilley dropped in. They couldn't stay long, but we had a nice time while they did. Gene's a dear. I wish this all didn't have to end so suddenly. But the family are leaving Friday. And then what happens to me? I'm just a plaything of circumstances, to be thrown from one extreme to the other. I want to be broad-minded and I want to not be selfish but I *do* want freedom and a car and leisure, and there you are!

Monday, August 19

Met Alyce downtown and we looked at pearls. I found some I was crazy about for $3.25[309]. Hope I get them. Perhaps I can keep the apartment from Thursday till Monday. I hope so.

Tuesday, August 20

Got my pearls. They are eatable. Also new shoes, stockings, hat, etc. Went to Fanny's to a tea to see K. Mansfield. Fun. This evening about 5 [p.m.], Fanny's [married sweetheart] Bud Anderson arrived. He came to talk about Fanny but we talked about everything in the world. Poor boy—he's not happy with the girl he married. It must be rather awful! He told me a lot of things about his life. He's good-looking and in love with Fanny. Jack [her brother] and I went to a show this evening. Had Packard.

Wednesday, August 21

Ran around in the car this morning. About 11:30 Bud came up again. We talked and had the bestest time. About 1 o'clock I drove him out to Oswego Country Club[310] to get his golf clubs. I have a feeling he could

---

309 Those luscious imitation pearls will cost $43 in 2012.
310 Across the Willamette from Oak Grove, Lake Oswego was about 10-12 miles from downtown.

teach me things—and yet. He's straight. I'm sure of it. There's nothing low about him.

This evening we went down to Mathis'[s] pre-opening and I tried on coats. I selected a scrumptious one and had it put away for a month. If I want to change my mind I can. About 10 o'clock tonight the folks' friend George Tift arrived. He's 24. Good-looking and modern. There's something different about him. I can't quite figure him out. I didn't get to talk with him much but we're going out to dinner Friday night together. Mother and Daddy are leaving tomorrow.

Thursday, August 22

My family left at five bells[311] this morning. I didn't think I could stand it at first. It left the most terrible blankness. Gee, but they are wonderful to me and I don't half deserve them, I know.

Bud came up and Fanny also this afternoon. Then I went downtown, saw my coat again. This evening we were going to have a party but it fell through. I didn't particularly want Bob, and Dick couldn't come. Damn him, anyway. So Fanny and Bud came for a while. Then they left. Alyce and I talked and were bored. Now she's gone and I'm all alone and lonesome.

Friday, August 23

Well! Various things have happened today. Bud phoned this morning. Bob came to lunch at 12. He brought it with him and we cooked it and sat across from each other and ate and were happy. Then we sat on the couch and he told me he loved me some more, and it was all very nice. Then Fanny arrived which was the cue for all of us to act silly. We read extracts of our diaries to Bob and he nearly split. About 3:30 Bill Adams came up and took Fanny and me for a ride downtown and around. This evening—my gosh! This evening! I went to dinner with said George.

It all began calmly enough. We ate at the Heathman—good food,

---

[311] 5 a.m.

soft music—and we got along perfectly. I could really talk to him and he apparently to me. He's engaged to a Sally in Denver. We talked about love. He said it was something that grew on you. I said it was something that happened. And then we talked about everything. Finally we left and drove around, then came up to the apartment and played cards. Then he began to say interesting things. That I was lovely—*I, lovely.* And once out of a clear sky, "I'll bet you're on a lot of boys' minds," and once, "You'll never have to worry about getting married." I [said], "Perhaps no one will ask me." He: "Well, if they don't, just let me know, and if I'm not married, I will."

We agreed to have next Thanksgiving dinner together. Also he said he was going to invite me to a Phi Schi[312] dance. All this was very interesting, but not particularly dynamic. Then suddenly he kissed me. And my worlds tumbled. It left me all breathless and funny. And then things happened. Big things. He sang to me, songs about, "You're an angel but your eyes are filled with devils," and, "My Sin."[313] Then he'd kiss me and say, "You're darling, you sweet, you adorable— you were made to be loved. Someday some man is going to worship the ground you walk on,"—Oh, perfect. It may be just his line, but gee whiz, it's effective. I was in a whirl. That he began to wonder if he loved Sally and finally he thought he didn't. He was afraid he more than liked me. Before we realized it was 12:30, then we couldn't say goodby. We stalled and talked. I'd open the door and he'd close it. Oh, we had an awful time. Finally, I fairly pushed him out. He's calling tomorrow at 5. I don't know what's happened to me. My bridges are burned. I haven't any will. I'm mad, mad, I'm a fool. But he does something to me. And yet—once—when I told him to "be careful," he said, "Darling—I wouldn't harm you for the world, don't you know it?" And I said "How?" And he said, "You'll just have to take my word for it."

---

312 Probably Phi Kappa Psi

313 "My Sin" was a hit in 1929 for Annette Hanshaw and others, including Fred Waring's Pennsylvanians.

Saturday, August 24

I wonder—could it be love? But surely not—yet—what? He took me to dinner again tonight. We went to Caroline's. Then drove up the highway. It was a perfect night. Just simply gorgeous. And we talked, and talked, and talked about everything. It's funny, just the quirk of his lips with a twinkle in [his] eye can make me tumble over inside. He's dynamite. We went to Crown Point[314] and the water was moonlit and the stars were sparkly. He told me he loved me—*loved me*. Also, he's written Sally that if she wants to, to send his fraternity pin back, and a ring, and he said if she did, I could wear the pin. I told him he didn't say he loved me as if he meant it. And he said, "Wait till I see what Sally has said and I'll tell you differently." And the way he kisses me! And when I told him again to be careful, he said, "I'll take care of you, dear. I respect you too much to do otherwise." He sang to me all the way home. And he keeps saying, "Doggone it, Doris—you *bother* me." Once he said, "I don't want to be in love with you. It wouldn't be good for me. But I can't seem to help myself."

Oh, dear! This can't go on. We had barbecue on the way home. And I didn't leave him till 2 o'clock, and it didn't seem as though I'd been with him any time at all. Because I'm afraid I love him. It's a terrible sort of love. It isn't nice. It makes my head reel and my will lax.

Sunday, August 25

He came up this afternoon at 4 [p.m.]. We had dinner at the Heathman. Then came up here. What he does to my heart isn't even funny. It's tragedy. But I'm not going to think about him anymore. It's so silly for me to behave thusly. He had to leave at 7 [p.m.] for Eugene. Won't be back until Wednesday. I could hardly let him go. But did, eventually. He's going to write me, maybe. Gee whiz, what's wrong with me?

I've had an awful time with Bob throughout all this. Royal Oliver and Alyce and Gordon came up this evening. We had a good time—all

---

314 A lookout point about 15 miles east of Portland, overlooking the Columbia River Gorge and Mirror Lake. Luther Bailey was involved in the building of Vista House at Crown Point in 1916.

of us talking at once and being silly. Royal kissed me and I didn't want him to, so soon after George's. It was so cute, the way he left (George). He'd go down the hall—reach the steps—come back and kiss me—go again—back again—and in the last time I ran to him, kissed him, and pushed him down. As he reached the second landing I leaned over the banister and he looked up and we threw a kiss. Then I ran into my room before I weakened again. And I have to wait until Wednesday!

Monday, August 26

Fanny and Bud were up all morning. Fanny was breaking up with him because I'm leaving my apartment and she hasn't any place to meet him. I sold my golf clubs at a funny secondhand store to a man that didn't know a damn thing about them. I felt mean but I had to have the money for a Permanent. Marjie came and got me about 4. So here I am, apartment gone and, with it, unconventionality. (Whew! That's a mouthful.) But I'm happy because I love Marjie and I'm in love with George. Fanny thinks he's funny looking, but I don't care. He has something else—oh! I want to see him. There's so many things that might happen between now and Wednesday.

Tuesday, August 27

Had my Permanent today. Don't know whether I like it or not. Dinner at Fanny's, then she brought me home. Love her!

Wednesday, August 28

This afternoon I got a letter from him, and it was all a letter could or should be. And I was happy. He said he'd phone me from Salem; if not, Portland. Last Sunday we planned to go to dinner tonight. But 5, 6, 7, 8 o'clock arrived and no George. By nine I was desperate and now at 10 I'm sick. Something happened, but what? He could have phoned me—if he knew he was going to be late. Perhaps there was an accident. Perhaps he heard from Sally. Perhaps any number of things. The point is I'm perfectly and wholly miserable. I was a fool to let myself care. I don't even know that I do. But, oh, it's the suspense and the uncertainty and the wondering that hurts, and hurts—and hurts.

Thursday, August 29

Met Fanny downtown. I asked if George had registered [at his hotel]—but he hadn't. I also asked if he'd had any mail. Yes, two letters, but they were forwarded to his office in Portland. So he can't have heard from Sally. Now what did happen? Is he afraid to see me again—or doesn't he want to? His letter sounded as if he did—though some way, I'd like to be mad and on my dignity. But somehow I can only feel leaden, and ask why. It will be all right, I'm sure. It was all too wonderful for it to end this way. Besides, he's too much of a gentleman just to kiss me over. I will hear from him, so I'll keep on hoping and hoping some more. I only hope he hasn't been in some terrible accident.

Friday, August 30

Well, it's all in accordance with my life anyway. I should have expected it. I phoned his firm in town. He's been through and went straight on to Seattle without stopping. One of those letters was from Sally, I know, saying she would keep him and he decided to be kept. So didn't even see me again. And probably never will—ended it all—just like that! He might have let me know. But he didn't. He didn't know how it would hurt me. I didn't, either. I never dreamed I could feel like this. It's hell. Went canoeing with Bob tonight, and I actually had to clench my fist to keep from crying out when he kissed me. They made me sick—but contact of his lips sent shivers of repulsion all through me. I've never been so miserable. Just a week ago tonight I met him, and loved him—kissed him—and now—it's all over.

It's life, I suppose, and not the first heartbreak I've had. But I never knew one could hurt like this. I just feel all crumbled up inside. Nothing matters. Nothing. I could almost die. I can't even feel very cynical. It's all too awful. Oh, God! What have I done to deserve this! Ever—it isn't fair. But it's happened, and he'll marry Sally and be happy and so will she. Since I can't have him it's better to end abruptly this way. Anyway, he's given me something I didn't know—a beautiful glimpse of love. A tender poignant vision of love, and I still think he meant what he said. It's just circumstances that have made this happen. So all I can do is thank Fate for giving me the bit it did—and try and forget. But, oh, how it hurts!

Saturday, August 31

Downtown all day. Saw a wonderful show. Left me—[unfinished line]

Sunday, September 1

A new month. New paper [in her diary], and a chapter of my life. School starts Tuesday so I've packed the rest of my diary away and am starting with a clean slate. All my summer's happiness and tears are tied with a rubber band. It will make it easier to forget. I'll not let myself be sentimental and tearful. I won't. This will be just a record of my school year—my last year at St. Helen's Hall, and it will be as complete and as treasured as the rest of the chapters. And I'm going to be happy, not morbid and cynical but happy. I'm glad I'm alive, and I'm glad I'm capable of loving. There! Bob phoned twice today. Wanted to go out this evening. I didn't.

Monday, September 2

Went out with Bob and Barry and Marjie. I decided to be nice to Bob since it was the last time I'd see him for a long time. I did try, and I thought I was, but Marjie says I treat him like dirt. We saw "Mme. X"—a perfect show, and then went to a thrilling, funny-looking Chop Suey place near Burnside[315] and ate some funny Chinese noodles. It was fun! And I got off with the Chop Sticks. Barry is just awfully good-looking but rude and

---

315 Portland's Chinatown. This was Doris's first time eating "foreign" food.

stingy, and second-class. I kept comparing them with George and the contrast was pitiful.

Tuesday, September 3

Oh, gee—everything's nice. There wasn't even anything wrong. It seems that he had wired me Wednesday and I didn't get it. I got an airmail letter today, just as nice as ever. Oh, bless his heart. I knew it wasn't a line. I knew he was different. Came to school today[316]. I'm all unpacked and we think we've the cutest room in the house, and Coie's so sweet. I know I'm going to be happy. How can I help it with such a perfect beginning?—oh, life!

The Senior Girls' House, the dorm where Doris lived, is the only remaining building of St. Helen's Hall. It's at SW 14th Avenue and SW Montgomery Street, overlooking the freeway at the onramp to Interstate 405 South.

---

316 Doris will board at St. Helen's Hall this year.

Friday, September 13

No letter today. Why that terrible ache? I can't let him make me feel this way.

Saturday, September 14

Downtown all day. Buying, spending, having fun. Then we saw the most perfect show. And the characters just fitted Sally, George, the Baron[318] and me. In fact, the whole thing was made to order. They even played "My Sin" and I thought I would scream. It ended as it should, though. Wonder, oh, I wonder how this will end. I have a feeling he hasn't gotten my letters. So I sent him one from the Heathman and mailed it myself. Now to see what happens. Oh, gosh, I can't let myself care like this, because it's going to be so hard not to let it get me.

Sunday, September 15

Church this morning. I'm crazy about Jeanette. She comes pretty darn near to being my ideal. She sees life. She isn't little or on the surface. She likes life, too—really, because she's traveled. This afternoon Homer and Art came up. Art's dumn. This evening Bob and Jimmy came up. It was good to see Bob again. He's a darling, really—Coie and I entertained them in the Parlor and Julia and Rosemary acted unbearably silly. It was fun, though.

Monday, September 16

Oh, I'm a fool. I'm five kinds of a damn fool. I got a letter from George—a nice long one. But there was about a page in it of Sally. The Baron is visiting her, and he sounded rather jealous and up in the air, and asked me what to do? He also said she didn't send the pin back and it sounded so nonchalant. "Oh, I've some news for you—Sally didn't send back my pin."

And instead of being sweet and lady-like about it, and trying to help

---

318 The Baron is apparently a rival for Sally's affections.

him, I wrote a cool, rather sarcastic letter, suggesting that perhaps life would be less complicated for him if I quietly stepped out of the picture. And [I] mailed it, before I changed my mind. It's gone now, gone. I can't get it back. Oh, why haven't I any sense? Why do I insist on being such a damned idiot? Oh, gosh!

Tuesday, September 17

I have the driest, burnt-out feeling. I keep telling myself not to think and not to worry—but I can't help it. I took his letter wrong. I acted like a jealous, silly little schoolgirl. I don't mean anything to him. I knew all along that nothing would ever come of it. That he'd marry Sally, that she had him first and that I didn't want to marry him anyway.

Yet, the first sign on his part of friendship and confidence makes me get huffy and proud and on my dignity. I'll bet he's disgusted. I'll bet he's laughing at me, thinks I'm a silly fool. I'll get a cool letter back. Either that or nothing at all. I don't know which would be worse.

Oh, this is awful. If it only didn't make me feel like running out into the night and dying. Oh, to get away by myself, where I can cry and cry and get it out of my system. I don't even know whether I could cry. I'm so choked up inside.

Wednesday, September 18

Went riding this afternoon. I had a sweet horse, but stubborn. But, oh, it was fun. We rode in the ring, formed figures and etc. I'm dead tired now, just weak and wobbly. And not so very happy.

Thursday, September 19

No letter today. I went all to pieces inside. I wanted to fall down and kick my heels and cry and cry. Instead I could just let a few tears trickle, then hide. I knew it would be this way. If I could only run from all humanity. The more I read his letter the sweeter it seems. He didn't mean anything.

Then my letter probably hit him like a dash of cold water. It's all my fault and I'm a fool.

The question is, should I write and apologize or just wait and see what happens? Whatever I do will be wrong. I never do the right thing. Oh, gosh! Why did he ever come into my life at all? I don't want anybody to control my happiness. I want to be independent of everyone. Master of my destiny and yet, a mere man can make me behave like this!

Oh, hell! What to do? If I don't love him, I wonder what sort of a weak, shameless character I'll be when I do meet the man I love. Oh! I'm afraid he's it, and he's gone. Because I haven't any sense and jump at conclusions. Will I never learn?

Friday, September 20
Still no word and I'm trying to be brave and philosophical, but it's hard. He means more every day. I think I'll write. I've got to do something. We had a surprise party for Julia this evening. That is, the seniors. We played cards and danced and ate. Jeanette and Rosemary and I played Poker. Fun and plenty of it. But, oh! How hard to keep my mind on the game!

Saturday, September 21
Went out with Marjie this afternoon. I felt so free and untrammeled. And we saw George Shade. It was thrilling and rather dramatic. Then out to her house—better left unsaid. Gee! I love her. We were both so silly because we were happy. Life is fun but I wish it weren't quite so complicated.

Sunday, September 22
Came in this morning—and! There was a phone call from Dr. Scott. I didn't know what to think. He left word for me to phone. Shall I? Do I want to? Wouldn't it be better not to? It's funny I'm not more thrilled. I'm afraid George is to blame—oh, what is he thinking of me? Does he care at all? Have I spoiled everything? Anyway I hereby make a solemn vow to

never act without thinking again. It's childish and senseless, and causes more grief than otherwise. Oh, damn!

"My love is almost anguish now—
It beats so strong and true.
T'were rapture could I deem that thou
Such anguish ever knew."[319]

Monday, September 23

Well! It's done now. I wrote and apologized. At least my side of it is clear. If he doesn't answer, it will be because he's filled with false pride, and who wants a man with false pride! Oh, gosh! I'm happy.

Oh—I almost forgot. I called Dr. Scott as per ordered. He said he had to talk to me and wanted me to come over. But I can't very well, and I don't very much want to. It seems that he is being fast eclipsed or something. He was darn nice and said when I didn't phone back, he was frantic. Not long ago that would've put me in turmoil. Now I even forgot to record it for two days. I'm nutty, I guess.

Sunday, September 29

We all went out to Oswego today to the most gorgeous home. [The homeowners] gave their house and canoes over to us and we swam and ran around and convinced ourselves that we were having a perfect time. Even though there were no men around. I was in the middle of the lake just at sundown and the water turned red and the sky blue-gold. And, of course, I thought of George.

---

319 From "Stanzas," by Charlotte Brontë

Monday, September 30 C.S.

Marjie pledged Kappa—nice! Check and letter from Mother and Daddy—and box of candy from my darling brothers. Sweet! Oh, I'm happiness personified.

Tuesday, October 1

I asked Ed Gerlinger to the Boarders' dance. Why did I do that? I can't imagine! Ed was darling when I found him and said sure. Well, anyway, he's a perfect dancer. I phoned Dick to ask him if he'd accept a blind date. He said he was going to Eugene. Why do I like that man? Because he likes the wind and stars.

Wednesday, October 2

Sweetest darn letter from Marjie. That's about all that's happened. Rosemary just walked in. I can't think, guess because I'm tired. I've eaten way too many peanuts.

Thursday, October 3

And life goes on! Letter from Fanny and Alyce. Fanny's so thrilled at Boston and all it has to offer, and Alyce is in love again. I'd like to get away from this place tonight. All the squabble and wrangle seem so futile. Oh, for the night and the stars and a fast car—and love. Yet here I stay in the midst of a mass of girls.

Friday, October 4

Wasn't on the Dinky[320]—I'm glad, because I've studied.

---

320 Dinky — slang for Deficiency list

Saturday, October 5

Well—Ed phoned at the last minute that he was leaving for Cal. So I phoned Bob and asked him to come to the dance. He said he would. He didn't! And here I sit in my finger wave and new pearl earrings. The music below—and me, jelled [*sic*]. Alone. It's the humiliation of it [that] hurts.

Now they're playing "My Sin." I could and would cry if it weren't that that's what I'm expected to do. My head aches like hell. Everything happens for the best. Perhaps I wouldn't have had a good time anyway. Oh, it's hard not to be blue. Haven't heard from George for a week (though I didn't answer his last letter). No man—dance—no fun. Have to write an essay tomorrow. Laughter outside, music. I want to be loved for myself. I *need* comfort. Isn't there anyone that needs me? That's crying for me? That wants me?

And here I am, being sentimental. I'll cry pretty soon. What's a man in a lifetime? Or a measly little dance? I'm out for the big things in life. And not the petty. The real, not the make-believe. It's the wind and stars I like. Not a flesh and blood human. Besides, I'll not be affected by exterior circumstances. My happiness comes from within. Mind over matter—there! Tears, stay—hell!

Sunday, October 6

Just bummed around and studied. Bored to death.

Monday, October 7

Oh—George phoned this evening! Actually I heard his voice, and oh—I'm still feeling all up in the air. It was awful! The way he says, "Now, listen, Doris," and rolls my name around on his tongue. I was in the recreation room and it was dark and I couldn't even talk. He said he had the darndest time phoning me. That it was a heck of an institution I was in. Also! He asked me what I was doing Christmas and I said I hoped Arizona. And he said, "That's where I'd like to go." And I said OK. My gosh! Wouldn't it be perfect? Maybe he's coming up tomorrow night. Maybe.

Tuesday, October 8

Went around in a daze all day today. He didn't come up. Neither did he phone. Probably because those darn little kids hung on to it all evening.[321]

Wednesday, October 9

Guess I'm done for. I'm not even very happy. It isn't fun to be this much in love. Where shall I begin? We went riding this afternoon in the woods. It was damp and the leaves were turning red and the smell of autumn was in the air. My sweet old horse kicked his little feet and pranced along the path, and the sky was blue and I thought and dreamed. And wondered mostly if I ever would see George again. Then we were in study hall at seven [when] Sister Superior called me out and said Mr. Tift was in the Parlor.

I simply froze up. Didn't have a chance to even powder my nose. I don't know how I ever got in there. But I did. And we sat on the couch. After these agonizing weeks of alternate turmoil and happiness he was actually sitting beside me. We talked about everything but what was most important—Sally. Finally he said, "I'm not going to Denver for Thanksgiving." And I said, "But I thought that was when you were going to announce your engagement." And he said, "I'm not going to get married. The Baron can have her. I don't care." And my heart stood still and he said it without a trace of regret or jealousy.

About that time Julia and Betty took it upon themselves to look at him. So they came in the Parlor and giggled and looked at pictures on the wall and behave like silly little schoolgirls. I was so darned mad. It was hard enough anyway. Finally they dispersed but they'd taken something with them. I hate that parlor. It cramps my style. Soon after that the bell rang, and he took my hands to say goodby, and suddenly I was in his arms and in that kiss was all that yearning and hunger of six weeks' torture. I gave him all I had. I reveled in that minute. I'll never forget it. He held me so close, so tightly, and just said one word— "Doris," with a sort of gasp. If I should die tomorrow, I've lived.

---

321 Other girls in the house were using the telephone.

Then I took him to the door and he disappeared into the night and I came back to Study Hall. Down to earth and fountain pens, brown desks and blackboards. But he said he given up trying to phone me. That the line was always busy. But he'd write. I'm going to Gearheart[322] Friday. He may not write. If not, I won't care. I'm going to quit being down and live in the nice things that have happened. And I'm so glad I feel like this. And my one aim in life—the shining goal, the light—everything is centered towards when I'll see him again.

Thursday, October 10
Work, work, work, when I want to dream. I'm not trying to control myself. Oh, gosh! I'm happy. And tomorrow, the beach.

"This isn't sunshine, this is storm. This isn't just a sunny pool. This is the ocean. This isn't the safe surface of life. This is the depth, the height. This is flood. This is flame. This is love!"[323]

Friday, October 11
Went to the beach this afternoon[324]. I've been for a run down by the ocean. It's glorious. Foggy and mysterious. And I'm in love with George. Wrote him not a very nice letter[325] and yet not so bad. I'll mail it tomorrow. Oh, I love this salt sea smell and wind. Everyone's so excited and happy.

Saturday, October 12
Gee! We're having a good time. Had our luncheon on the rocks by the breakers. Then took a long walk through the woods to a spring. After that we went in the ocean. It was cold—oh, so cold. But we jumped the white

---

322 Coastal resort town in Oregon, 81 miles northwest from Portland. The Bailey family once owned a beach cottage there, but sold it to pay for Rae's college education.

323 Appears to be Doris's original work

324 Field trip with the girls of St. Helen's Hall

325 She means flirty or sexy, not rude or cold.

crest and screamed and lived beneath the blue sky. And Coie and I got dinner, which was more of a joke than otherwise, considering the way I cook. The dinner having been swallowed, we all went to Seaside to a show. Then home to the fire and roasted marshmallows.

Sunday, October 13

All I've done since Friday is eat and dance and sing. Gee, but I've been happy. And flirted all the way home with the bus driver, and sat by an open window and looked at the moon. And fight with Nancy. We even stooped to hair pulling on the floor of the car. Oh, it's a great life! Now I'm dirty and dead-tired.

Monday, October 14

We both had the same impulse at the same time. He wrote me Friday night. His letter left me a little awed and breathless. It is something I'll keep forever. Oh, I'm so lucky. I can't believe that it is true. I'm really in love for the first time in my life. And he apparently feels the same about me. Happy, happy, happy. I hope my letter wasn't too cold—and we'll be together next weekend. Oh, I wonder what it will bring forth.

Love—yes, actually. There is something divinely beautiful about it. Everything in life, even the routine of eating has a new significance. As if it were almost flavored with love. Sweet. Oh, I'm glad that I'm capable of this. Somehow I can't be pessimistic. This isn't going to fall through because it's the real thing. God means for me to be happy and loving him. It isn't an accident. Fate had it arranged. He's the man I love. Oh, it's such a nice feeling inside of me. It seems to envelop me. Oh, gosh, I can't say what I mean.

Tuesday, October 15

I answered George's letter today, making definite arrangements for Friday. Marjie's coming home and I'm going out there. Till Friday—that's my slogan. To see him—talk.

Wednesday, October 16

Well! We never know what the morrow will bring forth. I'm in the infirmary. I fainted in Chapel. For no good reason except that a pain in my side threatens to get the better of me and the world turned black. Sister Superior took me out. Now I feel fine. Nice comfortable blue and white room, soft bed, plenty of attention, and nothing to do but listen to the rain and dream about George. Kathleen Jones is in [the infirmary] with me; she's talking in her sleep and rather telling secrets. She['d] better be careful. I nearly forgot. Bud came up Monday night. He's a darling. Too bad he isn't happy.

Thursday, October 17

I shouldn't be up but I am because I want to get out tomorrow. Oh, what will it bring forth?

Friday, October 18

"I have no wish to cry or saying
No least desire to pray or curse
The loss of love is a terrible thing
They lie—who say that death is worse."[326]

Yes—there it is in black and white. I don't know how it happened or why. Yes, I do, too. It's just that I'm too damned romantic and idealistic. It hurts, oh, so terribly. To discover there was nothing when I thought there was so much. It shakes all my foundations. It's hard to believe in anything now. Love—my vision of it must be out of all reason. Oh, no! Surely not! It can't be—this is it.

I left here at four after a mad last-minute rush and fight with my English teacher. Had a finger wave, and was to meet [George] at six, but didn't get there until 6:30. There was something wrong from the very first.

---

326 "The Loss of Love," a contemporary (to Doris's time) poem by Countee Cullen (he was born 1903), one of the Harlem Renaissance poets

Little things mattered so. We sat near the door—they forgot my cocktail fork. The coffee was cold; my gloves lay crumbled on the table instead of in a slim, slick pat.

Yet it wasn't so bad. Conversation was free enough, and we even discussed going to Arizona for Christmas. After dinner we drove up to Mrs. Taylor's and I ran in to see about Fanny. Then we drove out Terwilliger and down the valley. I contracted a silly mood and we rather enjoyed ourselves. Suddenly he stopped the car and crushed me to him. So hard, so fierce, almost savage. There was nothing tender about it or restful. We were in the middle of a white road, and a car honked past. It was all brittle and bright—tho pleasant enough for all of that. I was perfectly satisfied.

Then we drove on, slowly, and turned into a dirt road and parked. I was happy then. My head lay on his lap, and we talked about love and marriage and all such interesting things. Ourselves—then we suddenly let go. He made love as only he can, and I felt justified in letting him have as much as he did. I excuse myself because I thought I loved him and he me. I drifted. I reveled. I drank it in. His lips, his eyes, his strong arms. Oh, dear—how can I explain it? There was suddenly something wrong. And inexplicable intangible something.

Then it came upon me in a rush. He didn't care, he was simply out for what he to get. He—George—the man I thought I loved, that beautiful idealistic dream. It was all being crushed. He'd seen my soul. He had had a part of me no one else knew, and he consecrated [*sic*][327] it. Made it cheap—sordid. I felt dry, futile. "Let's go," that was all. We went, and he sang some silly songs while I huddled in the corner. The sky was stormy, the moon was tossed in a sea of fitful black clouds. A universe, an infinity of space. That scene is imprinted on my memory. I just stared dumnly.

Finally he realized something was wrong and asked. I couldn't speak at first. No one will ever know how I felt. He thought I was sulking because he wouldn't let me drive, and said, "Doris, you're just a pampered little child." Then something broke. I knew then that he'd never understand. That it wasn't in him to know. But I said, "Oh, it's just life. I've got to get over expecting so much from it. I'm always expecting something big

---

[327] She means desecrated.

and stupendous and then discovering nothing, thinking I found a golden dream, and then having a crash." And he said, "Do you mean that you thought life was beautiful until tonight, and that I spoiled it?"

"Yes."

And then he laughed. Laughed. Thought I was a fool, thought I was childish and silly, and probably anyone else would, too. Perhaps I am. But, no—I won't lose it! At the time I almost believed him and we dropped subject and chattered. We drove out towards Alyce's and our conversation was all that we might wish. Witty, bantering, slighting, kidding; in other words, nothing. Then we started home. Even stopped for a Coca-Cola. On the last stretch he became more serious. We talked about Sally. He said he was quite sure at times that he didn't love her. We almost got back into the old swing of things. And I, in a last desperate effort, suggested we drive down by the river. I thought perhaps it was my imagination.

It was beautiful. The moonlight filtered down to the trees. The water was black. The world was still and frightening. I stood by an oak tree, hung on to it and loved the river. I turned around and he held me, and kissed my eyes and lips, throat and said, "I love you tonight, Doris." But it was too savage. There was too much man in him. The starlight and moss called for tenderness and beauty. And he gave only passion. I knew then that it could never be. That he was not for me. I didn't want him. I wanted to run. That poignant moon; that spot where my dreams are laid. I'd taken him to it. I'd shown him my heart, and he hadn't seen. He didn't want to see. He couldn't.

We went home then. He knew, and I knew, that it was all over. He's phoning in the morning but I can't see him again. It would be a farce. It's too strange for me to try [to] figure out. It seems unbelievable that I should've been so sure. Will it always be that way? Will my dreams always so far outdistance reality? Won't I ever find the kindred spirit and the silver ball? Will I know it when I do?

Saturday, October 19

Yes, he phoned. He's going to Seattle for the rest of the weekend, more power to him. I don't even wonder how he feels. "How weary, flat, still, and unprofitable are all the uses of the world."[328] Marjie and I went to a football game. Oregon won, with a couple of thrilling touchdowns. Saw a mob of people we knew and had a good time. Show this evening.

"Oregon defending goal under shadow of posts. Held Idaho to 4 downs when this close to line." Rae Bailey took this photo of the Oregon-Idaho game Nov. 20, 1920.

Sunday, October 20

I'm glad my diary is my own, and no one else ever reads and judges me by it. I'd be accused of being over-tragic. Well, perhaps I am. But so long as no one knows about it, where's the harm? Because it is tragedy to me. It's as big a thing as losing a friend by death. To lose a dream. Because without our dreams, what is there to live for and build on? Without ideals and visions. Oh! The ideal of my life is gone. I can't stand it. And yet, why not? Others do. I want to be hard and pessimistic and maybe philosophical. I suppose I should say, "Well, at least I've learned some good pointers on necking." Well, what of it? I have.

---

328 "How weary, stale, flat, and unprofitable seem to me all the uses of this world!" Hamlet, 1:2:133-34

Monday, October 21
I buried myself in work today. After school Jeanette and I went downtown. Went to see Eddy. He was so darned sweet. He's a good egg. Really! Then we drank Coca-Colas by the score and ate crushed ice and whipped cream bars. Also bought peanuts. It's a great life. Wrote home for money.

Tuesday, October 22 C.S.
Letter from Fanny, and so darned much work to do. I'm swamped.

Wednesday, October 23
I wanted to go riding but needed to study. I have the most purposeful feeling tonight. I'm all seriousness and anything as trivial as a man has no chance. Which reminds me, I've had a phone call from Bob and Bill Adams. I'll have things to say to Bob.

Thursday, October 24
Had the annual "Old Girl-New Girl" party tonight. Jeanette and K[athleen] and I went as wild Spanish gentlemen with mustaches and a drunken air. Only toward 10 o'clock we were too tired to be anything but flops. Just try [to] act wild and thrilling when your feet and legs and back and head are one solid ache. The music was good, though. So it's not such a bad life.

Friday, October 25
A week ago today—why do I think? I hate him. Hate, hate. It's black and dirty. I see red. I hate him, with a terrible, violent awfulness. It scares me.

biggest was a trip soon—on land and sea. If it could only mean Arizona for Christmas, wouldn't I be happy?

Sunday, November 3

Church this morning, of course. Then studied all afternoon. I was out on the grass, and Jeanette and Herb came over and we ate ice cream. He's rather cute, but not good enough for her, I don't think.

Monday, November 4

Dragged around all day, feeling like the devil. And finally gave up and came to the infirmary. I'm a flop, a washout. Why do I have to always go under?

Tuesday, November 5

Dr. Baird came this morning. First he thought I had the Grippe, then he blamed it on my side. I really don't care what's wrong. Just so I get out in a hurry. Incidentally, I'm starved and he ordered no food. Now why did he do that? Food never hurt anyone, and gee, but I'm hungry. And he said he saw Dr. Scott at the hospital this morning, and that he's been asking about me. Funny what an appeal that man has for me when I'm sick. And yet perhaps not so funny. Two years ago last Saturday, I met him. The darling—I wonder if he's happy?

Wednesday, November 6

Still here, and oh, so darned hungry. Have had notes from Coie, Julia, and Jeanette. They are all such darlings, made me feel so good.

Thursday, November 7

And still I remain on my back. Had the nicest, most wonderful letter from Marjie. Life wouldn't revolve if I didn't have her. She's stuck, when the others have drifted.

Friday, November 8

Marjie sent me flowers. All pink and white and bunchy—a symbol of her sweetness. I cried, of course. Letter and check from Daddy. The letter certainly discouraged, or tried to, all hopes of Arizona for Christmas. The question is—what will happen to me? I can't very well just drift, or can I? Oh, I wish we'd strike a gold mine. Then there wouldn't be these continual "ifs."

Sunday, November 10

And still I remain. Now they're talking hospital. But I'll fight it with all the fight left in me. Don't see why they don't decide on what's wrong. Coie sent me a gorgeous deep rose plant. The darling. People are too good to me. I don't deserve it. I've acquired a sudden will and desire to write. But I haven't quite enough confidence in myself.

Good Samaritan Hospital, which is still located on NW 22nd Avenue in Portland.

Monday, November 11

Well! I seem to be at the hospital[335], regardless of all my fighting. Had an X-ray picture taken and I'm hoping for the best. I have an uncontrollable

---

[335] Good Samaritan again.

desire to see Dr. Scott. Guess it's the hospital atmosphere. It simply grips me. I know I'd feel much better if he were here. Coie and her aunt came to see me. They were both sweetness personified. Brought me magazines and made me feel as if somebody cared. It's gotten to the point where I want my mother.

Tuesday, November 12

I'm discovering the stuff that I made of. Vanity. I guess that's what it could be called. I've been stewing and fretting all day. I'm driving myself insane. I thought, of course, I'd see an intern and perhaps make this being in bed a trifle interesting. But do I? No! Damn it all. I'll be here in this 2 x 4 room and twist and turn and bite the sheets. I can hear their hearty laughs, and now and then get a glimpse of a white back. But otherwise I'm just a lonesome, neglected patient in room 363. It doesn't even occur to the poor pieces of tripe that a little attention or flirtation might be all a patient needs to inspire her on. Darn! Soon I'll run out into the hall and grab a man by his neck. I want to yell, scream, raise the general devil and attract some attention to myself. I can't keep my nose powdered for eons. And my blue jacket on. I'm disgusted. Guess I'll have to quit hoping and resign myself to the inevitable. Not even Dr. Scott has appeared. He might ask someone sometime if I am here. Which reminds me—my nurse said he had another baby last July. Funny, he didn't tell me about it. Flowers from Ruth and Aunt Lola and Bill Adams. Mrs. Taylor came to see me. Likewise, Sister KA and AS and AB. That's just in the way of news items.

Wednesday, November 13

Today is my Marjie's birthday. Wonder what she's doing. Ruth Crum and Dr. and Mrs. Parker and Bill Adams all came up after dinner last night. I thought Bill intended staying all night. Some men haven't any idea when to leave. Then this morning I had four doctors hovering around. They did their level best to push my stomach through to my back. Still they don't know what's wrong. I feel perfectly putrid today. I do so want to get well.

It's vitally necessary. I can't afford to be sick. Sister says to leave it in the hands of the Lord. That He knows what's wrong and will do what He thinks best. I wish He'd tell Dr. Baird. It would enlighten matters. But I guess she's right.

No live intern as yet. Hope is going. Guess I'll just have to live in memories and dreams. After all, they are less dangerous.

Thursday, November 14

Gang of doctors again this morning. Feel like hell. But there is an intern. He came in just when I waked [*sic*] from my after-lunch nap, and I was looking like heck. Nevertheless he stayed 45 minutes and has a black mustache and loves horses and the desert. So we both waxed intelligent on a good deal of horse talk. He's nice but not much sex appeal, although a darned entrancing laugh. They are going to give me gas tomorrow. The devil, I say. Bill came up last night. No mail. Rank food. I'd like to cry. I would.

Friday, November 15

[Weak handwriting] Dr. Scott came—just as I was coming out of the gas.

-- Lapse—15-22 --

Friday, November 22

It is strange—what this month brought forth. I had an operation last Saturday for abscesses. Felt rotten all week, of course, but better today. It's just like another appendicitis operation. Drainage tubes and all the pain that goes with it. Sitting up straight and not much food. Everyone has been wonderful to me. Coming and sending things. Bob and Johnny have been up and, of course, Bill Adams.

The big thing is though, that Dr. Baird says I can't go back to school this year. But I'm to go to Arizona and ride and get well. I can't help but wonder why Fate was so determined that I don't finish what I've tried so hard [to finish]. Perhaps I can take an examination and enter college in Arizona. Everything happens for the best so I'm waiting to see why this is. It will be fun going to Arizona again. It can't look too bleak. I guess Fate will work it out some way. But my destiny certainly is queer and mixed-up.

I won't let it down me, though. I'll keep fighting. I know what I want to do, and the obstacles simply make it more urgent. Besides—what is life without obstacles? Stale. So I'm getting my share and I want to be able to say: "In the fell clutch of circumstance I have not winced nor cried aloud; under the bludgeonings of chance, my head is bloody but unbowed."[336]

Saturday, November 30

Haven't felt like writing. It's so darned awkward. Things have been moving. Had a regular party in here last night. Everyone's home for the holidays. Marjie's been here since Wednesday night. It's going to be awful when she leaves, after having her. Gosh, but I love her. Maybe she'll go back to Arizona with me. Just maybe. Things have happened but it's too hard to try and go back. The intern affair is moving right along. He's engaged, but men seem to make a habit of doing that. Which reminds me. I got a letter from George. Never expected to hear again. He'll be in town Wednesday and wants to see me. He doesn't know I'm here. He seems to know that I might not want to see him but said to drop a note if I did. Haven't decided yet what to do. It would help my pride to ignore him. Still, it would be someone else to come and see me. I can't decide whether I even want to see him or not. It might hurt. Still, there is no harm in being friends. That's what we were meant to be. Oh, well—Fate will take care of it.

---

336 "Invictus," by William Ernest Henley

Sunday, December 1

November gone! Life is strange. Just terribly strange. My intern and I had the best time this morning. I exposed a lot of radical ideas about never getting married, as I do. It worked. He's a darling. The girl that gets him is lucky. He's so serious about life and yet has an amazing sense of humor. Wish things would get more personal. I like him. He fascinates me. Afraid he could do other things. Marjie's gone. It's lonesome and quiet. Coie came up this afternoon. Maybe she's going to write George. Just maybe. It's obvious that I couldn't write intelligently or legibly.

Monday, December 2

It's so lonesome and sorta awful. Finished all the good reading matter, so there's nothing to do but think. Want to be up. I want so many things, and here I lie. I am glad I'm alive, but the sooner I get out of here, the better. I'm afraid I'll get morbid, and cynical, and pessimistic. I might even lose my good disposition. Perhaps. It's time for lunch. Maybe something interesting will happen this afternoon. It just might. Jeanette was here late yesterday; so was Bill. I don't understand him. He told me I shouldn't go out with Rex. Boy, just give me a chance! That man has S. A.[337]

Later—Maloney and Ragsdale came up. They were out on a big party last night and both had hangovers and were afraid to go back to school. Maloney was all for making more Whoopee tonight and then going to California. To heck with the education. If he didn't dissipate so much, he'd be something. He's ruining himself, though, this way. A sweet kid. Makes me want to mother him. Guess he arouses my maternal instincts. What! Wouldn't he be surprised? He thinks he's so very sophisticated. Bill came up this evening. Likewise Coie and Phoebe.

Tuesday, December 3

Dr. Scott came in this morning. The sweet! We had the best time. That man appeals to me. I can't quite figure him out. I think he thinks I'm a lot

---

[337] Sex appeal

more "wise to the world" than I am. My intern[338] was in, too. But not for long. Dr. Rockey called him out. Damn. He's—things he shouldn't be. I could fall in love with him. But I'm not going to.

Later—the "other intern" Dr. Peterson came in this afternoon. He's just the opposite of Dr. Paulson. Silly, blond, modern—but fully as fascinating. He took my diary and calmly read it. What could I do? Then he laughed at my maternal instincts. Hereafter, this little book remains undercover whilst curious doctors are on deck. No, I guess I don't like him. He's crude and vulgar. His conversation is far from elevating. But then—one gets tired of hitting the ceiling and touching the heights. Oh, hell! Now why do I waste ink on him? Bob and Jimmy came up this evening. Nice little Bob, and to think I was once in love with him. My heart is inconsistent. I'm inconsistent. I wonder where I'll end. I wonder so many things. Is there really something big in the way of a love affair someplace for me? Is there love? You'd think with all my disillusionment, that I'd quit hoping and dreaming. Well, perhaps I shall, someday, and content myself with adventure.

Wednesday, December 4

Ross Bates[339] came in [to her room] on a stretcher this morning. Poor kid has been here five months and has two more to go. And he can still grin. That's courage for you. Good-looking rather, too. Dr. Peterson came in and my heart behaved foolishly. He hadn't been in long when Helen Hyde arrived, and scared him out. Damn it! It's funny, how some men affect me not a whit and others—this business of man and woman is a mixed-up affair anyway. I say to heck with the men, and yet one can appear, and even though I don't will it and fight against it, and have the strangest power over me. Funny.

There's been a little boy, somewhere, crying and moaning. It hurts. People in pain. Made me wonder which is the harder to bear—physical or

---

338 Dr. Paulson is Doris's new favorite.
339 One of the boys from Hill Military Academy

mental torture? We can cry with bodily pain. But if someone has wounded your heart, it hurts too deeply to even cry out.

Later—10 o'clock—Dr. Paulson has just been here. [340] That laugh—it does things to the inside of me. I know he's not as hard as he pretends to be. Not with those eyes. We agreed that the whole human race was shallow and that the only way to avoid being disillusioned was not to expect anything. True enough. I can't imagine him being overcome with passion. He has too stolid a control of himself. Nothing impulsive or daring about him, and yet, what is it that makes an appeal? His stability?

(My gosh! The most awful commotion down the hall. Sounded as if someone were being choked. That horrible, rasping, guttural sound. Why don't they do something for him?)

Thursday, December 5

Only one tube in me now. Nothing much happened today. Maloney came about six. He's having a hard time of it. Trouble, trouble, and more trouble. Perhaps he'll outgrow being so obstreperous. Ruth[341] and Bill were up all evening and we all acted very silly. Put my feet on the floor without anyone's permission. Must create some excitement.

Friday, December 6

Whoopee! Tubes all gone! Wheelchair this afternoon. Been reading a book that makes me wonder, maybe there's something in "free love." [342]

Later, very much—well! I had my wheelchair ride. Went down to see Ross. We had a great time. But he told me about the girl Dr. Paulson's engaged to. He said she was affected and common and slangy. I don't

---

340 Doris seems to be falling into a rescue-romance again.
341 She says Ruth Crum when she means Rae's girlfriend; otherwise, Doris's friend Ruth.
342 The idea of "free love" did not originate in the 1960s. The modern definition is an offshoot of both anarchism and the women's suffrage movement in the 1800s. Free love means, essentially, having sex with whomever one wants without need for marriage, so common in 2013 that hardly anyone remarks upon it.

understand why he—who could have the pick of most anyone—should show such poor judgment? About 5:30 [p.m.] Dr. Peterson arrived, and in a few minutes, Dr. Paulson. Seeing them both together, I couldn't help comparing them. The one's so very fine and straight, and the personification of all that should be admired, and the other almost gross in his display of modernism, yet strangely fascinating for all of that. But one will go so much further than the other, if only he isn't misled by some darn fool woman. Gee! I don't know why I'm so concerned about his welfare. But I am. It must be his eyes. Anyway, despite all that, we had an uproariously good time. The one so silly, the other so filled with strength. It made me feel slightly morbid and disgustingly philosophical—this problem of character.

Saturday, December 7

The day dawned, as days will do, and with the dawn before bath or bed made came Dr. Paulson. A smile, a chuckle, a twinkle from his eye. The less I see of him, the better, for my sense of security and independence. We argued. I, as usual, not knowing or caring what we were arguing about. Enough just to talk to him. Enough to know he was there. Then nurses and various and sundry things shooed him out and left me with an odd sensation of buoyancy. And he's going to marry someone who doesn't see those finer qualities. I'm sure of it. For her, he's a conquest. A new trophy to brag about, to dangle before her friends' eyes. Oh, hell! Anyone would think I was in love with him.

Anyway, about 2 o'clock old Bill arrived and proceeded to tease me. Dr. Peterson stuck his head in, perceived Bill's feet, made a face and went out. What I can't understand is, I blushed and became confused when he means so very little. Bill stayed and stayed and stayed. About four I mounted my chariot and started to see Ross. But the room was full of men, so I contented myself with the sun room. Later friend Kelly dropped by. He's a flop. These dissipated children—will they never learn?

Sunday, December 8

Doctor says in 10 days I should be on my way to Arizona. Christmas at home—what could be sweeter? Yet leaving my Portland, my school. I wish I wouldn't think about it. Leaving Marjie and the gang, I mean. Then, strangely, there's someone else I don't seem to want to leave. Someone who shouldn't matter a bit. I feel blue today. I don't like feeling that way. I shouldn't. With life before me and always the promise of adventure. I won't be sadder. I will be happy and then, I love Arizona and besides, it's adding another chapter, another episode of action and experience to my life. So quit brooding, you fool—and read.

Later—I didn't read. I slept and when I woke up, company came in, and brought me candy, books, and gossip about school. Then about four I went to see Ross. He's the sweetest kid, and so easy to talk to. We bat conversation back and forth like old friends. I even ate my dinner in here with him. Then home and to bed to fight with my nurse. I'm happy now. Perhaps I'm destined for something big. I feel that way tonight.

"Oh, life and little people, stand aside, give way."[343] Never mind—just a bit of egotism. But happy, happy with the night and life and the ability to see beauty. I want to live amidst beauty. I want exquisiteness and softness and moonlight always. Music gentle, star dust, and love like something ethereal. Oh, nothing sordid and ugly. I hope not, that I don't want to see life. It's my aim, but [to] see it with an eye for the silver and gold, and not the grays and blacks. The shades, the shadows, the mysticism. But not the glaring white and daylight.

Still later, again—9:30 [p.m.]—Dr. Peterson came in and sat on the bed. He needed a shave, and he's too quick, nervous, high-strung. Yet when he'd start to leave, I'd want to yell, "Don't go, please." I hated him at the same time wanting to be nearer to him. To touch his hair or something. Everything I'd say would sound childish. He makes me feel like an amateur. I feel now as if I almost don't want to see him ever again. He cramps my style. He has the upper hand and still I don't like him. I don't admire him, and yet—underneath it all, it seems to me virtually impossible that he likes me. Hell!

---

343 Not clear if she's quoting someone else, or herself

Thursday, December 12

Ashes to ashes, dust to dust. But what could I expect? He came about 11 and in an attempt to be unconcerned I was cross and rather rude to him. Then the nurse asked him to do a spinal puncture. Up he got and out he went, having stayed about 10 minutes. He hasn't been back. Oh, I can't leave without seeing him again. My eyes are glued to the door. Every step toward my room sends my silly heart all over the place. Everyone who comes in my room finds me flushed and expectant, because I thought they might be ~~him~~ he. Not seeing him is so very much worse than seeing him.

Went to the beauty parlor in the wheelchair this afternoon. Fun!

Friday, December 13

It's Friday the 13th but I saw him. Oh, gee! I felt foolishly elated all day, even though it was for just such a very few minutes. I'm in the sun room now and the wind is howling and the rain's pounding on the building. The trees swish and blow and the sky is leaden. Just the sort of evening I love. Tempestuous. Anything might happen—just anything.

[Written in large print on two blank pages:] ~His eyes, hair, mouth— pages that I could write about him. They are saturated with things I cannot write.~

I'm leaving tomorrow, for [the] Davidsons'. Then, eventually, Arizona. Glad, happy, he seemed unwilling to say goodby, but had an engagement. He lingered. I want him. But then I wanted other things. Hearts and flowers, romance—and rain weeping down the wet street in a fury of passion. There are so many people I haven't met yet, and there will always be the sky and trees and flickering smiles that come and go. He said he'd come in to say goodby tomorrow. I don't want to tell him goodby. Just *au revoir.*

Later—Dr. Peterson bounced in and out again. Change my opinion about him. His flippancy is a mask. He's really earnest and sincere beneath at all. I'm sure. Mostly because there must be something good about him if he's a pal of Herbie['s].

Saturday, December 14 C.S.

And on to the next thing. But it's going to be hard to forget immediately. Dr. Paulson—Herbie—my intern. Well, anyway, he came about 10 o'clock and we launched into a big football argument. I was wonder afterwards how I could talk coherently. Dr. Baird came to the door and said, "Now, now," and I said, "I'm behaving myself." And Herbie blushed. First time he ever seemed ill at ease. It was, oh, nice. When it was time to leave he got up and wandered around the room. Finally he said, "I'll come back later to say goodby." About two hours hence he strode in again. We talked about a score of things, all pushed and jumbled up together. His future, his dreams, Arizona, idealism, and yet all the time I was really unconscious of talking. I was too vitally aware of his presence. He seems different, too. Eventually he had to go. Stood up. I wanted to stop time. He couldn't actually be going. Oh, so far above me, mouth serious, eyes sincere, black hair, all man and strength of character. Oh, kiss me, kiss me, I wanted to scream it. My heart showed it. He took my hand—the contact was ecstasy incarnated. "I'll have to say goodby, Doris—and I'm glad to have known you. Have a good time in Arizona. Good luck," mere formalities. Those all jumbled together. "Oh, you won't forget me altogether, will you?" "Of course I won't forget you." My hand lingered in his. His eyes held mine. Words—what are words when eyes can speak like that? Then he was going. "Goodby," over his shoulder. Goodby—weakly into the pillow. And that ends that little episode. But his eyes are in my soul, and I can't help but think if *she* hadn't been, things might've been different.

Then Miss Linsley came to say goodby. I've been so wrapped in him, I haven't mentioned the others. She was floor supervisor and we both had our dreams of travel. We agreed to write and tell the other at the first fulfillment of a dream come true. And, of course, the floor orderly—a replica of Lon Chaney in his queer, halting way—said goodby almost tearfully, and said he hoped we met in heaven. I couldn't laugh. That strange, unkempt derelict really liked me. Then I dressed and trotted up to see Ross. Darling boy, half man, half child. He—oh, so casually—asked me to write him from Arizona. Eventually the Davidsons arrived, and I drove away from the hospital knowing I was leaving my heap of ashes. No matter how many people circulate around, there will always be a bright spot for having known him and his philosophy of life, and a dark spot, for not having known more. I shall dream of his eyes holding mine almost sternly, as if demanding me to say what I was thinking. His eyes flecked with gold, and his chin—noble. Dr. Paulson, I salute you are being what you are, when you could have been cheap. Oh, gosh!

Sunday, December 15

I'm happy in dreams. He's my dream because they were so many things he might have done and I'd have been disappointed. As it is, I can think about them, and they are still all silver and gold. I'm glad he didn't kiss me because it would've brought him down to the level of material things. He seems now like a god. I want to always remember him as such, standing straight and tall above me, holding my destiny in his eyes. I'll always be able to weave my dreams around him and they shall never grow stale because they can't be tarnished or soiled with actualities.

Monday, December 16

Just lazy today, and full of thoughts about ever so many things.

Tuesday, December 17

Now I know why my life has been stirred up into such a mixture. Why I haven't stayed on the beaten path and why my life chose to be varied. My obstacles were thrown in my way and why I'm still striving for a goal. Fate meant it to be that way for a reason. It was so that I might have a broader outlook on life, so that when I write, my mind won't be narrow and limited to certain things. If I'd stayed at home and sailed merrily through school, I would have thought I was seeing all and in reality only skimming the surface.

But as it is, I've had the veneer scraped off. I steered clear of the rut, and in seeing and living what I have, I'm able to stand away from myself and see what I'm doing. It isn't egotism that makes me say this. It's a subtle something inside of me that tells my inner self that I have lived for a purpose. But I've been placed in the position I have because of a reason, and someday I'll do something big. I'll give something to the world's poor—oh, hell. I can't explain it, but I mean that destiny has a surprise in store for me.

I was going to a show with Bill tomorrow, then Dr. Baird said no go. Mrs. Davidson thought I wanted to see him especially so she invited him to dinner for tomorrow night—and now I have to appear interested in him and grateful to her because humanity doesn't "understand" me.

Wednesday, December 18

My school—my alma mater. I went up to pack my trunk today. Got there just as the boarders had gone to lunch, so no one expected me and everyone talked and yelled, and well—I was the cynosure[345] of all eyes. I'll never forget that minute. Made me feel as if I'd really come into my own at last. I ate lunch with them (only I was too excited to eat) and oh, it was perfect. Afterwards I was kissed and hugged and squealed at from all directions. Coie was so darn nice. Every time she talk about my leaving she'd cry. I hadn't realized that she cared like that. It struck a tender spot. And made a lump in my throat. Then Rosemary, and Julia, and Jeanette, and Phoebe, and Betty, and all the rest. Gosh! But I love them, and when it came time to leave, I couldn't stand it. I bore up pretty well till Sister said, "Don't forget us." Forget them? That was the last straw, when I cared so very much. Yes, I cried then. I got away, finally, and oh! It was hard. I never talk so fast and furiously before.

Bill came to dinner this evening. It wasn't so bad. He was very amiable and the Davidsons liked him. We went in the den and played the Victrola. I felt in a terribly romantic mood. An irony of Fate, since Bill is the least romantic person there is. I pretended he was Herbie and what he would do and say under the circumstances.

---

345 The center of attraction.

Thursday, December 19

Just a day. Bill phoned. Bought and addressed Christmas cards. S'all.

Friday, December 20

Marjie came this morning. Don't know when I've been as glad to see anyone. We ate lunch at The Cottage. Talked and talked and talked. Then drove out to her house and monkeyed around the neighborhood. Then to Hill Villa[346] for more food where we met Rus [Marjie's beau]. He looked terribly tragic because he does love Marjie so, and she was so damned offhand. But, of course, she can't help not loving him anymore than he can help loving her. It's cruel—but it's life. Afterward we came back home. Rae came over this evening with Ruth. I felt very silly and behaved likewise.

---

346 Hill Villa was a Portland restaurant known for its fine cuisine. It's called The Chart House today, located up on Terwilliger.

Arizona
(1929)

Saturday, December 21

"Parting is such sweet sorrow—etc." I didn't think I could leave Marjie when the time came. It's stupendous what she means to me. But here I am in my little berth, and happy now that the first awful hurt is going. I'm going home, home, home.

Sunday, December 21 [*sic*]

Events have progressed. Train's too damn jerky to write. College kids. Fun till late this evening.

Monday, December 22 [*sic*]

Changed trains at L.A. and said goodby to all the new-made friends. It seems to me I'm always having to say goodby to people. Rode all day across the desert. There were two New York boys on the train and we had a great time. Played silly games on the observation car. Phoenix at 11:20 [p.m.] and now I'm home in my own little room. So cozy and comfortable, and Mother and Daddy looked so good.

Tuesday, December 24

Went downtown and viewed the city. Bunch of good-looking men. Fun seeing people.

Wednesday, December 25 —Christmas Day

Sunshine and blue skies. Nevertheless, it's Christmas. Ate dinner at Aunt Florence's with the Richards. I like them all. They are good sports. The hell of it is they knew George so well and they keep talking about him. It hurts. I don't want to think about him.

Sunday, December 29

Lost glasses. Will write more when I find them.

Monday, December 30

George, George. What is wrong with me? I thought it was all over. He didn't like the moon and stars. I hate him. I had it all decided. So why do I find myself thinking and dreaming and wondering? He's 1,500 miles away, yet there's a ghost that's always here. Perhaps because my room was his room. He sat by these windows and ate at the same table. Someone is always telling me something he said or did. I'm actually fighting an inclination to write him. Perhaps it's just because I'm lonesome. It's going to be hard down here, so far from Portland and all that it means. No horse in sight, and my goal so far in the distance. I feel futile and almost like saying what's the use?

Daddy says there's no money, and maybe no school [college] next year. I don't want to have to worry and be materialistic. I want to dream and be able to stand by my sentiments and give into my impulses. To avoid all my pet aversions and not be tied to facts. I want to create a certain atmosphere to develop my artistic temperament. But all that can't be done when I'm recovering from an operation and business is poor and there are dishes to be washed. I'm afraid—of slipping into a rut and being (as my English teacher would say), "Just another of life's little tragedies who had the ability to do something worthwhile but not the will." Oh, I won't! I'll hold onto my dreams and I'll make it if I can't find adventure in life. This is just a test to see how easily I can be beaten, and I'll climb it as I've climbed the other obstructions.

And eventually I'll reach the other side and the pot of gold will be all the more precious for having had to fight for it. George? He's a luxury and weakness. A shortcut to happiness, avoiding the rocks. It's my lesser self that asks for him. The self that is willing to sacrifice idealism for materialism but I won't give in. I'm still hunting the fire and strength and ethereal beauty of my love. Of love as I see it. And somewhere there is a man who lives in dreams and worships the night wind. And if I have long enough, I'll find him.

Tuesday, December 31—New Year's Eve

The end of another year. I've learned a lot, lived a lot, and lost a lot. But it's in the cards. I'm glad I haven't done anything to be ashamed of. I hope I'll always be able to hold up my head and know I'm as good as the next person. Everything I've done might not be approved of by the public. But I know I've been right.

Some way I feel that this year is going to mean something special. I've been preparing myself. I wanted to take the car and drive off by myself tonight but Daddy wouldn't let me. He couldn't see the reason for it. It's no fault of his for not understanding. I guess it will always be that way. There is a something in me that has never been satisfied. It would have meant so much to usher the new era in, by myself in the desert beneath the stars. It would be almost a good omen. Oh! I wanted it. The answer to so many dreams. It's 11 now. Just an hour, a new beginning.

I'll go out alone anyway.

125 SPRINGTIME ON THE DESERT IN ARIZONA

*

Appendix I: Glossary of Doris's Slang

Bachelor lady (girl): A single woman living alone or with other women, working for her living

Batching it: A man living as a bachelor, with no woman to take care of him (housekeeper, relative, wife), is "batching it."

Bell-hop: Errand boy employed by a hotel to carry luggage, etc.

Bestest: Best

Beta: Beta Theta Pi fraternity

Blab: Gossip or conversation

Blooie: When everything goes to pieces, an explosion. Also, **Flooey, Flooie**

Bloomers: Underpants, but very loose and puffed out

Blotter: Something used to absorb excess ink or other liquid, especially a sheet of blotting paper with a firm backing

Bosh: see **Bunk**

Bummed (around): Stayed in, at home; lazy

Bunk: Nonsense, foolish, dumb

Cat: Bitch

Cattish: Gossipy, mean, backbiting, bitchy

Cheap: Of little account or value, shoddy, low-class

Co-eds: Female college students; young women of college age, regardless if they were in school

Collegiate: Characteristic of college students; neat and proper; a desirable man

Common: Vulgar, cheap, inferior

Coolie: Derogatory for Asian or Chinese; a **"coolie coat"** was a satin Chinese jacket

Course: Schedule of classes, class load

Cram: Study hard before an exam

Cut up: Act silly

Dinky: Deficiency list at school with names of students who are in academic danger

Dumb bunny; bunnies: someone who is very foolish, clumsy, stupid

Dumn: Doris's misspelling of **Dumb**

Egg, Good: A pal, a good sport

Fast: Amorous, horny, aggressive

Feature it: Believe it, tell it (a story or gossip)

Flooey, Flooie: See **Blooie**

Gay: Happy, lighthearted

Grip: Suitcase

Hammer: Hang around, spend time

Hammy: Ridiculous; overly humorous or dramatic

Hard: Tough, street-smart; see **Common, Cheap**

Heavy: Unpopular

Het (up): Heated, excited

Hick/hicky: Unsophisticated; like a country bumpkin

High-hat: Snobbish, haughty; to act superior to another person

Hoof it: Walk

Hot: Spectacular, wonderful, sophisticated, sexy

Hot dog! Exclamation of joy. Also **Hot dawg, Hot diggity, Hot ziggity dog!**

Hotsy-totsy: Pleasing, wonderful

Hunky-dory: see **hotsy-totsy**

"It": Sex appeal (see **Sex Appeal**)

Kappa: Kappa Kappa Gamma sorority

Kerflunk: A sudden muffled thud or sound, like an explosion or flat tire; ruined or wasted

Kid: Soft white leather, from a baby goat skin; see also **Some kid!**

Knickers: Loose-fitting short trousers gathered at the knee; a style for men, sometimes worn for golf; girls wore them for riding horses or under a dress.

KO: OK

Line: Patter or way of speaking

Loge: Seats in the mezzanine at the theatre, sometimes within theatre boxes or enclosures.

Low: see **cheap, common**

Make love to: Pitching woo, to engage in amorous speech and caressing (not intercourse)

Marcel: To put waves/curls in the hair, a woman's hairstyle (named for the inventor of the marcel curling iron); finger wave.

Merry ha-ha, the: This expression seems to mean to give someone the cold shoulder or other brush-off, the colorful equivalent to "flipping someone off"

Namby-pamby: Weak and indecisive; lacking in character

Necking: Passionate kissing

Nifty: Cute, cool, nice, fun

Not so worse: Not bad, wonderful

Paint: Facial make-up such as lipstick, rouge, or more; also **Painted**: Wearing make-up

Pamy-wamy: see **namby pamby**

Peck: A large quantity, a lot; technically, 8 dry quarts measurement

Pep/Peppy: Energy or high spirits

Petting: Heavier necking, "feeling up"; also, **petting party**: one or more couples engaged in petting

Pie-eyed: Drunk

Pitty pat skid skid: The noise your heart makes when you see a handsome man or pretty lady

Rate: Count as worthwhile, popular or likeable

Sap: A loser, a fool

S.A.: Sex appeal

Shot: Drunk

Show: Usually a movie (silent film), but occasionally a live play, Vaudeville performance or light opera

Snappy: Smart, lively, slick

Snub: To rudely avoid

Soaked: Drunk; **Soaks:** drunks

Some kid! Expression meaning adorable person, cute; expressing admiration; see also: **You kid!**

Spizzed: Went, hurried

Step-ins: Female undergarments, also known as tap pants; under-shorts for women

Stewed: Drunk

Swell: Wonderful

Rave, raving: Enthuse, talk excitedly

Technique: Used as an adjective, "the right way," or "how it's done"

Tough: Wild, unchaperoned (a party); uncivilized, of a lower social class (a person)

You kid! "You're swell!"

Zowie! Wow!

Appendix II: Pop Culture

Movies

Beau Geste: In this 1926 silent, Michael "Beau" Geste leaves England in disgrace and joins the infamous French Foreign Legion. He is reunited with his two brothers in North Africa, where they face great danger. The film starred Ronald Colman.

Breakfast at Sunrise, released in 1927, starred Constance Talmadge as Madeleine in this romance based on the French play *Le Dejeuner au Soleil* by Andre Birabeau.

Captain Swagger, starring Rod La Rocque, opened in 1928. Hugh Drummond goes broke living too high and turns to crime in order to pay his bills. Sue Carol and Richard Tucker also starred.

Don Juan, the first of at least ten adaptations of this story, starred Sir John Barrymore as the misogynistic skirt-chaser who falls for a convent girl. Released in 1926. After watching this movie, Doris declares, "I hate men."

Fazil, also known as *Neapolitan Nights*: An Arab prince born and raised in the desert and a beautiful Frenchwoman from Paris fall in love and marry, but their differences may tear them apart. This was released in 1928 and starred Charles Farrell and Greta Nissen.

339

The Goose Hangs High is a 1925 comedy film based on a play by the same name, featuring Constance Bennett, Myrtle Stedman and George Irving. Redone in 1932 as *This Reckless Age*. Doris may have seen the play at the Heilig; the Heilig was primarily a stage and vaudeville house until 1929.

Hula, the silent film, was based on the novel *Hula: A Romance of Hawaii*, by Armine von Tempski. The movie was directed by Victor Fleming, starred Clara Bow and was released by Paramount Pictures. It was one of the top-10 grossing movies of 1927.

The Iron Mask starred Douglas Fairbanks in his "fond farewell to the swashbuckling silents," in 1929. King Louis XIII of France is thrilled to have born to him a son and heir to the throne. But the queen delivers twins, and Cardinal Richelieu sees the second son as a potential for rivalry.

The King of Kings: A 1926 Cecil B. DeMille picture about the life and death of Jesus. Mary Magdalene becomes angry when Judas, now a follower of Jesus, won't come to her feast. She goes to see Jesus and becomes repentant. From there the Bible story unfolds. Doris said that even atheists couldn't help but believe in God after seeing this film.

Madame X: A young lawyer unknowingly defends his mother who abandoned him when he was three. This 1929 movie starred Ruth Chatterton, Lewis Stone and Raymond Hackett.

Metropolis, a 1927 film, tells of a futuristic city, Metropolis, sharply divided between the working class and the city planners. It's a Utopian society where wealthy residents live a carefree life, but the underclass lives in horror. A longer movie, 153 minutes, compared to 70 minutes for *Orchids and Ermine*. Stars Brigitte Helm and Alfred Abel.

Oh Kay! came out in 1928, starring Colleen Moore, Lawrence Gray and Alan Hale as a short, silent-film version of the Gershwin musical of the same name. The silent has none of the songs, alas. Lady Kay is engaged to marry, but she tries to escape on her boat, which nearly sinks, and is saved by a shipload of bootleggers.

Orchids and Ermine: A 1927 romantic comedy starring Colleen Moore, Jack Mulhall and Sam Hardy. A poor telephone operator who dreams of marrying rich, and falls for the wrong guy—but with a case of mistaken identity, is he really Mr. Wrong? It all comes right in the end, of course.

Seventh Heaven, starring Janet Gaynor and Charles Farrell, came out in 1928. A street cleaner saves a young woman's life, and the pair slowly fall in love until war intervenes.

The Smart Set starred William Haines as a snazzy polo player who has to redeem himself after getting kicked off the U. S. Team. It was a 1928 Metro-Goldwyn-Mayer picture and also starred Jack Holt and Alyce Day.

Speedy: "Speedy" loses his job as a soda-jerk, then spends the day with his girl at Coney Island. He becomes a cab driver and delivers Babe Ruth to Yankee Stadium, where he stays to see the game. This 1928 film stars Harold Lloyd and features lots of slapstick comedy and crazy car rides.

The Student Prince is an operetta in four acts with music by Sigmund Romberg. It opened December 2, 1924, on Broadway in New York. Doris saw it on stage with her brother Rae in May 1926, and again with Marjie March 21, 1928, possibly on screen, both times in Portland. It was made into a movie in 1927 called *The Student Prince of Old Heidelberg*. A cloistered, overprotected Austrian prince falls in love with a down-to-earth barmaid.

Trooping Co-eds: The Universal Pictures movie for which Doris auditioned in Phoenix. The movie was apparently never made.

The Venus of Venice, released in 1927, starred Constance Talmadge, Hedda Hopper and Antonio Moreno. A slick caper movie about a petty thief (Talmadge) falls for a wealthy American artist.

Wings is a 1927silent film about two World War I fighter pilot friends, both involved with the same beauty, produced by Lucien Hubbard, directed by William A. Wellman and released by Paramount Pictures. Wings was the first film to win the Academy Award for Best Picture, and the only true silent films to do so; starred Clara Bow, Charles "Buddy" Rogers, and Richard Arlen.

Celebrities

"See Barnum," Doris's would-be lover was a descendent of circus magnate PT Barnum. With no sons to inherit his fortune, Barnum offered $25,000 to his grandson, Clinton H. Seeley, if "he shall habitually use the name of Barnum, either as Clinton Barnum Seeley, or C. Barnum, Seeley, or Barnum Seeley in his name, so that the name Barnum shall always be known as his name." Clinton readily agreed, accepting Barnum's second choice, C. Barnum. Unfortunately, Clinton was not especially fond of or good at the family business. The only other male heir at the time of P.T.'s death was Herbert Barnum Seeley, Sr. He eventually succeeded in suing his aunt and brother for his share of the estate but died relatively young in 1914. "See Barnum" may have been his son Herbert Barnum Seeley, Jr., born in 1911, using the moniker of See/C. Barnum per his great-grandfather's wishes. [347]

Lon Chaney (Sr.), known as "The Man of 1,000 Faces," was an American actor in Hollywood during the era of silent films. He was famous for his frightening but pathetic parts in horror films, for roles such as Quasimodo in *The Hunchback of Notre Dame* and *The Phantom of the Opera*. He made only one movie with sound, a 1930 remake of his 1925 film *The Unholy Three*.

---

[347] With thanks to Denise Shelton for the sleuthing.

Charles Lindbergh: On May 20, 1927 Charles Lindbergh took off from Long Island in The Spirit of St. Louis. Thirty-three and a half hours and 3,500 miles later, he landed in Paris, the first to fly the Atlantic alone. Flying the "Spirit of St. Louis," he touched down in 49 states, visited 92 cities, gave 147 speeches, and rode 1,290 miles in parades. Lindbergh flew his Spirit of St. Louis into the Portland Swan Island Airport on September 14, 1927. He dedicated the airport, which operated until 1940, when Kaiser began building ships there.

Harold Lloyd was one of the most popular and influential film comedians of the era. Lloyd made nearly 200 comedy films, both silent and "talkies," between 1914 and 1947. His movies often had extended chase scenes and daredevil tricks.

Anita Loos was the author of *Gentlemen Prefer Blondes.* She was one of Hollywood's early successful screenwriters. She began writing screen scenarios for the Biograph Company at an early age. Her book became a bestseller worldwide, though not very successful as a silent movie. The tale was later remade with Marilyn Monroe and Jane Russell, and was a smashing success on screen and on Broadway. Doris wanted to be an author like Anita Loos.

Colleen Moore, prolific silent film star and Hollywood beauty, was in *Oh Kay, Smiling Irish Eyes, Why Be Good? Synthetic Sin,* and *Footlights & Fools* in just 1929. Moore was from Michigan and attended the Detroit Conservatory for acting. She got into movies with the help of her uncle Walter Howey, the Chicago newspaper editor who inspired the character Walter Burns in *The Front Page.* By 1927 she was the top box-office draw in the US, pulling in the phenomenal sum of $12,500 a week.

George Stoll, born in 1905, was a violin prodigy who became a music conductor. He played with his jazz trio and quintet around the U.S., clearly spending some time in Portland in the late 1920s conducting the orchestra at The Broadway Theatre. He soon left Portland for Los Angeles and the bright lights, where he was music director, conductor, and composer on any number of musicals for MGM Studios. He worked on the music for *The Wizard of Oz*, among others. Toward the end of his career, Stoll worked with Elvis Presley. Stoll died in 1985.

Constance Talmadge was blonde where star sister Norma Talmadge was brunette. Constance was a buoyant comedienne, one of silent film's most popular and enduring stars of romantic comedy. Both sisters left the industry with the advent of sound; their "pronounced and rather squeaky Brooklyn accent did not prove all that suitable for talkies," according to IMDB.

Norma Shearer: When Doris wants to be "less silly and more charming and elusive," she wanted to be like Norma Shearer. Shearer is quoted as saying, "It is impossible to get anything made or accomplished without stepping on some toes; enemies are inevitable when one is a doer." Doris wasn't alone in admiring Ms. Shearer: She is one of the celebrities whose picture Anne Frank placed on the wall of her Amsterdam bedroom in the "Secret Annex" while in hiding during the Nazi occupation, according to IMDB.

Portland Theaters

The Organ at the Broadway: The Wurlitzer in the Broadway Theatre was installed in 1926 and played in its prime by Oliver Wallace, with George Stoll conducting the orchestra. The organ itself still exists, though not at the Broadway. It was moved and reinstalled at the Oaks Park roller rink in 1955. It is the only large Portland theatre organ that is still complete and intact.

Broadway Theater: Originally located at 1008 Broadway. The Broadway Theatre opened in 1926. The Broadway Theatre operated into the 1980s, but was demolished in 1988.

The Heilig Theatre: The second "Heilig" in Portland, opened on October 10, 1910, this theatre was located at Broadway and Taylor Street. It was designed by architect Edwin W. Houghton. The Heilig operated primarily as a stage and vaudeville house until 1929, when it reopened as a movie house called the Hippodrome. During the 1930s it underwent three more name changes, operating as the Rialto, the Music Box, and finally the Mayfair. The house was purchased by Evergreen Theatres in 1953 and, after being extensively remodeled, reopened as the Fox Theatre in August, 1954. The theater building was demolished in 1997.

Hollywood Theatre: The Hollywood Theatre is a central historical point of the Hollywood District in northeast Portland. It was built in 1926 at 4122 NE Sandy Boulevard and still stands today.

The Music Box Theatre: The Music Box was a popular name for theatres in Portland; one source says there were as many as six theatres with that name over time. The one Doris likely attended was on Alder Street. It opened in 1911 as The People's Theater, was renamed the The Music Box and The Alder Theatre. It had a two-keyboard, nine-stop Wurlitzer organ.

Orpheum Theatre: Built in 1913 on the corner of SW Broadway and Yamhill as the Empress Theater; remodeled in 1926. It closed April 25, 1976, when it was razed for a Nordstrom store.

The Pantages Theatre: There was a Pantages Family Theatre in Portland in 1915; it offered live shows, Vaudeville performances, and even circus acts. In the 1920s it began to show silent films. The Pantages Theater was located at Broadway and Alder Street. Doris may have seen the circus here. She also saw Babe Ruth here in 1926.

The Portland: The Portland Theatre opened in 1928. After about a year, the theater was sold and renamed The Paramount. In the mid-1980s, the Paramount was restored and renamed The Portland. The Portland Theatre is located at 1111 SW Broadway, still extant today as the Arlene Schnitzer Concert Hall, Portland Center for Performing Arts.

Publications

The Saturday Evening Post began in 1728 as Benjamin Franklin's *Pennsylvania Gazette*; it became known as *The Saturday Evening Post* in 1821. It was the first magazine in the United States to reach a circulation of one million. The magazine has been synonymous with Norman Rockwell, who, for years, painted Americana for its covers.

Music

Annette Hanshaw's signature song was "Under the Moon," with the lyrics, "The skies are starry and bright. The birds are sleeping at night. And there is no one in sight, under the moon." First recorded by vaudevillians Aileen Stanley and Johnny Marvin, 1927.

"My Sin," was also a hit for Annette Hanshaw; it was also a #2 hit for Ben Selvin in 1929, and #7 for Fred Waring and the Pennsylvanians. This was written by Lew Brown, Buddy DeSylva and Ray Henderson. The flip side contains, "I Get the Blues When It Rains."

"Reaching for the Moon," the title of this book, is the title to a song written by Irving Berlin in 1930. It was the title song to a film of the same name (though recorded without lyrics); the film starred Douglas Fairbanks, Sr. It was recorded a number of times in 1930. Its melancholy lonesome tune seems to fit Doris's mood when she's moon-gazing. Ella Fitzgerald does a lovely rendition of the song. "I'm just the words looking for the tune, reaching for the moon and you."

Appendix III:
About the Doris Diaries[348]

The Doris Diaries are a lifetime's worth of diaries kept by Doris Louise Bailey (later, Doris Murphy), a Portland, Oregon, native (1910-2011). Doris Bailey Murphy was my great aunt. She began keeping a daily record of her life as a 15-year-old in Portland in 1925.

The diaries themselves are enchanting at first glance—filled with pen-and-ink-scrawled daily gripes about school, catching the street-car, buying a new hat, and joyous outings with friends. But very soon, her use of contemporary slang (*pep, swell,* and *hotsy-totsy,* for example) and her daily occupations bring to life the rapidly changing world of the 1920s. Doris talks on the telephone with boys, she plays tennis and golf, and dances to music on the Victrola. Her parents are bastions of the white, Protestant, upper middle-class of Portland; they were born and raised in Alabama in the post-Civil War era, with Victorian morals. But times were changing in the 1920s, and Doris constantly pushes the boundaries of acceptable behavior for a young girl. She dances, kisses, and rides in cars with boys; she sneaks out, breaks curfew, and engages in "petting parties."

Her disdain for being conventional is evident in every entry. She is privileged, vain, judgmental, fickle, passionate, fashionable, consumerist, horny, untamed, and very romantic, imagining herself in love and out of it with each passing day. And yet, she knows when her behavior is "not very nice," calling herself out, in effect, when she knows she's pushed too far. In her room, at her desk, she soars into flights of fancy with her pen.

---

348 Introduction to *I've Got Some Lovin' to Do: The Diaries of a Roaring Twenties Teen (1925-1926),* edited for space.

Doris's interest in politics and culture has not yet awakened in her teen years, as is evident by her attitudes and essentially shallow thoughts. But in later diaries (college years in Portland and Arizona), her sense of injustice against the oppressed (her transformation from oppressor to liberator) grows, and she continues her growth from Portland debutante to literary publisher (*The Dilettante*, a literary magazine in 1934) arts champion (at the Skidmore Arts Center, another pet project, 1935), and enlightened student.

Doris studied social work, shocking the Reed College community when she interviewed prostitutes in Portland for her thesis (the dean called her parents for a conference to discuss the scandalous behavior). She graduated from Reed in 1938. She left Portland that year for San Francisco, where she worked with World War II refugees at the Red Cross, and became active in the labor movements that were burgeoning across America. She flirted with joining the Communist Party, and began an affair with a married man. He eventually got a divorce from his wife; Doris and Joe Murphy were wed in 1948. They lived in San Francisco where Joe was in labor leadership until the 1960s, when they retired to Occidental, California, a small town in the redwoods and vineyards of Sonoma County. Joe died in 1987 and Doris wrote her autobiography, which was published when she was 96.

Doris died at home, with her dog and cat nearby, at age 101 in March of 2011, and upon her death, her trustee, my mother (daughter of Doris's brother Rae) discovered another surprise—the box of journals, kept so many years in a closet. I received these with joy and surprise, never having known of their existence. Discovering the charming entries in these diaries and their historical significance compelled me to seek publication for these gems of Americana—a glimpse at the twentieth century from a girl/ woman who would not be quiet and behave. A growing following on social media further encouraged me toward publication of these diaries.

While the life of one young woman may or may not have an impact on the historical context or future introspection of Portland, the daily views from a young person from 1925 through 1930 will certainly offer insight into local happenings and events, as well as cast light on cultural, societal and technological changes, including early twentieth century gender roles and feminist perspectives.

My Great Aunt Doris attended Reed College and left a small legacy to Reed in her will. Sales from the first volume of *The Doris Diaries* have already gone toward funding a scholarship at Reed, and I will continue to fund that with subsequent volumes. In doing so, I hope to honor her original wishes.

Photo Credits

All photos courtesy of the Bailey family unless otherwise noted.

1   Front cover photos: Doris, 15, with (unnamed) kitten and Jack, 7, in backyard of the Bailey home at 1320 The Alameda, Portland, 1925. Rae took this photo on the last day the family lived there before moving to Culpepper Terrace. Postcards, public domain. Cover design by Eric J. Kos.

2   The Bailey men. Rae was taking photos that day and handed the camera to either Doris or his mother. Taken at the same time as the cover photo of Doris and Jack, in August 1925, the last day at their old house on The Alameda.

3   Marjorie Dana, Doris's best friend, known as Marjie.

4   Portland, Oregon, with Mt. Hood in the distance. Postcard, public domain.

5   Downtown Portland, Fifth Street north from Morrison, with streetcars. Postcard, public domain.

6   The house on Culpepper Terrace. Photo by Mia Romero.

7   Broadway in Portland. Postcard, public domain.

8   St. Helen's Hall moved into the former Portland Academy, pictured. Photo courtesy of the Architectural Heritage Center, Portland, OR.

9   The Loop, about 1918. Photo by Rae Bailey.

10 Doris and Jack on a horse, about 1924. Photo by Rae Bailey.

11 Doris in a party dress, about 1928.

12 Good Samaritan Hospital. Postcard, public domain.

13 Here lies Micky: Doris's original doodle. Scanned from diary.

14   Long Beach Pier: Panorama showing auditorium and Pleasure Pier, Long Beach, Cal. Postcard, public domain.

15   Winter scene of East Lake Park, Los Angeles, Cal. Postcard, public domain.

16   Hollywood Union High School, Hollywood, Cal. Postcard, public domain.

17   Los Angeles traffic. Postcard, public domain.

18   Wood and Florence Upshaw lived in Tucson in this house, before moving to Phoenix to work with Luther Bailey. Photo by Rae Bailey, circa 1924.

19   Wood and Florence Upshaw in the entry of their home. Photo by Rae Bailey, circa 1924.

20   Doris and Marjie on horseback in Arizona, 1928.

21   Roosevelt Dam. Postcard, public domain.

22   Camelback Mountain, Phoenix. Postcard, public domain.

23   The corral: Doris's original doodle. Scanned from diary.

24   Head crack: Doris's original doodle. Scanned from diary.

25   Jefferson Hotel, Phoenix, Arizona. Postcard, public domain.

26   Horse races in Phoenix. Photo by Rae Bailey.

27   Rae riding two horses. Photo caption says "El caballero y dos caballos." Circa 1924.

28   Central Avenue, showing Adams Hotel, Phoenix, Arizona. Postcard, public domain.

29   Cortez and Gurley streets, Prescott, Arizona. Postcard, public domain.

30   Kaibab Trail, Grand Canyon, Arizona. Postcard, public domain.

31   Ruthmary Burroughs and the gypsy children; photo taken outside Portland. Photo by Rae Bailey.

32   Newspaper clipping and photo from *The Morning Oregonian*, Sept. 12, 1928.

33   Ruth Darlyn Crum, 1928.

34   Hazelwood Cream Store. Postcard, public domain.

35   The New Heathman Hotel. Postcard, public domain.

36   Studio portrait of Doris, circa 1928.

37   Ruth Crum and Rae Bailey, circa 1929.

38 Doris on her way to a party, circa 1929.

39 Union Depot, Portland, Oregon. Postcard, public domain.

40 Horses at Mt. Hood Lodge, circa 1924. Probably taken at the lodge that Luther designed or built.

41 The Oaks, from The Chutes, Portland. Postcard, public domain.

42 Senior Girls' House, Portland Heights. Photo by Julia Park Tracey.

43 Oregon Football, University of Oregon vs. Idaho, Nov. 20, 1920. Photo by Rae Bailey.

44 Good Samaritan Hospital, Portland, Oregon. Postcard, public domain.

45 Springtime on the desert in Arizona. Postcard, public domain.

46 Doris and her horse, Ruffian, about 1980. Photo by Elizabeth Bailey Park.

47 Author photo, back cover: Julia Park Tracey, by J. Astra Brinkman, 2012.

Corrections

The following errors were made in identifying people or places in *I've Got Some Lovin' to Do: The Diaries of a Roaring Twenties Teen (1925-1926)*, and should, for posterity, be recognized as incorrect. Any errors in transcription or misidentification are mine.

Mary Lois Dana was noted as the given name of Marjie Dana, Doris's best friend, based on Doris's own scrapbooks and files. Further research has shown that Marjie was, in fact, Marjorie Dana. Mary Lois was Marjie's younger sister.

The photo (page 33) showing the view from Culpepper Terrace is, in fact, the view from The Alameda. Thanks to Geoff Wexler of the Oregon Historical Society for examining the photographs and clarifying this misidentification.

The item Doris called "a Dixie" has been identified as an ice cream pop, not a candy, thanks to Suzanne McKereghan.

Index

Pages

Appendix/appendicitis   85, 98, 101, 186, 189, 190, 200, 220, 311

Arizona   100, 108-110, 114, 119, 130, 134, 137, 139, 144, 146-147, 151, 159, 186, 189, 206, 218, 220, 229, 233, 246, 248, 260, 297, 302, 308-309, 312, 317, 320-321, 331, 348

Atheist   121, 331

Bailey family (relatives)   3-5, 8-12

Bailey, Elizabeth (Elizabeth Lee Bailey)   4, 8, 10

Bailey, Jack (John Upshaw Bailey)   8, 11, 12, 14, 59, 74, 86, 97, 100, 118, 171, 190, 264-265, 282, 350

Bailey, Joe (Joseph A. Bailey)   1, 8, 11, 12, 25-27, 29-30, 42, 46-47, 49, 58, 66, 69, 72, 74-75, 77, 79-80, 108, 114, 120-121, 126, 132, 155, 172, 176, 185, 190, 194, 195, 219, 226, 229, 230, 232-235, 238-239, 260

Bailey, Luther R. (Daddy)   3-4, 8-11, 12-13, 21, 22, 25, 26, 28, 34, 38, 47, 50, 52, 54, 55, 61, 75, 79, 82, 86, 92, 96, 97, 100, 101, 102-106, 108-110, 114, 117, 126, 130, 141, 170, 171, 179, 180, 186, 190, 195, 201, 208, 210, 212, 213, 219, 220, 248, 250, 263-267, 281, 283, 285, 296, 309, 351-352

Bailey, Rae (William Raeford Bailey)   8, 10, 12, 13, 22-23, 38, 68, 135, 139, 166, 169, 170, 172, 185, 186, 209-214, 247, 250-253, 260, 299, 304, 324, 326-328, 341, 348

Bailey, Willie Doris Upshaw (Mother)   4, 8-10, 12, 14, 22, 23, 25, 31, 37, 38, 40, 41, 45, 49, 52, 54, 55, 58, 60, 68, 82, 85, 86, 88, 92, 96, 97, 100, 108, 110, 126, 130, 162, 172, 174, 176, 186, 189, 190, 191, 201, 202, 233, 234, 238, 247, 264, 265, 266, 267, 271, 279, 281, 283, 296, 306, 310, 326, 350

Barnum, See   15, 193-194, 197, 204, 342, 353, 356

Bates, Ross   314, 315, 316, 317, 319, 321, 331

Beach   15, 42, 92-96, 167, 173-174, 277, 299, 351

Berg's   14, 170, 191, 222

Billy Taylor   147

Birthday   4, 38, 102, 104, 233-234, 262, 310

Boat   62, 269, 341, 343

Bridge (cards)   122, 126, 129, 130, 178, 213

Bronco   15, 122, 124, 125-126, 150

Cadillac   61, 70, 87

California   2-4, 14, 36, 43, 79, 86, 94, 96, 100, 103-104, 137, 218, 223, 313, 329, 348

Camelback   123, 124

Candy (making)   107

Canoe   37, 274, 275-276, 277, 287, 295

Catlin's   75

Chapel   175, 301

Chev(rolet)   22, 39, 52

Chinatown   38, 167, 251, 288, 307

Church   9, 49, 54, 66, 75, 111, 117, 176, 177, 239, 253, 270, 271, 292, 308

Christian Endeavor (C. E.)   16, 49

Christmas   203, 208, 209, 210, 211, 212, 297, 302, 308, 309, 317, 324, 326

Cigarette   5, 166, 268, 271, 307

Circus   139, 194, 258, 342, 345

Coca-Cola   105, 107, 188, 192, 303, 306

Coffee Dan's   166

College   3, 8, 9, 15, 16, 17, 58, 150, 168, 175, 177, 181,
                                     182, 185, 188, 191, 193, 194, 198, 223, 236,
                                     239, 269, 271, 290, 299, 312, 326, 327, 331

Columbia (River, beach)   56, 67, 263, 269, 272, 277, 285

Compact   130

Costume   76, 79, 185, 252

Coupe   140

Cowboy   4, 15, 118, 125, 150, 158, 159, 193, 218

Crash of 1929   306

Cross-dressing   79, 148

Crum, Ruth   12, 185, 210, 211, 231, 310, 315, 351

Culpepper Terrace   3, 15, 26, 37, 47, 53, 58, 60, 75, 103, 350,
                                     353, 357

Curl (curling iron, curled hair)   27, 38, 42, 53, 87, 97, 100, 102, 122, 180,
                                     187, 249, 272, 336

Daddy: see *Bailey, Luther R.*

Dana (family)   3, 5, 13, 22, 52, 88, 171, 173, 187, 195, 196,
                                     204, 207, 210, 212, 214, 218, 220, 224,
                                     233, 235, 238, 251, 254, 262, 266, 257

Dance   6, 61, 65, 76, 79, 106, 114, 138, 149, 150, 156,
                                     173, 176, 193, 204-205, 222, 227, 248, 250,
                                     253, 258, 262, 264, 269, 270, 277, 279, 280,
                                     284, 294, 296, 297, 300, 307, 347

Desert   4, 7, 42, 114, 118, 120, 123, 140, 147, 155,
                                     157, 159, 189, 218, 233, 247, 311, 326, 328,
                                     339, 352

Diary   2-4, 24, 50, 84, 85, 89, 186, 221, 288, 304,
                                     307, 314, 318, 350, 351

Diphtheria   1, 32, 38, 354

Doctor   1-5, 14, 23, 25, 29, 31, 35, 36, 44, 46, 49, 50,
                                     53, 80, 85, 86, 98, 100, 104, 105, 106, 110,
                                     111, 118, 119, 121, 123, 143, 144, 151, 155,
                                     168, 171, 178, 180, 181, 189, 201, 207, 220,
                                     235, 236, 238, 239, 242, 245, 255-256,
                                     310-311, 314, 317

Dressmaker	46, 241, 275-277
Ether	1, 151, 152, 311
Financial harships (for Bailey family)	2-4, 7, 10, 21, 46, 79, 86, 213, 220, 306, 327, 331
Flu/influenza	89, 171, 208, 233
Football	193, 205, 223, 304, 321, 352
Ford	43, 45, 46, 49, 93, 128, 140, 176, 205, 225, 241, 353
Fountain pen, trouble with	37, 57, 102, 111, 172, 194-195, 197, 299, 347
Fraternity (pin)	106, 173, 262, 284, 285, 291, 292, 333
Fur(s)	27, 42, 70, 197
Garage	54, 93, 105
Gin	107, 166, 224, 226
Glasses	68, 70, 110, 184, 262, 272, 326
Golf	56, 195, 263, 267, 281, 282, 286, 336, 347
Grand Canyon	153, 156-158, 218, 351
Grant (High School)	13, 32, 43, 45, 49, 58, 98, 103, 171, 194
Grippe	308
Gym	24, 186, 194
Gypsies	170, 171
Hazelwood (Cream Store, district)	175, 192, 200
Heathman Hotel	169, 170, 191, 203, 212, 218, 220, 223, 233, 235, 238, 240, 283, 285, 292, 356
Hike (hiking)	52, 53, 55, 58, 59, 123, 158, 174, 194, 201, 202, 203, 208, 214, 226, 239, 250, 254, 269, 271, 280, 299, 306
Hill Military Academy (HMA, the Hill)	16, 30, 39, 49, 52, 73, 138, 307, 314
Hollywood (city)	3, 94, 96, 97, 99, 102, 108, 342-343
Hollywood (theatre)	169, 345
Holy Rollers	134, 138, 140, 148, 156, 160
Homesick	31, 96, 98, 99, 120, 122, 137, 186, 205, 263
Horse	2, 4, 12, 15, 74, 109, 110, 114, 115, 117-119, 121, 122, 124-128, 130-136, 139-144, 146-148, 150, 152-156, 159-161, 181, 196, 218, 246, 248, 259-260, 269, 272, 293, 298, 307, 311, 327, 329

Horse race	128, 131, 135, 144
Horse show	196, 307
Hospital	1-5, 14, 21, 24, 25, 36, 53, 73, 85, 86, 104, 105, 116, 141, 150-151, 155, 162, 202, 207, 238, 308-310, 321, 331
Infection	1, 85, 98, 110, 151, 207, 311
Job	67, 68, 109, 129, 236
Kiss(ing)	1, 5, 24, 27-28, 34, 47-49, 57, 58, 65, 69-70, 87, 92, 107, 119, 132-133, 136, 140-143, 149, 151, 158, 173, 176-181, 194-199, 201-202, 218, 222, 243-244, 254-258, 269, 271-273, 276, 278, 284-287, 298, 303, 321-323, 336
Lake Oswego	52, 259, 282, 295
Lincoln (High School)	13, 15, 46, 261
Lindberg, Charles	66, 343
Maid	9, 53, 55, 74, 186
Marcel (finger wave); see also *curl*	38, 104, 336
Marriage/married	2-6, 13, 14, 70, 106, 128, 131-133, 138, 140-142, 153, 162, 168, 179, 181-184, 185, 202, 210, 225, 230, 243-244, 247, 261, 278, 281, 282, 284, 298, 313, 348
Meier & Frank	16, 46
Montavilla	14, 16, 178, 200, 207, 255
Moon	5, 37, 48, 132, 134, 140, 144, 147-151, 154, 158, 161, 171, 189, 218, 227, 247, 269-270, 273-274, 276, 285, 300, 302-303, 317, 327, 346
Mother: see *Bailey, Willie Doris Upshaw*	
Movies (by name)	Beau Geste, 62; Breakfast at Sunrise, 45; Captain Swagger, 259; Don Juan, 57; Fazil, 166; The Goose Hangs High, 59; Hula, 61; The Iron Mask, 236; The King of Kings, 121; Madame X, 281; Metropolis, 59; Oh, Kay! 171; Orchids and Ermine, 38; Seventh Heaven, 161; The Smart Set, 110; Speedy, 118; The Student Prince, 107; Trooping Co-Eds, 129; The Venus of Venice, 45; Wings, 177
Mt. Hood	9, 28, 67-68, 260

Multnomah Club   204, 258

Mustache   42, 45, 49, 58, 79, 185, 278, 305, 311

Northwestern Bank   8, 46, 79

Nurse(s)   21, 23-24, 29-30, 105, 151, 310, 316-318, 320

Oak Grove   52, 88, 168, 183, 190, 226, 238, 241, 256, 259

Oakland   14, 36, 38, 102, 108, 167

Office (Daddy's)   126, 131, 137

Operation   85, 143, 151, 152, 162, 167, 200, 220, 234, 311, 327

Oregon Agricultural College (OAC)   16-17, 174, 204

Oregon Normal School (Western   193
  Oregon State University)

Packard   54, 167, 212, 245, 265, 282

Permanent (wave)   286

Phoenix   3-4, 8, 108-109, 114, 117, 123, 131, 135, 145,
                                     160, 163, 326, 331

Picture (film, photograph)   60, 121, 129, 160, 166, 167, 171, 207-209,
                                     212, 233, 253, 275, 277, 298, 309, 319

Pneumonia   31, 35

Poetry/poem   63, 89, 156, 217, 246, 276, 295, 301, 318

Poker   34, 40, 61, 179, 210, 294

Portland   1-5, 8-11, 13-15, 25, 27-29, 32, 39, 53, 59, 62,
                                     64, 66, 73, 75, 86, 88, 94, 97-99, 102-106,
                                     122, 138, 141, 144, 151-152, 159-160, 168-
                                     171, 175, 184,/ 196, 203-204, 210, 223,
                                     226, 231-232, 251, 258, 262, 267, 275, 285-
                                     288, 309, 317, 319, 324, 326, 331

Prescott (Arizona)   4, 124, 133, 149, 150, 152, 157

Radio   5, 15, 25-26, 197, 235, 254, 258

Rain   4, 37, 40, 60, 62, 64, 75, 93, 99, 103, 157,
                                     161, 180, 183, 192, 194, 196, 201, 237, 242,
                                     245, 259, 280, 301, 318, 320, 346

Ranch   24, 133, 193, 196

Record (phonograph, on Victrola)   5, 87, 226, 227, 272, 323, 347

River   10, 22, 29, 52, 56, 67-68, 128, 131, 134, 135,
                                     140, 144, 154, 157, 161, 168, 189, 206, 238,
                                     243, 259, 260, 263, 277, 285, 303

Roadster	49, 50, 59, 70, 101, 116, 128, 176, 250, 271, 275
Rodeo	4, 124-125, 138, 149-150, 264,
San Francisco	22, 38, 103, 166-167, 331, 348
Saturday Evening Post	21, 346
Scarlet fever	1, 21, 23, 25
Scott, Dr. Abel D.	2, 14, 86, 105, 109, 110, 115-117, 122, 130, 141, 143, 148, 151, 153-155, 162, 176-179, 182, 184, 191, 195, 197, 198, 200, 201, 206, 207, 211, 213, 214, 219, 223, 227, 228, 233, 235, 239, 240, 242, 244-245, 279, 281, 294, 295, 308, 310, 311, 313
Secret Sorrow	266, 270
Sellwood (Portland)	44
Sex appeal	17, 222, 311, 313
Show (go to the; a film)	1, 38, 44, 45, 53, 56, 59, 60, 61, 62, 66, 70, 75, 82, 88, 96, 99, 100, 101, 104, 105, 106, 107, 109, 111, 151, 166, 169, 171, 175, 177, 179, 181, 185, 190, 191, 194, 196, 200, 210, 211, 213, 214, 219, 220, 223, 224, 231, 232, 233, 237, 238, 240, 242, 246, 249, 254, 255, 259, 261, 263, 266, 267, 270, 271, 274, 276, 279, 281, 282, 288, 292, 300, 304, 323
Snow	27-29, 222-226, 248
Sorority	263-264, 296, 331, 336
Soul	66, 70, 142, 153, 184, 228, 239, 244, 248, 269, 275, 277, 280, 302, 321
Spending money/allowance	3-4, 62, 82, 105, 129, 167, 171, 185, 191, 195, 203, 204, 208, 213, 219, 220, 230, 237, 248, 250, 261, 267, 275, 282, 286, 296, 305, 306, 307, 309, 327
St. Helen's Hall	3, 14, 17, 25, 50, 64, 68, 76, 137, 169, 173, 174, 175, 181, 185, 190, 197, 220, 223, 225, 226, 240, 241, 242, 248, 250-251, 259, 265, 273, 288, 289, 296, 298, 299, 301, 306, 310, 311, 323
Stadium	66, 129, 188, 258

Stars (in the sky) 118, 132, 146, 149, 270, 275, 276, 285, 296, 297, 327, 328

Stevens, Micky 15, 20, 23, 26, 32-34, 37, 38, 41, 43-48, 52-53, 56-59, 62-69, 71-72, 75-77, 80-82, 86, 89, 106, 124, 127, 155, 195, 197, 240, 249, 275-277

Stoll, George 15, 53, 169, 172, 175, 226, 254, 343

Streetcar 39, 52, 56, 60, 66, 80, 178, 186, 187, 193, 199, 202, 204, 206, 220, 223, 224, 229, 235, 238, 251, 347

Sumner, Bishop 14, 175, 231, 253

Swim 60, 93, 120, 136-138, 140-146, 151, 153-156, 174, 262, 277, 280

The Loop 67-68, 282

The Oaks 95, 262

Train 67, 92, 102, 163, 166, 168, 183, 190, 238, 261, 274, 326

Train station 100, 130, 163, 183, 236, 238, 251-252

Treatment (medical; for ailments, appendix) 1, 30-31, 35, 85, 98, 110, 151, 189, 207, 255, 311

Ukulele (uke) 38, 58, 155

University of Oregon (U of O) 16-17, 198

Upshaw family 9-10, 12, 92, 97, 100, 114, 117, 130

Victrola (see also *records*) 87, 272, 323, 347

Washington (Seattle, etc.) 50, 53, 56, 58, 65, 110, 188, 271, 273-274, 277, 287, 304

Westover (streetcar, W.O.) 17, 37, 55, 60, 77, 186, 189, 210, 225, 240

Whiskey 139

Willamette (River) 22, 29, 52, 269, 282

Woods 52, 53, 194, 202, 208, 214, 239, 250, 256, 259, 277, 291, 298, 299, 307, 348

CPSIA information can be obtained at www.ICGtesting.com
Printed in the USA
LVOW06s0523200813

348639LV00002B/5/P

15.3.22

MAI

KT-445-134

the downright weird. From cursed
'ghost' ships and disappearing cities,
to real-life mermaids and invisible
ships, you'll be stunned at some of
the strange and spooky goings-on
around the worl

C333668613

All these mysteries have baffled the experts and left investigators clueless. My mission is to find out the truth. And I need your help.

Together, we'll weigh up the evidence, look at all the explanations — then you decide which is the best solution. You can even keep track of your solved mysteries by turning to page 101 and recording your verdict!

A word of warning: If you're the nervous type, put this book down now. Some of the mysteries we'll be investigating are pretty scary. The kind of things that might make a person a bit, well, jumpy . . .

What was that?

Did you hear something?

OK, I'd better calm down . . . and breathe . . .

Let's go. Time to explore the world's greatest mysteries!

Richard Hammond

RICHARD HAMMOND'S

GREAT MYSTERIES OF THE WORLD

WEIRD WATERS

RED FOX

RICHARD HAMMOND'S GREAT MYSTERIES OF THE WORLD: WEIRD WATERS
A RED FOX BOOK 978 1 849 41712 9

Published in Great Britain by Red Fox,
an imprint of Random House Children's Publishers UK
A Random House Group Company
1 3 5 7 9 10 8 6 4 2

Bind-up edition published by The Bodley Head 2013
This Red Fox edition published 2014

Copyright © Richard Hammond, 2013
Cover illustration copyright © Donough O'Malley, 2014
Inside illustration copyright © Donough O'Malley, 2013
Author photographs copyright © Joseph Sinclair, 2013
Text design by Lizzy Laczynska and Rachel Clark
Picture research by Liane Payne and Random House Children's Publishers

The Random House Group Limited supports the Forest Stewardship Council® (FSC®),
the leading international forest-certification organisation. Our books carrying the FSC label
are printed on FSC®-certified paper. FSC is the only forest-certification scheme supported
by the leading environmental organisations, including Greenpeace. Our paper procurement
policy can be found at www.randomhouse.co.uk/environment

Set in Baskerville Classico 12/17.5pt

RANDOM HOUSE CHILDREN'S PUBLISHERS UK
61–63 Uxbridge Road, London W5 5SA

www.**randomhousechildrens**.co.uk
www.**totallyrandombooks**.co.uk
www.**randomhouse**.co.uk

Addresses for companies within The Random House Group Limited can be found at:
www.randomhouse.co.uk/offices.htm

THE RANDOM HOUSE GROUP Limited Reg. No. 954009

A CIP catalogue record for this book is available from the British Library.

Printed and bound in Great Britain by
CPI Group (UK) Ltd, Croydon, CR0 4YY

With special thanks to Amanda Li

CONTENTS

Deep-sea Diving Kit List   1

1. The Lost City of Atlantis   5

2. The *Mary Celeste*   27

3. Mythical Mermaids   49

4. The Bermuda Triangle   61

5. The Philadelphia Experiment   89

Want to Know More?   99

Decision Time   101

DEEP-SEA DIVING-KIT LIST

All water investigators know one thing. They're going to get wet. So I'm going to need some serious training – and some serious equipment – to help me on my mission to explore these weird watery mysteries. Here are a few of the basics:

 DIVING WET SUIT – keeps you from freezing in a cold sea

 DIVE SKIN – only for warmer waters, it protects you from jellyfish stings and sunburn

 FLIPPERS – help you move faster and more efficiently through the water

 DIVING MASK, OXYGEN TANKS AND REGULATOR – you need to be able to breathe!

 DIVING WEIGHTS – to get down really deep. Weights attach to the body and help you descend

 DIVING KNIFE – if you get caught up in weed or fishing line, this could be a lifesaver

 WHISTLE, LIGHT OR SIGNALLING DEVICE – in case you're lost or swept out in a current

BCD (BUOYANCY CONTROL DEVICE) – wear it like a vest. You control the flow of air to move up or down once underwater

 UNDERWATER FLASHLIGHT – it's really dark down there! Best to have a headlight too

 BOAT – to take you to the diving location. The boat should have a red and white 'diver down' flag to alert others that divers are underwater in the area

 BUDDY – no one should dive without a buddy to help them out

 UNDERWATER CAMERA – to get the best shots possible. My model has a 100m depth rating and a macro lens for crystal-clear close-up shots. It also has a power flash for those dark, murky waters

Know your diving signals

Hand gestures are the best way of communicating when you're underwater. It's really important to know some basic signals – your life could depend on it!

1. *Are you OK?*

2. *Yes, I'm OK.*

3. *Not OK, something's wrong.*

Hand moves from side to side

Right, so now I'm fully kitted up, join me on my first mystery hunt . . .

3

The Lost City of Atlantis

THE MISSION ...

... to search for the legendary lost city of Atlantis.

BURNING QUESTIONS

- 🔥 Was Atlantis swallowed up by the sea more than 9,000 years ago?
- 🔥 Can an entire city disappear without trace?
- 🔥 Did Atlantis ever exist?

MISSION DETAILS

I'm looking for Atlantis – an ancient city built by an advanced civilization on a mysterious island. According to legend, Atlantis disappeared under the sea long, long ago. No trace has ever been found of its buildings or its people.

One of the reasons people find Atlantis fascinating is because it was supposed to have existed more than *10,000 years ago* (probably around 9600 BC). This, if you need reminding, was the time of the Stone Age. The humans we know about were still chipping away with sharpened bits of flint and trying to make fire!

But the Atlanteans – which is what you're called if you live in a city called Atlantis – were busy being brilliant architects, talented engineers and having intelligent discussions about politics and art. So if we ever found Atlantis, we would literally have to rewrite the history of human civilization . . .

THE EVIDENCE

There have been hundreds, maybe thousands, of investigations into Atlantis. Books have been written about it, divers have searched for it, films and TV programmes have been made about it.

But no one's ever found any trace of Atlantis. So how do we even know about it?

It's because Atlantis and its history were described in detail by none other than the famous Greek philosopher, Plato. In about 360 BC he wrote a long essay about an incredible island nation. His description has fascinated people ever since. Here are some of the things he said:

- Atlantis was ruled by ten kings
- The island of Atlantis was located close to the Pillars of Hercules
- The Atlanteans were clever, wealthy and powerful – an ancient superpower with a fleet of warships and more than a million soldiers
- They fought against Europe and Asia. They also tried, but failed, to invade Athens
- They were incredible engineers, architects and artists

Here is one of Plato's descriptions:

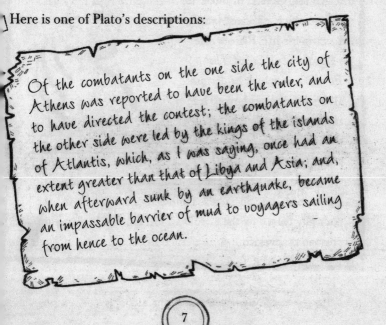

Of the combatants on the one side the city of Athens was reported to have been the ruler, and to have directed the contest; the combatants on the other side were led by the kings of the islands of Atlantis, which, as I was saying, once had an extent greater than that of Libya and Asia; and, when afterward sunk by an earthquake, became an impassable barrier of mud to voyagers sailing from hence to the ocean.

Ever since Plato's time, people have wondered where this amazing place could have been – and if we can find it.

Was Plato making it all up? Or was Atlantis just an impressive work of fiction, Plato's own *Harry Potter*?

Potted Plato

Philosophers are people who think a lot about the big questions in life – a bit like me, really. Questions like 'Why are we here?' and 'What is wisdom?' – or, in my case, 'Why does my hair always stick up in the morning?'

Plato thought a lot about questions like these (except the last one, of course). He was born in Athens, Greece, in about 429 BC, to a rich, educated family. Later in his life, Plato wrote a famous book called *The Republic*, in which he discussed all his ideas about how to lead and govern people. He was thoughtful, wise – and extremely clever (again, the similarity!).

Plato – looking a bit stony-faced?

Plato spent a lot of time with his older philosopher friend, Socrates. Socrates is famous too, because he was the poor guy forced by the Greeks to kill himself by drinking poisonous hemlock.

We know all this because Plato wrote it down. And we believe him.

Plato is thought to have been one of the greatest philosophers of our time, admired and respected for centuries. So why shouldn't we believe his account of Atlantis?

As we can't ask him, we'll never know!

Atlantis – the Place

Amazing Atlantis!

COME TO THE DREAM CITY OF ATLANTIS! ENJOY SCENIC VIEWS FROM THE HARBOURS, RELAXING IN BEAUTIFUL SURROUNDINGS, WORSHIPPING IN THE FINEST TEMPLES AND WATCHING THE INCREDIBLE WILDLIFE ON THIS STUNNING ISLAND.

Atlantis sounds like a brilliant place to live. Plato says that it was made up of a large central island surrounded by three huge harbours. The harbours were in the shape of concentric circles – a series of circles that radiate outwards from one centre. There was a canal and tunnels for ships to pass through. On the island, there was a huge city of beautiful buildings, a large palace, temples, fountains, bridges, gardens, ports and docks.

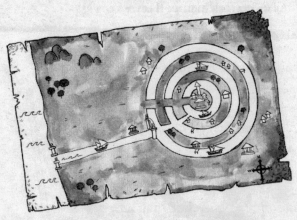

The Atlanteans had everything they could possibly need. The islands were full of exotic plants, fruits and animals, even elephants. There were precious metals too. The people made stunning gold and silver statues and displayed them around the city. There were large resources of a metal called *orichalcum*, which 'glowed like fire' – now thought to be copper. This lost treasure is another reason why adventurers seek Atlantis – whoever finds it could get *seriously* rich!

On top of the most central hill – called the Acropolis Hill – the Atlanteans built two huge temples. The most important was in honour of Poseidon. Inside this temple was a golden statue of the sea god on a chariot being pulled by winged horses. The Atlantean rulers came here to discuss important issues and to worship the powerful Poseidon.

All around the temples, bulls ran free. Bulls were really important to the Atlanteans – they regarded them as sacred, worshipped them and sometimes sacrificed them to the gods.

The Atlanteans had it all. But one day it fell apart . . .

What Happened?

Atlantis disappeared – literally overnight. What could have wiped out these beautiful islands and the people that lived on them?

Plato said that a 'terrible night of fire and earthquakes' was sent by the gods as a punishment to the badly behaved islanders, who had become too powerful and corrupt for their own good. Modern-day investigators think a natural disaster, most likely a tsunami, could have hit the island, destroying Atlantis and its people. If so, the island could now lie deep under the sea, undiscovered for thousands of years.

Tsunami Terror

'Tsunami' means 'harbour wave' in Japanese.

A tsunami is a gigantic wave caused by a massive underwater disturbance, usually an undersea earthquake or a volcanic eruption. Deep in the ocean, movement on the sea floor pushes the water above it, causing fast-moving waves. Once these waves reach shallower waters near the shore, they slow down but get bigger. This is when they can get to terrifying heights – as much as 40 metres.

A tsunami can wipe out everything in its path once it hits land, destroying entire cities, towns and villages. The speed and power of the water is unbelievable.

© AFP/GETTY IMAGES

The town of Otsuchi in Japan, following the devastating earthquake and tsunami of 2011

Certain parts of the world are prone to earthquake activity and tsunamis. One of these areas is called the 'Ring of Fire' and includes much of Asia and the Americas' Pacific coast.

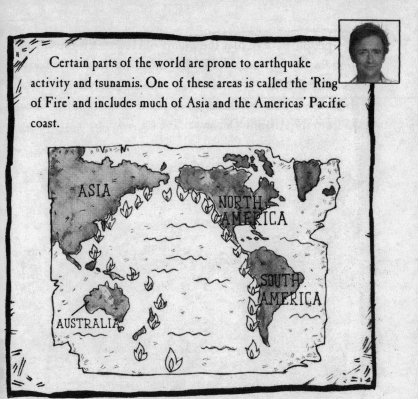

THE LOCATION

We're not short of potential locations for Atlantis. It's a hot topic and there are lots of ideas out there: Egypt, Cuba, the Canary Islands, England, even chilly Antarctica, among many others.

Plato said that Atlantis was located *just beyond* or *in front of* the Pillars of Hercules, depending on your translation of ancient Greek. (I don't know about you, but my ancient Greek's just a little bit rusty . . .)

Most people believe that the Pillars of Hercules is the ancient name for the two huge rocks that lie on each side of what we now call the Strait of Gibraltar (one is called Gibraltar, the other Jebel Musa). They mark the entry point to the Mediterranean Sea from the Atlantic Ocean.

So all we have to do is dive down around the Strait of Gibraltar and we'll find Atlantis there? Well, if things were that straightforward, they would have found Atlantis years ago. Not everyone agrees about the location – and as you'll discover, trying to find Atlantis is anything but straightforward. There are countless 'experts' out there with different ideas and theories – and everyone makes mistakes.

Whoops!

It's easy to get carried away when you're mystery hunting. When excited researchers found an image with what looked like a grid of ancient roads under the Atlantic Ocean, they thought they had struck Atlantis gold. But the sunken 'city' was just an illusion. The 'roads' were actually lines reflecting the path of a boat as it was collecting data for maps!

Not everyone gets it right!

MY MISSION

Judging by what Plato said, the Mediterranean Sea and the Atlantic Ocean seem to be the obvious places to begin my investigation – but where exactly?

🌐 *A wetlands area in Southern Spain*
Satellite photographs from space show images of large circles buried underneath the mud at Doñana, Europe's largest wetlands. I'm going to find out more about these circles and what they might mean. Some serious techie gadgets will be required!

🌐 *The Greek island of Crete*
There are lots of similarities between an ancient civilization called the Minoans (who once lived on Crete) and the Atlanteans. I'm going to check out the Minoan history to see what it's all about. Digging and mapping involved.

🌑 *An area of sea close to the island of Cyprus*

There are rumours that man-made structures have been detected on the ocean floor southeast of Cyprus. I'll be diving down to take a look.

Note: There has been a suggestion that Atlantis is buried deep under a notorious area of ocean in the western part of the north Atlantic. Find out more on this in 'The Bermuda Triangle' (pages 61–88).

See you when I get back!

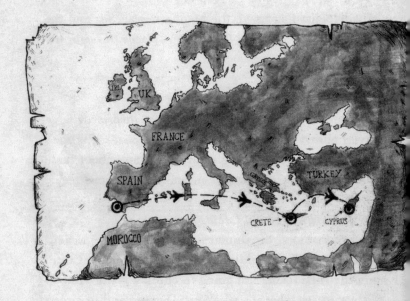

EXTRA KIT

Deep-sea diving kit is perfect for exploring water, but what if you're trying to find something buried underground? Guess what? – I'm going to need a gadget.

🌐 *The GPR* – a machine that transmits high-frequency radio waves through the earth. OK, it may look a bit like a lawnmower, but in fact this is a high-tech piece of kit that can scan areas deep underground to detect what lies below. This is also called 'sonar imaging'.

A 'wheely' fun way to find out what lies underground...

Digging Deep

Deeply buried sites have always been hard for archaeologists to deal with. It's pointless trying to dig up the earth with a shovel, if the site you're looking for is a kilometre underground and you're not even sure of its exact location.

GPR – Ground Penetrating Radar – has changed all that. It was first developed as a way of collecting information about the structure of the moon. The technology has proved really useful for archaeologists as well as astronauts, as it can be used to help find ancient remains deep below ground. The data it collects is then processed by a computer and turned into maps.

MISSION COMPLETED

Well – I've dived into the deepest oceans . . .

Spent hours surveying the land with my GPR machine . . .

Talked to lots of experts . . .

I haven't discovered the city of Atlantis yet – but I do have some very interesting information for you.

WHAT DO YOU THINK?

1. The Minoans and the Atlanteans Were One and the Same

When Plato wrote about the 'Atlanteans', was he describing a real group of people called the Minoans? They were a Bronze Age civilization who lived on the Greek islands of Crete and Santorini (and in other regions). We think the Minoans died out around 1500 BC, but they were around for hundreds of years before that.

The coincidences I have found are pretty amazing:

- Like the Atlanteans, the Minoans were very advanced for their time. They were the first Europeans known to have used a written language. They had hot and cold running water and were highly skilled plumbers –

18

archaeologists believe that Minoan Crete was home to the world's first flushing toilet!

🌀 Their king, Minos, lived in a huge 150-room palace in Knossos. Plato described a great palace on Atlantis – could they be the same?

🌀 Bulls were important animals in Atlantis. They were in Crete too. Archaeologists have unearthed paintings of Minoan bullfighters wrestling and jumping over bulls

A Minoan wall painting showing the incredible things you can do with bulls!

🌀 Both civilizations were excellent shipbuilders and had powerful naval fleets

🌀 The Minoans disappeared, just like the Atlanteans. Around 1500 BC, a volcano erupted on the island of Santorini (then called Thera), not far from the island of Crete. It was a massive eruption, blasting out red-hot ash, gas and rocks, and it could have caused a later tsunami

 To back this up, archaeologists have found micro-organisms in the local soil that could only have come from the ocean floor. How did they get there? They're most likely what's left of a massive tsunami from long ago. So, did a tsunami wipe out the Minoans (who were really the Atlanteans)?

Not everything fits. Crete, though in the Mediterranean, is not very close to the Strait of Gibraltar. Also, the Minoans lived thousands of years *later* than Plato's Atlanteans. Some people think that the translations of his writings might not be exact, which could possibly explain the differences in date and location. For example, Plato said that Atlantis existed about 9,000 years before his time – but if that translation was wrong and it was actually *900* years before, then that would tie in with the Minoans nicely. Hmmm . . .

2. Atlantis Is Buried under Mud Flats in Spain

This is a really interesting one – and also the most recent of our theories. The images from satellite photos certainly indicate that there is *something* buried deep in the wetland area of Donaña, on the Atlantic coast of Spain. What it is exactly, no one can be sure, as the images can only show a vague outline.

What we do know is this:

 The wetlands were once a huge bay, but the ocean has receded over many years, leaving behind marshland

 The shapes discovered do look similar to the famed

circular harbours of Atlantis. There are also some rectangular shapes which the investigators think might be the remains of the Atlantean temples. Why not dig it all up and find out for sure? Well, the area is part of a National Park and one of Europe's most important wetland reserves – so that's not an option

- Plato said there was a plain and a range of high mountains behind the island Atlantis. In this area, there is a plain that runs from Spain's southern coast up to the city of Seville. The high mountains could be those of the Sierra Morena and Sierra Nevada

- Copper, another feature of Atlantis, is found in the mines of the Sierra Morena

- A research team, headed by Professor Richard Freund, found a large piece of stone with a carved symbol on it. It shows three concentric rings with a line in the centre, like a channel, and what looks like a simple human figure next to it. Could this carving represent the harbours and people of Atlantis?

Even though the stone is not old enough to have come from Atlantis itself, the research team think it may have come from a 'memorial city' nearby – a city built years later by a group of Atlanteans who managed to escape the disaster that befell their island. Professor Freund thinks these survivors could have moved inland and built more cities. Perhaps they made the stone symbols in tribute to Atlantis, their true home. More than a hundred of these stone symbols have been found in central Spain – do they prove that the real Atlantis is here?

3. Atlantis Was Once Part of Cyprus

Everyone got very excited in 2004, when an archaeologist called Robert Sarmast found what appeared to be two large man-made structures beneath the ocean, close to the island of Cyprus in the Mediterranean. Sonar data images taken 1,500 metres below sea level showed what were possibly two straight, two-kilometre-long walls, sitting on a flat-topped hill. Sarmast studied Plato's measurements of the walled city and said they matched up. He is convinced that he has found the legendary Acropolis Hill that was at the centre of Atlantis.

Could Cyprus once have been part of Atlantis? Here are some reasons why:

- Sarmast thinks that part of the landmass sank under the sea thousands of years ago
- Plato said there were elephants on Atlantis. Well, surprisingly, there used to be a species of dwarf elephant on Cyprus (now sadly extinct)
- According to Plato, copper was abundant on Atlantis And what is the island of Cyprus named for? – you've got it – copper! Cyprus was once very famous for its copper reserves

- Every year in Cyprus, the people celebrate a Festival of the Flood – but no one knows why. Does the tradition go back thousands of years, marking the sinking of Atlantis under the sea?
- The highest mountain on the island is named Olympos. Could this be the original Mount Olympus, the sacred mountain of the Greek gods?

4. It's Just a Story

As everything we know about Atlantis comes from Plato, we only have his word for it. He may have been making it all up. Perhaps he was describing his fantasy, his ideal world. But if it *was* made up, why would Plato have brought his perfect world to an end? Seems a bit of a shame, doesn't it?

Well, Plato may have been trying to help people learn that actions have consequences. The people of Atlantis had everything, but they lost their way, became greedy and behaved badly. As a result, they were punished by the gods. This could have been an allegory – an important lesson told through a story. Was Plato's story made up for this reason?

5. Aliens on Atlantis

Some people believe that the Atlanteans weren't human. They think that Atlantis was populated by 'extraterrestrials'

– aliens from outer space! Could a group of advanced, intelligent aliens have landed on Earth and formed their own colony, thousands of years ago? If so, what happened to them? Maybe a natural disaster killed them or perhaps they destroyed themselves accidentally – with a nuclear bomb or with a weapon so weird and technologically advanced we can't even begin to imagine it!

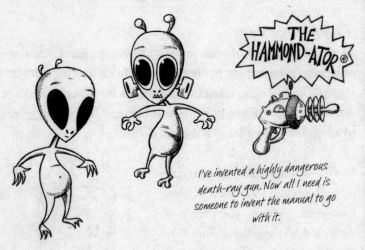

THE HAMMOND-ATOR®

I've invented a highly dangerous death-ray gun. Now all I need is someone to invent the manual to go with it.

The alien believers think that this idea could solve some big unanswered questions – like, for example, how (and why) did the ancient Egyptians build the pyramids? And why are similar pyramids found in Central America and other far-away parts of the world? Some think that the knowledge needed to build them came from intelligent pyramid-loving aliens who passed it on to the ancient cultures of our world.

There is no scientific evidence for this idea that I know of – but it's certainly 'out of this world'!

YOU DECIDE

So, now we've come to the end of our Atlantis adventure, do you think it was a real place – or a just myth?

Why not turn to page 101 and vote for your favourite theory, or write your thoughts about the Atlantis mystery in the notes section.

The great Atlantis debate will continue – and the watery hunt will go on . . .

The
Mary Celeste

THE MISSION...

... to find out why the passengers and crew disappeared from a ship called the *Mary Celeste*.

© HULTON ARCHIVE/GETTY IMAGES

The ghostly, abandoned Mary Celeste

BURNING QUESTIONS

♦ How can ten people just vanish into thin air?

♦ Did the crew abandon their ship – and why?

MISSION DETAILS

I'm trying to get to the bottom of one of the biggest ever maritime mysteries, one that has had people scratching their heads for more than a hundred years.

On 5 December 1872 a ship was discovered drifting in the Atlantic Ocean – in good condition, with no signs of any major problems. Just one odd thing: the crew had completely disappeared.

What could have happened? Did the passengers panic and leave the ship for some reason – or was there a more sinister explanation?

THE EVIDENCE

The mystery of the *Mary Celeste* has fascinated people ever since the infamous 'ghost ship' was found silently floating alone, all those years ago. People have come up with all sorts of ideas about what could have happened, from attacks by bloodthirsty pirates to the entire crew being abducted by aliens.

The famous mystery writer Sir Arthur Conan Doyle even made up his own 'explanation' – more on that later.

But even though there was a full investigation at the time, we

really don't have that much to go on. Just a spooky, empty ship and the eyewitness accounts of the sailors who found it.

The facts we know for sure are:

- There were ten people on board the *Mary Celeste*: Captain Benjamin Briggs, his wife, Sarah, their two-year-old daughter, Sophia, and a crew of seven men
- A small rowing boat, called a yawl, was missing. The railings on one side of the ship had been lowered so the yawl had probably been launched
- All the cargo (hundreds of barrels of alcohol) was intact, apart from just nine barrels, which were found to be empty
- The ship's clock wasn't working and the compass was destroyed
- The stove had been moved
- The sextant and chronometer were missing. (In the days before sat nav, these instruments would have been essential for navigating the ship)
- The ship's navigation book was missing – but the log book was still there
- The halyard (the rope used to hoist the sail) was broken and part of it was missing

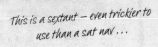
This is a sextant – even trickier to use than a sat nav . . .

- There was some water slopping around between the decks, and one of the pumps was broken. Two of the ship's hatches had been removed

Fact or Fiction?

Sir Arthur Conan Doyle – who later went on to create the brilliant violin-playing detective Sherlock Holmes – loved a good mystery (me too!).

Take a look at his photograph. Here's another mystery for you – how did Sir Arthur get his moustache to twirl upwards in that gravity-defying way? (I admit I don't have the answer to this – yet another great unsolved mystery of our time.)

Conan Doyle was fascinated by the *Mary Celeste* case and decided to write his own story about the ghost ship. His gruesome version was published in 1884.

In his story:

- The ship is named the *Marie Celeste*
- Among the crew and passengers is a strange-looking character named Septimius Goring. Septimius has lost all the fingers on his right hand, leaving just a thumb, but no one knows why. (Sounds like he could do with a trip to a second-hand shop . . . ?)
- Turns out we were right to be suspicious about Goring – he's a bad guy. He shoots the captain, takes control of the *Marie Celeste* and sails her to Africa
- He then murders most of the crew and is last seen disappearing into the Sahara desert . . .

30

The story caused a lot of confusion as people weren't sure if it was the truth. And many still think the real ship was called the *Marie Celeste*. Even more confusingly, over time, other details about the real-life case have been exaggerated, or made up. For example, lots of people believe that the ship was found with half-eaten meals at the table and half-drunk cups of coffee. If this were true, it would have meant that the passengers had left the ship incredibly fast, without even having time to finish their food. But, just like the Conan Doyle story, it's pure fiction!

THE LOCATION

The *Mary Celeste* set sail from New York, USA, on 7 November 1872, bound for Genoa in Italy. She was a brigantine – a ship with two masts. (By the way, ships are always referred to as 'she' – an old sailor's tradition.)

On board was a cargo of 1,701 barrels of pure alcohol, used to fortify wine and destined for the vineyards of Italy.

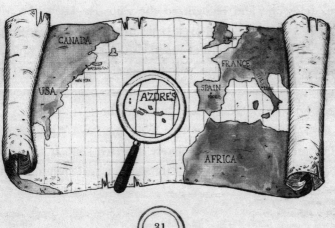

The log book's last entry was recorded on 25 November and described nothing unusual. At this point, the ship was just six miles away from the island of Santa Maria. Santa Maria is one of nine Portuguese islands called the Azores, in the North Atlantic Ocean.

When she was discovered, the *Mary Celeste* had drifted 400 miles east of Santa Maria and was heading towards the Strait of Gibraltar.

What Happened?

A Canadian ship called *Dei Gratia* had left New York harbour a few days after the *Mary Celeste*. On 5 December the *Dei Gratia* crew were puzzled to see a ship in the distance, apparently unmanned (that means no one was on board). They could tell this because of the way the *Mary Celeste* was moving. She was doing something sailors call 'yawing', which is swinging around to the right and left – clearly not under a captain's control.

Captain Morehouse of the *Dei Gratia* looked carefully through his telescope and recognized the ship. He knew the *Mary Celeste*'s captain – he'd even had dinner with Captain Briggs the night before she had sailed. After a couple of hours of observation there were still no signs of life on board and absolutely no response to their signals. So Morehouse decided to send out a boarding party in a small boat.

The men boarded a completely deserted ship. It must have been a really spooky sight – the ship's wheel spinning round with no hand to guide it, the deck and rigging creaking, but not a soul on board to reply to the men's shouts and calls. From the look of things – the sailors had left behind their boots and pipes and the captain's wife hadn't taken any of her jewellery – the crew had left the ship in a bit of a hurry.

Rather appropriately for a ghost ship, Captain Morehouse put a 'skeleton crew' on the *Mary Celeste*, and both ships were sailed back to Gibraltar.

Spooky Ships

Would you have volunteered to be the first to step aboard the scarily silent and empty *Mary Celeste*, not knowing what had happened? It's enough to literally 'shiver your timbers'! But it seems there might be even spookier ships out there, according to sailors' tales. Take the legend of the ghostly *Flying Dutchman*, for example.

Sailors are petrified of spotting this ghostly glowing ship. Why? Because anyone who sees it is supposed to die an awful death. This is what is known as a 'bad omen'. And, as omens go, seeing the *Flying Dutchman* is a really, really bad one.

The story goes that in 1641 a Dutch ship was caught up in a terrible storm near the Cape of Good Hope (on the Atlantic coast of South Africa). As the ship crashed into rocks and began to sink, the captain screamed out that he would *never* give up – that he would keep sailing round the Cape until Doomsday! (Quite a long time, then.) Unfortunately, the captain then drowned, along with the rest of his crew. But, according to legend, his phantom ship carries on, doomed to sail the seven seas for eternity ...

Years later, in 1881, the Royal Navy ship *Bacchante* was sailing round the Cape, when – yikes! A terrifying sight came into view. Yes, you've guessed it: it was the *Flying Dutchman*, glowing with a ghostly red light, as if she had sailed from the depths of hell itself. The crew were understandably terrified and panic broke out amongst the men. Soon afterwards the ship vanished from sight. Everyone breathed a sigh of relief. But worse was to come ... the sailor who had first spotted the *Dutchman* later fell from a mast to his death. Eek!

MY MISSION

After hearing that story, I'm a teeny bit nervous about spotting any kind of ghost ship. Fortunately, the *Flying Dutchman* is supposed to haunt oceans in South Africa – a very long way away from where I'll be sailing to search out the wreck

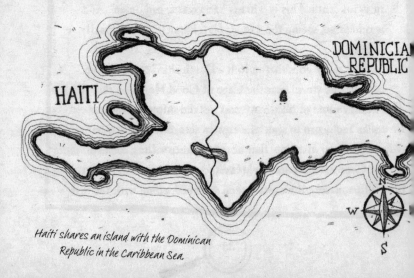

HAITI

DOMINICIA REPUBLIC

Haiti shares an island with the Dominican Republic in the Caribbean Sea.

of the *Mary Celeste*. I'm off to the Caribbean! But what is the *Mary Celeste* doing there?

In 2001 a team of divers found the remains of the legendary ship lying on a coral reef, just off the coast of Haiti. The poor old *Mary Celeste* had been abandoned by her last owner and left to rot.

I'll be diving down to the *Mary Celeste*'s final resting place to inspect the wreck. I'll need my full deep-sea diving kit to have a good old look around. Luckily, the Caribbean is one of the warmer seas of the world, and the coral reef should be full of amazing sea creatures. I'm just off to get a book and check out exactly which ones . . .

. . . OK, so there's good news and there's bad news. The bad news is that I now know what lives in coral reefs in the Caribbean Sea – the Caribbean reef shark!

Large carnivorous teeth!

The good news is that, apparently, shark attacks are extremely rare. In fact, most sharks only attack humans by mistake, thinking they are big fish. So – just in case a wandering reef shark mistakes me for a fish, I've invested in a whopping bit of kit to take along:

EXTRA KIT

A shark cage. This super-strong submersible cage is constructed from marine-grade aluminium. It's not big – with a height of 3 metres and a width of just 2 metres, it's going to be cosy, but, most importantly, it should – hopefully – protect me from the fiercest reef shark!

MISSION COMPLETED

Back from my diving adventure – and you'll be pleased to hear (I hope!) that I wasn't eaten by a Caribbean reef shark. Even better – I found the *Mary Celeste*! She's not looking her best, though. Having been underwater for so many years, much of her wood has rotted and her sails have completely disintegrated. She is pretty much unrecognizable as a ship and is almost completely covered in coral. It's a sad sight . . .

I couldn't get right inside the wreck because the shark cage was, well, a bit limiting. And there was no way I was getting out of that cage to take a closer look!

It was fascinating to see the old wreck of this mysterious ship . . . but it couldn't really tell me anything new about the mystery. So, like the legendary detective Sherlock Holmes, we will have to use our incredible powers of deduction . . .

WHAT DO YOU THINK?

There are lots of theories, ranging from the ridiculous to the realistic. There was once even an episode of TV's *Doctor Who* (from 1965 – the Doctor really is ancient!) that blamed the *Mary Celeste* crew's disappearance on a rogue group of Daleks! Well, wouldn't *you* jump overboard if a bunch of one-armed metallic monsters suddenly appeared on board your ship?

Hmm – maybe best to 'exterminate' that idea and move on to some others . . .

1. Sea Monster Attack

Were the passengers devoured by a giant octopus? Perhaps 'squidnapped'?

Many people at the time believed that some kind of huge sea monster attacked the ship. This theory depends on a few other things. Firstly, believing that sea monsters actually exist. Throughout history, sailors have told tales of horrible monsters such as the Kraken, a gigantic squid-like creature with writhing tentacles that attacks ships at sea.

This artist painted a picture of the Kraken in 1801, based on real sailors' descriptions at the time. Not something you'd want to encounter on a relaxing boating trip . . .

'Mmm – fish and ships for dinner tonigh

But if a hungry Kraken was responsible for the disappearance, surely the passengers would have had to be on deck for the monster to attack them? (I don't know about you, but I'd get *below* deck very fast if a massive monster with waving tentacles suddenly rose out of the waves.)

Also, why – and how – would a sea monster take the yawl, sextant, chronometer and ship's papers? Those great big tentacles aren't exactly made for picking up delicate objects, are they? Surely there would have been some bite marks in the deck, or at least some signs of a struggle?

2. Plundering Pirates

Yo ho ho! In days of old, posses of plundering pirates sailed the oceans on the lookout for ships to raid. Given their liking for a bottle of rum, the *Mary Celeste* – which was carrying barrels of alcohol – should have been an ideal target for a group of thirsty pirates. They might have got rid of the passengers and crew by throwing them overboard – or perhaps making them walk the plank!

But if pirates *had* attacked the ship, why would they have left all those valuable barrels behind? Plus, again, there were no visible

39

signs of an attack or a struggle. Could pirates really be to blame for the crew's disappearance?

3. Foul Play

Was there a cunning plot to make a fortune out of the *Mary Celeste*? In those days, you could claim a very nice amount of cash – 'salvage money' – if you rescued a ship that had valuable cargo on board. Some believed that the captains of the two ships involved planned to do exactly this.

In Gibraltar, where the *Mary Celeste* was eventually taken by the *Dei Gratia*, the Attorney General, Mr Solly Flood, made some serious accusations against Captains Briggs and Morehouse. He suggested that a plot had been hatched between the two captains to get rid of the crew and claim the salvage money for themselves.

Mr Flood later accused Captain Morehouse and the crew of the *Dei Gratia* of murdering everyone on board the *Mary Celeste*. None of these accusations of 'foul play!' were ever proved, but they did have a big impact. People everywhere heard about the rumours and everyone got talking about the mysterious case. That's been going on ever since.

4. Mutiny!

If you were a captain of a ship, the one thing you would dread (apart from pirates, sea monsters and terrible storms, obviously) was mutiny. A mutiny happens when the crew takes over the ship and gets rid of the captain because they don't like him very much. Any group of sailors would have had to

be really desperate to do this – because the punishment for mutiny was dire. If a mutineer was captured, it would be a case of 'Hang him by the yardarm!' – a particularly nasty way to die (the yardarm being a horizontal timber mounted on the mast of a ship).

Did a mutiny take place aboard the *Mary Celeste*? Were the crew so upset about something that they murdered the captain and his family, threw their bodies overboard, then escaped in the yawl, never to be seen again?

Mutinies always happen for a good reason – perhaps the sailors are badly treated, or suffering horribly on a very long voyage. As far as we know, Captain Briggs was a well-respected leader and there were no known troublemakers among the crew. Also the voyage was just a few weeks long, and there were plenty of food and water supplies on board. There was no obvious reason for the sailors to take over the ship. Was there something going on that we don't know about?

Mutiny on the *Bounty*

One of the most famous mutinies of all time – which had nothing at all to do with a chocolate-covered coconut bar – happened in 1789 in the Pacific Ocean. HMS *Bounty* was a British ship which sailed to Tahiti in 1788 on a voyage to collect breadfruit plants. Her captain was William Bligh, a brilliant and experienced sea man – though some say he was a harsh and difficult captain to work for.

After ten tough months at sea, the crew were delighted to spend some relaxing months on the beautiful island of Tahiti. So much so that, when the time came to start the long voyage home, most of the men decided that they would rather stay. This wasn't an option – and that's when the trouble started.

Life on board ship was always hard and the months at sea could seem never-ending. The diet of maggot-ridden 'ship's biscuit' (a kind of rock-hard bread, sadly; nothing at all like a custard cream) and harsh punishments of flogging didn't make the trip any more appealing. It was too much for some of Bligh's men.

On 28 April 1789 the captain's second-in-command, Fletcher Christian, along with twelve others, burst into Captain Bligh's cabin and dragged him up on deck. According to his log book, the men 'came into my cabin while I was fast asleep, and seizing me, tyed my hands with a Cord & threatened instant death if I made the least noise'.

They set the captain adrift in a seven-metre boat, along with eighteen of his loyal crew members. The merry mutineers then sailed straight back to the good life on Tahiti.

Now, things weren't looking too good for Captain Bligh and his men. They knew that they had very little chance of surviving on the open sea without any supplies. But incredibly – despite being chased by cannibals and stoned by the locals when they finally found an island – most of the sailors *did* survive. It was tough – they had to catch fish to

eat and find rainwater to drink. But they eventually
made it to the island of Timor (east of Indonesia). It had
taken them seven weeks and they had travelled more than
3,600 miles. Whatever you think of Captain Bligh, it was
an incredible achievement!

5. A Curse?

Some superstitious people think that the *Mary Celeste* was
cursed. From the moment she was launched in 1861, the *Mary
Celeste* (who was originally called *Amazon*) seemed to have
nothing but bad luck. In fact, even being renamed is supposed
to be bad luck for a ship!

A few examples:

- 🌐 Her first captain, Robert McLellan, was taken ill and
  died
- 🌐 Under the command of her second captain, John
  Parker, she ran into a fishing boat, was badly damaged
  and had to return to the shipyard for repairs
- 🌐 A fire broke out on board while she was at the shipyard
- 🌐 The *Mary Celeste* later collided with another ship in the
  English Channel and needed further repairs
- 🌐 In 1867 she ran aground during a storm off the coast of
  Nova Scotia
- 🌐 In 1872 she was found empty and all ten people on
  board had disappeared (our mystery)

After she was found abandoned, the *Mary Celeste* sailed for a further twelve years. She had many different owners during this time and, unfortunately, lost money for most of them. She came to a sad end when she was run aground off the coast of Haiti. Her final captain, Captain Gilman Parker, had loaded her with a worthless cargo of rubber boots and cat food, then tried to sink her, hoping to claim the insurance money. He died three months after his trial.

David Cartwright, one of her owners, said:

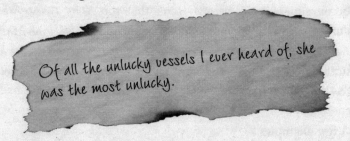

Of all the unlucky vessels I ever heard of, she was the most unlucky.

Could the *Mary Celeste* really have been cursed? And if so, what happened to the people on board?

Abandon Ship!

Captains only abandon their ships for a very good reason. What kind of emergency could have forced everyone off the ship?

6. A Sea Quake or Spout?

A sea quake is an earthquake that happens underneath the sea. One theory is that a sudden sea quake hit the *Mary Celeste*, dislodging the ship's stove and some of the barrels of alcohol, which leaked as a result. (Remember from the evidence that the stove had been moved and nine barrels were found empty?) As you probably know, fire – in the form of sparks from the stove – combined with alcohol would have a very 'explosive' result! The crew knew this too. Might they have panicked, jumped into the yawl (a small boat) and left as quickly as they could?

Another strange sea phenomenon is called a waterspout. This is the result of a whirling tornado moving over the sea, which pulls a long slim 'spout' of water many metres up into the sky. If a waterspout had suddenly hit the ship, it would explain why there was water sloshing between the decks. It could also be the reason why the two hatches blew off.

In either case, Captain Briggs would probably have thought that staying on the ship was too dangerous. He might have had enough time to grab a few important things like the sextant, chronometer and log book, but left everything else behind.

7. A Potential Explosion?

Now I didn't know this – and I'm pretty sure you didn't either – but apparently barrels for holding liquid are usually made from white oak. Why? Because white oak is watertight and keeps liquid intact. If you were a half-decent barrel maker, you'd *never* use red oak for a wine barrel because it's, quite frankly, useless for the job.

All the barrels on board the *Mary Celeste* were made of white oak – except for nine, made of red oak. For some reason, the wrong wood had been used. All very interesting, you might think, but what does it matter?

It matters because it explains the mystery of the empty nine barrels of alcohol on board, which were not, as many people at the time thought, drunk dry by the crew. What's much more likely is that the alcohol leaked through the red oak. In any case, raw strong alcohol is not at all drinkable and would have made the crew very ill if they'd tried it!

The leaking barrels would have begun to smell quite strongly. Is this why the deck hatches were removed – to get rid of the smell and the fumes coming from the cargo?

Alcohol is highly flammable – it catches fire incredibly easily – so with the strong smell of alcohol in the air, perhaps the captain and crew were worried about an explosion or fire breaking out – not a barrel of fun (sorry) on a wooden ship! Maybe they decided to get everyone to 'safety' in the yawl.

So let's imagine that all ten of them *did* get into the yawl. What became of them?

The fact that the halyard (rope) was broken might have been because they had used it to tie the yawl to the ship, and the rope snapped under the strain. The yawl may have capsized and they were drowned, or perhaps it drifted away and they eventually died of hunger and thirst. But nothing was ever found – no yawl and no bodies.

8. Alien Abduction!

Some have suggested that, because everyone vanished without trace, the ten people on board must have been kidnapped by

aliens. This sounds like a crazy idea, but there are certainly people out there who believe that aliens visit our planet. They also believe that aliens sometimes kidnap the occasional human for further inspection. So far, no one has actually proved  the existence of aliens or UFOs (Unidentified Flying Objects) and there is no concrete evidence that human beings are being spirited away by creatures from outer space. But that doesn't mean it's not happening!

Do you think it's possible that a group of aliens swooped down in their spacecraft to capture the crew and passengers of the *Mary Celeste*?

YOU DECIDE

It's a tricky one – maybe the only people who will ever know what really happened are the ten people on board the ship?

In the meantime, you need to make a decision. Which do *you* think is the most likely explanation?

Turn to the back of the book to record your findings!

Mythical Mermaids

THE MISSION ...

... to find out if mermaids really exist.

© HULTON ARCHIVE/GETTY IMAGES

A painting of a mermaid by John William Waterhouse.

BURNING QUESTION

Are mermaids just characters in fairy tales and myths?

MISSION DETAILS

No sailor's tale would be complete without a beautiful mermaid.

We all know what mermaids look like – they're a cross between a human and a fish, with the upper half of a woman and a large scaly fish's tail.

According to legend, mermaids live in the ocean and swim like fish. Though lovely to look at, in many stories, mermaids are sinister creatures who bring nothing but trouble to humans.

Tales of mermaids are told around the world and go back for many hundreds of years. So is there any truth in the mermaid myth?

THE LOCATION

Only one condition – it's got to be wet. Mermaids live in oceans and seas all over the world. Stories from some countries say that their mermaids live in rivers, lakes and pools.

When not in water, mermaids can usually be found sitting on rocks, combing their long hair and singing. They swim off quickly if they think they're in danger, so they are pretty impossible to catch. Slippery as a fish, one might say! (A group of fisherman said they once managed to catch a mermaid, however – read their story on page 53.)

THE EVIDENCE

Stories about mermaids appear as far back as 1000 BC.

- 🌐 The ancient Assyrians told tales of a goddess who fell in love with a human, but accidentally killed him. She tried to hide in a lake and became half fish, half human – the first mermaid

- 🌐 In Greek and Roman mythology, evil sea nymphs called sirens lured sailors to their deaths on the rocks. The sirens were half bird, half woman, the daughters of the sea god Phorcys. They had such sweet voices that anyone who heard their singing couldn't help themselves – they had to go closer. The Greek hero Odysseus got round this problem by making all his sailors plug their ears with wax so that they couldn't hear a thing. A great tip for any upcoming rounds of *X-Factor* auditions!

Grab your ear plugs, the Sirens are coming!

The evil side of mermaids is well-documented. Even Blackbeard, the legendary and not-very-easily-scared pirate, told his crew to avoid certain waters in case there were mermaids around. Mermaids were thought to bewitch sailors, take their treasure and then drag them down to a watery death.

Mermaids appear in the folklore of China, Japan, Africa, Scandinavia, Britain and many other places. One of the most famous stories about mermaids – 'The Little Mermaid' – was written in Denmark by Hans Christian Andersen in 1837. You'll probably know this one as it was made into a famous movie of the same name. In the story, the mermaid of the title falls madly in love with a human.

The statue of the Little Mermaid – as seen in Copenhagen Harbour.

She is so desperate to join him on land that she uses a witch's spell to exchange her mermaid's tail for human feet. Unfortunately, the feet are incredibly painful and she feels like she's walking on knives. That must have been a stabbing pain . . .

Mermaids have since featured in countless books, films and TV programmes. But has *anyone* actually seen one? Well, there are certainly a few people who think they have.

Here are some of their eyewitness accounts:

🌐 In January 1493 the explorer Christopher Columbus saw three mermaids playing together in the sea, just off the coast of Haiti. He said the mermaids had human faces, though he was surprised that they were not as pretty as he had expected – in fact, he said that their faces were 'more like a man's'! A group of mer*men*, perhaps, Christopher?

🌐 In 1608 explorer Henry Hudson set out for the chilly waters of the Arctic in search of a north-east passage. During the voyage, two of his crew shouted that they had spotted a mermaid in the water. All the men hurried to the side to see the mermaid, who had long black hair and white skin. In the log book, Hudson described her as having the 'tail of a porpoise and speckled like a mackerel'. A bit of a fishy tale, maybe?

🌐 A 1947 sighting took place on the Scottish island of Muck (great name!). An 80-year-old fisherman called Alexander Gunn said that he had seen a mermaid sitting on a lobster trap quite close to the shore, combing her hair. When the mermaid realized she was being watched, she immediately disappeared into the waves . . .

🌐 In the summer of 1833 six fishermen sailing off the Isle of Yell (another great name!) in the Shetlands said that a mermaid had got caught up in their fishing

lines. They hauled her aboard and kept her on their boat for several hours before returning her to the sea. Apparently, she had bristles running from her head to her shoulders, which she could raise or lower, like a crest. Hair-raising stuff! The creature 'offered no resistance nor attempted to bite, but she moaned piteously'

A much more recent encounter also describes the sad sound of a mermaid. In 2008 newspapers reported the experience of a man and his family in the Western Cape area of South Africa. They were walking by a local river when they spotted what they thought was a mermaid in the water. She had black hair, strange hypnotic red eyes and made a sound like a woman crying. The family believe it was a South African Kaaiman, a legendary creature, half fish, half human, that is supposed to live in deep pools

In the summer of 2009 the people of a town in Israel reported seeing a mermaid jumping out of the water like a dolphin and performing stunts! Despite a $1 million reward for finding the mermaid, the aquatic acrobat has never been seen again

There are many, many more accounts of mermaid sightings, from ancient times to the modern day. Could all these people be mistaken? Or are they making it all up?

Freaks and Fakes

The famous 'Fiji mermaid' was exhibited as part of P. T. Barnum's Travelling Show in the nineteenth century.

Other oddities in the show included:
- Tom Thumb – the smallest man on earth (about 60cm tall)
- A bearded lady
- A dog-faced boy
- A giant mummified man called the Cardiff Giant

Now, you probably haven't seen many bearded ladies or dog-faced boys in your neighbourhood recently (if I'm wrong, please let me know) – but in those times, travelling circuses and 'freak' shows full of weird and wonderful characters were pretty common. Thankfully, television was invented in the 1900s, so the freak shows gradually died out.

Just as well – many of Barnum's exhibits were later exposed as fakes. The Fiji mermaid was found to be the upper half of a monkey sewn to the lower half of a fish! But despite its weird appearance, the Fiji mermaid became one of the show's biggest attractions. Proving that people would believe anything in those days . . .

In 2004 a similar photo circulated on the internet, claiming to be that of a mummified mermaid body. It convinced a lot of the people who saw it – but it too was a fake. Proving that some people will *still* believe anything!

MY MISSION

So how does a person go about finding a mermaid? Go on a mer-mission, of course! All you have to do is set sail for a few years, hang around some rocks and wait to hear the sweet sound of singing . . .

Hmm – rather than spend years sailing the seas (I'm a busy man, you know – people to see, TV programmes to make . . .) I've decided to keep a careful eye out for all kinds of merpeople while I'm investigating the oceans for the other mysteries in this book. Here's what I'll be taking along on all my missions:

EXTRA KIT

- ⊛ EAR PLUGS – in case the singing starts! I really don't want to be mesmerized (or should that be mer-smerized?) by an evil mermaid
- ⊛ A VERY BIG NET – mermaid-sized, of course
- ⊛ A HUGE WATER TANK – to be filled with fresh sea water, for keeping a captured mermaid in
- ⊛ A SET OF HAIRBRUSH AND COMBS – to keep her happy; I might even throw in a few hair slides

MISSION COMPLETED

While I've been travelling around the oceans, lakes and rivers of the world, I've collected many more tales and sightings of mermaids. However, the same 'explanation' keeps cropping

up again and again – and it involves a creature which definitely isn't a mermaid. Intrigued? Here's more:

WHAT DO YOU THINK?

1. Mermaids Are Sea Cows

Is it possible that the whole mermaid idea is a mistake and that, for hundreds of years, sailors have been seeing an animal in the water? We are talking about a creature called a dugong – also known as a 'sea cow'.

So what is a dugong? It's a mammal that lives in warm coastal waters from East Africa to Australia, including the Red Sea, the Indian Ocean and the Pacific. Dugongs look a bit like big-nosed sea lions. They can live for up to 70 years and they are powerful swimmers. They spend much of their time alone or in pairs, though they occasionally gather in larger groups.

Here's one:

Now, a dugong doesn't look much like a mermaid to me – but you can see how the shape of the body and the tail swimming through murky water might confuse people (especially extremely short-sighted sailors).

But what about the mermaid's beautiful singing voice? Dugongs make a kind of weird high-pitched chirping – I've heard it on my travels – and, to be honest, it's not exactly tuneful. As well as this, you may have noticed that sea cows *don't* have long flowing hair.

So why the mix-up? Perhaps it's because of the dugongs' unusual behaviour? As they are mammals, they have to breathe air (though they can stay underwater for several minutes before surfacing). Sometimes they 'stand' on their tails in shallow water, with their heads above the surface to breathe. From a distance, a dugong's head could arguably be mistaken for a human one.

What do you think? Could all those mermaids really be sea cows?

2. Mermaids Are Real

Many people say they have seen a mermaid – so why would all these stories be around if mermaids didn't exist? The trouble is, we're lacking hard evidence – probably because those pesky merpeople just don't want to be caught! If only we could actually capture one to prove their existence, once and for all. But, as far as we know, no fish-tailed female has ever been brought to shore. And to this day, not a single photo or video has ever been taken of a real living and breathing mermaid. Maybe one day, a sailor will finally bring home a fishy friend.

3. Mermaids Are Made Up
The only other alternative is that all the stories and tales over the years are just that – fictional stories and tales. Perhaps they're a leftover from the days when many cultures believed in sea gods and other powerful water spirits. Or maybe the stories were just a way for sailors to entertain themselves during those long, boring sea voyages?

YOU DECIDE

After reading this, do you still believe in mermaids? There are only three choices and it's up to you to pick one . . .

The Bermuda Triangle

THE MISSION ...

... to find out about the mysterious disappearances of ships and planes in the Atlantic Ocean.

BURNING QUESTIONS

🔥 Why have so many people disappeared in this particular area?

🔥 What other weird stuff happens here?

MISSION DETAILS

The 'Bermuda Triangle'. What could it be?

An exotic three-sided shape?

A new kind of musical instrument?

The real Bermuda Triangle is much scarier than either of these. It's a large area of sea. Nothing too nerve-racking about that, you may think. But this stretch of ocean is a weird place; a place where large numbers of planes and boats seem to vanish into thin air. And nobody knows why ...

Some think strange and mysterious forces are at work – aliens, time warps, even death rays emanating from Atlantis have all been suggested. Others put the disappearances down to more rational reasons like bad weather, mechanical failure or poor piloting.

Whatever's going on, weird happenings go back to the time of Christopher Columbus, who sailed across the Atlantic from Spain in 1492. He reported seeing strange dancing lights on the horizon and a ball of fire falling into the sea. He also said that the ship's compasses wouldn't work properly – a phenomenon which has been widely reported by captains and pilots ever since.

A painting of the Santa Maria – which Christopher Columbus captained in 1492.

Stories of unexplained disappearances in the Bermuda Triangle started to circulate widely in the 1950s and '60s. Since then, it has become one of the most talked-about mysteries in the world. There's even a song about it! (If you're a fan of good music, don't bother downloading it.)

Time to find out more about the so-called 'Devil's Triangle' . . .

THE LOCATION

You won't find the Bermuda Triangle on any map. The Triangle in question is an imaginary one that is pinpointed on an area of sea in the Atlantic Ocean. There are three 'points' to the Triangle: the island of Bermuda, the island of Puerto Rico and the city of Miami in Florida, USA.

THE EVIDENCE

Though it's hard to put an actual number on the craft that have run into trouble in the Bermuda Triangle, some reports say that as many as 100 ships and planes have vanished in the last 25 years.

Very often, no distress or SOS signal is sent out before the disappearance. The plane or ship just goes right off the radar.

Of all these, Flight 19 is the most well-known and -documented disappearance.

The Mystery of Flight 19

On 5 December 1945 five Avenger torpedo bombers took off from Fort Lauderdale, Florida, on a standard training mission. There were fourteen men on board the five planes. After two hours of flying, a series of panic-stricken radio messages started to come through to HQ.

According to the chief pilot, Lieutenant Taylor, the in-flight compasses had stopped working and he wasn't sure of his location. Remember, this was long before the time of GPS, and pilots relied heavily on compasses for directions.

Part of the conversation between the pilots and crew and the military base went like this:

'We can't find west. Everything is wrong. We can't be sure of any direction. Everything looks strange, even the ocean.'

After some confusion, the last message was heard:

'It looks like we are entering white water... we're completely lost.'

Soon afterwards, contact was lost. A rescue plane was quickly sent out to find the bombers. Unbelievably, it exploded in mid-air and was also never seen again. (Let's not blame this on the Bermuda Triangle, though – the plane was apparently faulty.)

The bombers of Flight 19 were never heard from either. No trace of the five aircraft has ever been found.

There was a full investigation, but in the Navy's final report, the disappearance was put down to 'causes or reasons unknown'. Clearly, they didn't have a clue what had happened.

What could have happened to five planes to make them vanish completely?

Equally puzzling are these well-known disappearances:

🌍 A huge ship called the USS *Cyclops* went missing in March 1918 after leaving Barbados. She was heavily loaded with cargo and had a crew of more than 300. When she failed to arrive at her destination

(Baltimore in the United States), a huge search was conducted but not a thing was found. As this was towards the end of the First World War, people thought that the *Cyclops* could have been torpedoed by a German submarine. However, no SOS signal was ever sent, and no debris or wreckage was found. Spooky . . .

In 1963 the *Marine Sulphur Queen*, a large carrier ship with a huge cargo of – take a guess . . . sulphur! – disappeared near the southern coast of Florida. Some items were eventually found from the missing ship – these included a few life jackets (some were ripped; by sharks, it was thought), a piece of oar, a fog horn and a piece of broken board with part of the ship's name on it. To this day, no one knows if the ship's disappearance was down to leaking sulphur causing an explosion – or something more sinister

In January 1948 a British South American Airways plane called *Star Tiger* – containing 25 passengers and six crew – disappeared during a flight. No bodies, debris or wreckage were ever found and no emergency message was sent. The investigation said ' . . . no more baffling problem has ever been presented'. Yep, definitely baffling

Spookily, in the same month of the following year, January 1949, the *Star Tiger*'s sister plane, the *Star Ariel*, also vanished, somewhere between Bermuda and Jamaica. Again, there were no emergency messages or

calls for help – it just seemed to disappear in mid-air. Weird . . .

A Douglas DC-3 aircraft containing 32 people went missing in December 1948. It took off from Puerto Rico, headed for Florida – right into prime Bermuda Triangle territory. The pilot sent a routine message when he was about 20 minutes away from landing. After that the plane was never heard of again. No one in the area heard or saw an accident and, again, searches found no wreckage in the water. This is beginning to sound very familiar!

In the spring of 1974 a large luxury yacht called *Saba Bank* sailed from Nassau in the Bahamas on a test navigation. She and her crew never arrived at their destination

In October 1991 a Grunman Cougar jet heading to Tallahassee vanished and has never been found. The pilot made a request to increase his altitude – nothing unusual in that – and soon afterwards the plane disappeared from the radar. Guess what? No debris was found

The *Genesis* cargo ship disappeared on its way from Trinidad to St Vincent in April 1999. Before she vanished, a radio message was sent out, saying there was a problem with one of the pumps. Despite extensive searches, the ship and crew were never seen again.

There are many similar stories. However, before you make the mistake of thinking that the *Mary Celeste* could also have been a victim of the Bermuda Triangle, let me put you straight. The *Mary Celeste* was not sailing anywhere near the Triangle – she was many hundreds of miles away.

Back to the main story. Just what on earth is going on in the Bermuda Triangle?

More Strange Stuff ...

Not only do things seem to vanish into thin air, there are other kinds of freaky phenomena occurring. All these weird things have been reported by people travelling through the area:

- Disturbances and turbulence happening mid-flight
- Unusual-looking fog and cloud – sometimes yellowish in colour
- Compass and instrument failure or machinery behaving strangely
- Being unable to see the horizon properly
- A sense of weightlessness, or other strange physical feelings

A Near Miss

In 1966 a tug called *Good News* was heading towards Florida from Puerto Rico. Weather conditions were good and everything seemed normal until the crew noticed that the compass was spinning around crazily – in their words, 'going

bananas'. Nobody could understand why. Then the captain, Don Henry, noticed something really odd. He couldn't see the horizon (the line between the sea and the sky). It seemed as if the ocean and the sky had blended together and were the same colour.

If that wasn't weird enough, when he checked a cargo barge (which was attached to the ship) he couldn't see it – the barge was completely immersed in a strange cloud of fog! At the same time, the ship felt as if she was being pulled backwards by a very strong force. The shaken captain quickly ordered the engine on full power and the boat sailed on. Five minutes later, the fog cleared and the compass began behaving normally again. No one on board could explain what had happened. To this day, the captain and crew think they almost became victims of the notorious Bermuda Triangle. A close shave . . .

Lost in Time?

December 1970. Bruce Gernon and his father were mid-flight in their small plane, headed for Miami. They flew into some unusually dark clouds, which seemed to move and change shape around them. The clouds quickly formed a huge tunnel! Meanwhile, all their electronic equipment stopped working and the pair began to experience an odd feeling of weightlessness. When Gernon glanced behind the plane, he was stunned to see that the tunnel walls were collapsing in on them! He flew out of there as fast as he could . . .

The plane eventually came out the other side of the cloudy 'tunnel' into a blue sky with the familiar sight of Miami beach below them. After landing, Gernon realized something very strange. It had taken them just 47 minutes to make what was normally a 75-minute flight. Where did the missing 28 minutes go?

To this day, Gernon is convinced that his plane travelled through time, flying through some kind of time warp or time slip. He has even written a book about his experience.

The 'Dragon's Triangle'

In the Pacific Ocean, not far from the coast of Japan, is another strange area of sea where ships, boats and planes are said to disappear. Like the Bermuda Triangle, this region doesn't appear on any maps – but it does have a scary reputation. So much so that the Japanese have named it *Ma-no Umi* or the 'Sea of the Devil'! It is also known as the Dragon's Triangle.

In 1989 a writer called Charles Berlitz (famous for his books about the world's mysteries) said that five Japanese military vessels, and a total of 700 people, had disappeared here during the 1950s. He also said that the Japanese government had declared the whole area a danger zone after 100 scientists on a research boat had vanished in the Triangle. Others have scoffed, putting the disappearances down to the high level of volcanic activity and earthquakes in the area.

Interestingly, both the Bermuda and the Dragon's Triangle are said to be among the world's 'Vile Vortices'.

Electromagnetic fields

These are twelve points on the Earth's surface where mysterious disappearances are said to take place. If these are marked on a map, you can see that they are spread out equally in twelve parts across the Tropic of Cancer, the Tropic of Capricorn, and the North and South Poles. Some people think the vortices are the sites of ancient energy lines or unusual electromagnetic fields.

Sounds convincing. But is it true . . . ?

WHAT HAPPENED?

Things just don't disappear, do they? OK, my socks frequently do, but I'm fairly sure that there isn't some kind of invisible force over my house, sucking them up. Well, actually, you never know . . . perhaps there's a 'Bermuda Sock Triangle', a place where all the odd socks of the world end up?

OK – back to the real Triangle. What are the logical explanations?

One possibility for Flight 19 – and perhaps other missing planes – is that the planes simply got lost and were forced to ditch in rough seas after running out of fuel. Poor navigation by the pilots could be to blame, and their equipment may also have been faulty.

In the case of Flight 19, Lieutenant Taylor admitted that he was completely lost. From the garbled conversation he had with HQ, we know that he saw an island below the plane. He assumed that the planes were flying over a group of islands called the Florida Keys, so he decided to head north to the Florida peninsula, where the planes could land.

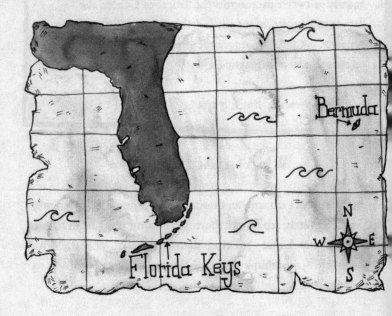

However, many people think that he was mistaken and his aircraft were actually *north* of Bermuda. If so, his decision meant they would have flown *further out* into the Atlantic Ocean. Eventually, the planes would have run out of fuel. The bombers were old-fashioned heavy military craft. If they ditched into the sea, they would probably have sunk very quickly.

Could this explanation account for all the missing planes on record? And what about all those missing ships and boats?

MY MISSION

Venturing into the Bermuda Triangle zone is a pretty nerve-racking experience. Even though thousands of people fly or sail through the 'danger zone' every year with no problems (as I keep reminding myself), I'd rather not take any chances.

So, in order to keep my name off the 'vanished without trace' list, I've got a strategy. Rather than zooming across the Triangle in a small plane or boat, I've decided to super-size all my modes of transport – in the hope that, the larger the craft, the less chance there'll be of it disappearing. So I'll be flying through the Triangle on one of the largest passenger planes in the world – a massive Airbus A380, which seats more than 500 passengers.

I've got a window seat, and my nose will be pressed against the window looking out for weird fog and any other strange goings on. I'm headed for Miami, Florida, a buzzing city and holiday destination. On the way back, I'm taking to the water and boarding a huge cruise ship – another massive craft that accommodates around 3,000 passengers. Try making that vanish into thin air, Bermuda Triangle!

EXTRA KIT

I'll be taking along:

 FLUORESCENT YELLOW LIFE JACKET – so if anything happens I will hopefully be spotted by rescuers

 WHISTLE – to attract attention in the above scenario

 VOICE RECORDER – I'll be recording my thoughts along the way, like a captain's log. If anything goes wrong, maybe they'll find the recorder and work out what happened

EXTRA COMPASSES – so if anyone's compasses start playing up, I will have several back-ups!

MISSION COMPLETED

Phew – back on dry land at last. I survived the Bermuda Triangle! To be honest, apart from being constantly on the look out for alien spaceships, strange fog and compass mishaps, the cruise was very relaxing. There was a great show every night, as much food as you could eat and . . . Sorry, I'm going off the point! But I'm relieved to say that I didn't see any sign of a spaceship, or fog and all my compasses worked fine. The outward flight was uneventful too. Seems like my 'make it big' strategy worked . . .

It was eerie at times, though, peering over the edge of the ship as we sailed through the ocean, and thinking about those watery depths and what they might hold. Are there hundreds of wrecks of ships, boats and planes down there?

And now, after reading piles of books and talking to lots of people on my journey, I've collected all the theories that might explain the Terrible Triangle:

1. Electronic Fog

Some of those who have experienced 'Triangle Terror' describe a strange greyish or yellow mist surrounding their plane or ship. It isn't like normal fog. This cloudy mist seems to have a spooky life of its own. It is said to move along with the craft and to make electronic equipment malfunction. Could this fog be the reason why so many pilots and captains lose their way – and does it eventually swallow them up?

In the 1970s a man called John Hutchison tried to prove that the spooky fog was real. He did various experiments to show that a force called electromagnetism was causing the fog. His theory (and it is just a theory) was that if electromagnetic fields of different wavelengths bounced off each other, it could cause objects to behave strangely – even ships.

Hutchison claimed that he had recreated the mysterious 'electronic fog' cloud at his home – and that it had produced some incredible results. Apparently, the fog caused everyday objects to literally defy gravity. A copper pipe was said to rise up and disappear, a bar of steel levitated (rose on its own), and samples of tough aluminium fell apart like jelly.

I'd pay good money to see a show like this, but unfortunately, very few people have been able to witness this amazing phenomenon. And no other scientists have been able to

76

produce the so-called 'Hutchison Effect'. In fact, the existence of the fog has never been proved in a proper lab test. Some in the scientific world have even accused Hutchison of faking his experiments using wire and magnets.

Others think that powerful electromagnetic storms could be the cause of the frightening fog. Bruce Gernon (see page 69), a 'fog survivor', came up with the idea that storms from within the Earth could penetrate the atmosphere in the form of electronic mist. According to Gernon, there is scientific evidence that the magnetism (a force which occurs all over the Earth) is weaker in the Triangle area than anywhere else. He thinks there is a connection.

If the fog *does* exist, does it cause people to lose their way, ships to sink and planes to crash into the sea? Or does it hold some other weird secret? The electronic fog theory lingers on . . .

2. Aliens!

Another suggestion is that aliens have discovered a passageway to Earth via the Bermuda Triangle and are using it as a kind of 'collecting station' for human beings. Are creatures from another planet capturing our planes and ships? And taking these interesting, possibly valuable, objects back to their planetary homes?

The alien theory would tie in with the fact that this area does seem to have a

large number of UFO sightings (Unidentified Flying Object – another way of saying 'flying saucer' or 'alien spacecraft'. You can read more about these in my *Great Mysteries of the World: Alien Encounters*).

In 1971 members of the crew of USS *John F. Kennedy*, an American aircraft carrier, witnessed something very strange: a glowing circular object hovering above their ship . . . It was large, about 60–90 metres in diameter, and yellowy-orange in colour. Whatever the thing was, it hovered silently for about 20 minutes, then *ping!* Disappeared. The strange thing was that during the entire time the UFO was above the ship, the ship's compasses stopped working . . . Sound familiar?

This is just one of many strange sightings in the area. No one knows if aliens are responsible or if the UFO sightings are caused by natural phenomena, such as ball lightning.

Did this spaceship enter through a Star G

Some alien believers think that the Bermuda Triangle is a 'Star Gate' – a doorway used by aliens for intergalactic space travel. This leads us on to another popular theory. That the Bermuda Triangle is what's called a portal to another world . . .

3. A Time Portal

There has been plenty of speculation that the Bermuda Triangle area contains some kind of unknown opening or passageway. Another idea is that the opening is a 'rip in time', where planes and ships are transported to another dimension, time or place. Or they are caught up, trapped in a kind of weird no-man's-land between different worlds. If you're thinking this all sounds like an episode of *Doctor Who*, you'd be right – it does!

People who believe this idea think it explains some of the strange variations in time reported by Triangle survivors, such as Bruce Gernon's lost 28 minutes. He could have experienced what's called a 'time slip' – when people are said to have moved backwards or forward in time.

A more scientific explanation is that these openings in time are things called wormholes. We're not talking about the little pink creatures that burrow through the soil, by the way, but something much, much bigger.

In physics, a wormhole is a passage in space-time – like a short cut between two regions of space or time. It's a big, big idea (and entirely theoretical at the moment), but world-famous brainy scientist Professor Stephen Hawking takes the idea of wormholes very seriously indeed. He has spent years working

on the physics behind wormholes (I've got a GCSE in Science, but this is a just a tad more advanced).

Put very simply, if wormholes did exist – and if humans could work out a way of travelling through them without being flattened like a pancake – they could potentially act as time machines. That could be incredibly useful. Especially for those times when you've done or said something silly – imagine being able to go back in time and change it!

Wormholes, time slips, portals – whatever you call them . . . is time travel the explanation for the Bermuda Triangle?

4. Wild Weather

The disappearances could be down to something very simple, yet completely beyond our control – that favourite subject of the British, the weather. The Caribbean-Atlantic region is well-known for violent storms, hurricanes and tornadoes. They can be very sudden and very unpredictable – so sailors and pilots can easily be taken by surprise. Any of the following weather-related events could sink a ship, or even crash a plane . . .

🌀 Destructive hurricanes
Massive swirling storms that gather up heat and energy from warm sea water, hurricanes usually begin in the Atlantic (near the Equator) and move north into the Gulf of Mexico and the Caribbean. A hurricane can spell disaster for both pilots and mariners as it is probably the most destructive weather event that exists. Boats can be capsized and planes very badly damaged

A satellite photo of a hurricane from above.

🌀 Rogue Waves

Satellite research has shown that a single wave can reach as high as 35 metres in open ocean areas. A wave like this could damage or destroy even the largest ship

🌀 Waterspout

A tornado (a whirling mass of air) at sea can create a waterspout, a kind of water twister. It travels over the water like a long funnel, sucking up water from the sea. The spouts vary in size and speed, but they can be huge, spiralling hundreds of metres into the sky and moving at up to 80 miles an hour. The spout usually disappears on reaching land – but can cause huge damage at sea

A whirling waterspout in action...

🔍 Lightning

During a storm a lightning bolt can contain up to a shocking one billion volts of electricity! No wonder it can damage planes or ships or set fire to their fuel supplies. The electric current can also produce a magnetic field, which causes problems with communications and compasses. A phenomenon called ball lightning is a circular mass of light which can move around on its own. Could this explain some of the UFO sightings reported in the Triangle – and the 'dancing lights' that Columbus once saw?

Add into the mix the effects of fast-moving currents, like the Gulf Stream, which can whisk debris away very quickly, some would say, is it any wonder that planes and ships disappear leaving no trace behind them?

5. A Flatulent Ocean?

Did you know that the ocean suffers from gas? Methane gas is created by ancient forests and organisms that have slowly rotted away over hundreds of years. It is trapped under the ocean floor and occasionally, such as during an underwater earthquake, the methane gas erupts violently into the water. (A bit like a fart in a bath, but a lot, lot bigger!)

These large bubbles of gas can hit ships and cause huge problems. They can also cause a temporary dip in the water, which can sink a ship.

And it gets worse. As gas is lighter than air, it continues moving upwards and could affect the lift of aircraft flying above the sea. The gas mixes with the atmosphere and changes the gas-to-oxygen ratio going into the plane's engine. It could be enough to make the engine stall and crash the plane.

How often does this kind of gas eruption take place? No one knows for sure.

6. Death by Atlantis?

Some people believe that the lost city of Atlantis is located deep underwater in the Bermuda Triangle – and that it is having a strange effect on the surrounding area. (See pages 5–25 for more on Atlantis and other possible locations.)

The writer Charles Berlitz wrote a famous book about the Bermuda Triangle in 1974. He thought Atlantis could be near an island called Bimini, to the west of the Triangle. In 1968 a 'road' of stones was found on the sea floor close to Bimini. Some scientists, however, think it is a completely natural stone formation, rather than a man-made Atlantean relic.

Atlantis, if it existed, was supposed to be an incredibly advanced civilization – and some think that the Atlanteans may have created a weapon that ultimately destroyed their own city. Could this unknown weapon, if it ever existed, still have the power to destroy modern-day planes and ships? Is there some kind of technology under the sea whooshing out harmful death rays or laser beams?

Another Atlantis theory is that the ancient people harnessed the power of energy crystals. Some claim that these crystals still rest on the seabed, sending out waves of energy that destroy ships and planes or, at the very least, confuse compasses and other instruments. Is there any evidence for this? As far as we know, no one has yet found any ancient weapons of destruction.

7. Accidents Will Happen

One very simple explanation is that the Bermuda Triangle area is incredibly busy – in fact, one of the busiest shipping lanes in the world goes right through it. It is also a major flight route for aircraft heading towards Florida, the Caribbean and South America. Perhaps there is absolutely nothing weird going on at all – simply that there are bound to be more accidents where there is more traffic?

It's also interesting that many of the big Triangle disappearances happened some years ago. In the 1950s and '60s planes and ships were not as reliable as they are today, and their fuel tanks weren't as large. Could this account for the higher number of disappearances in the past?

It's estimated that the Bermuda Triangle took more than 1,000 lives in the twentieth century. That averages about ten people per year. Some would say that is pretty normal for an area of such busy traffic.

Perhaps it's down to a combination of factors. Could faulty or old-fashioned planes, bad weather and poor navigation together form the big answer to the mystery of the Triangle?

8. The Environment

The environmental conditions in and around the Bermuda Triangle are unusual, to say the least:

- A huge current called the Gulf Stream moves through the Triangle. The Gulf Stream is an incredibly strong,

swift current that moves warm water from the Gulf of Mexico north into the Atlantic. The movement can throw boats hundreds of miles off course, and sailors need to be aware of it when they are navigating. The Gulf Stream can also quickly carry wreckage away from a disaster, making it impossible to find

There is also a strange area of water within the Triangle called the Sargasso Sea. It is the only sea in the world without a shoreline, bounded by sea currents on all sides (including the Gulf Stream). Christopher Columbus was one of the first to note the area, which is covered by a kind of thick mat of floating seaweed (called *sargussum*). The seaweed can cause problems for boats, as well as the fact that the Sargasso Sea is incredibly flat and still. Many sailing ships entering the

area become completely motionless. In fact, Columbus got stuck here for so long that he thought he might have a mutiny on his hands!

🌐 The sea floor under the Bermuda Triangle contains some of the deepest underwater trenches in the world. One is called the Puerto Rico Trench and dips at one point to a whopping 8,229 metres below sea level. Anything heavy sinking into the sea would fall a long way down, never to be seen again

🌐 Did you know that there are *two* North Poles? (Yep, news to me too!) Apparently, the needle of a compass will always be drawn to the *magnetic* North Pole, which isn't fixed, and moves over time. The *geographic* North Pole, however, is several hundred kilometres away from the Magnetic Pole and is always in the same place. Interestingly, the Bermuda Triangle area is one of only two places on Earth where true north and magnetic north line up together on a compass. (The other place is the Dragon's Triangle, off the coast of Japan – see page 70.) Some people think that this phenomenon is what's causing compass confusion and making instruments malfunction. Others disagree. Could there possibly be a connection?

🌐 Another reason for compass confusion could be the effect of magnetism in this area. In some areas of the world there are super-strong magnetic fields, created by magnetic rocks, electrical storms or magma flowing

near the surface of the Earth. The magnetic fields can have a chaotic effect on compasses and other equipment

Does this environment have anything to do with the weird goings-on? Many people believe so.

YOU DECIDE

Which do you think is the best solution to the Bermuda Triangle? Make your choice, then answer my next big question – having read all these stories, would *you* be brave enough to travel through the Bermuda Triangle?

Don't forget to record your thoughts at the back of this book!

MYSTERY 5
The Philadelphia Experiment

THE MISSION ...

... to find out if the ship, the USS *Eldridge*, was actually made invisible.

BURNING QUESTIONS

🔥 Can objects be made to vanish into thin air – and then return?

🔥 Was the experiment a cover-up?

MISSION DETAILS

There are two things immediately obvious about the Philadelphia Experiment. One, it was an experiment. Two, it took place in Philadelphia. Other than that, details are a little thin on the ground. Some think this is because the whole incident was covered up by the government (who didn't want anyone to know what had happened). Others think it is because it never actually happened. So who is right?

The experiment was supposed to have been performed by the United States Navy, back in 1943. So why are people still talking about it now? Well, what happened made everyone who heard the story *very* excited. It still does. Because unlike the cases

89

of the *Mary Celeste* and the Bermuda Triangle – where things that disappear are put down to mysterious forces beyond our control – it seems that the Navy actually made a ship disappear. It's more mind-boggling than Harry Potter's cloak!

The idea of being invisible is very appealing. I'm sure we could all think of some useful ways to deploy everyday 'invisible technology'– you could make your annoying sibling or super-strict teacher vanish whenever you fancied, for example!

The US Navy, however, denies everything.

Let's find out more . . .

THE LOCATION

The place where the experiment was supposed to have taken place was a naval shipyard in Philadelphia, Pennsylvania, USA.

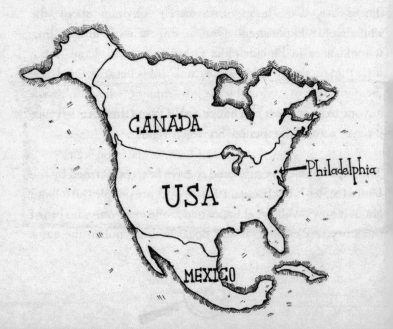

What Happened?

October 1943. It's the time of the Second World War, and the United States government, one of the Allied powers (which include Britain, France, the Soviet Union and China), is looking for new ways to help defeat the enemy.

The USS *Eldridge* is a large destroyer, built earlier in the year to escort soldiers and supplies to important locations around the world. With 1,000 Allied ships torpedoed and sunk in 1942, it's vital to improve defences against enemy submarines and ships.

The US Navy need the best brains in the country. So they employ the brilliant physicist Albert Einstein to work on developing ammunition and explosives.

But some think Einstein was working on a different project for the Navy . . . a top-secret one. And, let's face it, making your whole ship invisible would be the perfect solution for avoiding wartime attacks.

The Incredible Mr Einstein
Do you recognize this man? Underneath that wild hair is one of the finest brains of the twentieth century – it's Albert Einstein.

One of the most famous scientists of all time, Einstein was born in Germany in 1879. At the age of five, his interest in science was sparked when his father showed him a pocket compass. Albert was fascinated by it. Why did the needle always point in the same direction, whichever way the compass was turned? He realized that an unknown force was acting on it. This interest in forces continued throughout his life, as Einstein's most important work is about energy, the speed of light and gravitational forces.

In 1905 – his 'wonderful year' – Einstein rewrote Newton's laws of gravity when he came up with his theory of relativity, probably the most famous scientific equation ever known.

Here it is:

$e = mc2$ (in case you didn't know, that's energy equals mass multiplied by the speed of light squared!)

Apparently, it shows that matter and energy are different forms of the same thing. Matter can be turned into energy, and energy into matter. When his theory was proved correct in 1919, Einstein became incredibly famous, and in 1921 he received the acclaimed Nobel Prize for Physics.

In 1933, when Adolf Hitler became Chancellor of Germany, Albert Einstein left the country and emigrated to the United States. He never returned to Germany and in 1940 became a US citizen.

Einstein famously said: 'Imagination is more important than knowledge.'

There's no doubt that Einstein *did* work for the US Navy during the war – but was he responsible for the Philadelphia Experiment? This is what is supposed to have happened:

- Using large generators, naval scientists unleashed a powerful electromagnetic force around the USS *Eldridge*, creating a kind of 'force field'. The ship disappeared!
- The invisible vessel was then 'teleported', in true *Star Trek* style, from the naval yard in Philadelphia to a place called Norfolk, in Virginia. Then it reappeared back again in Philadelphia – all in all, 'travelling' a distance of about 350 km!
- Some say the men aboard the ship were also made invisible, with disastrous consequences. Some were never seen again, while others suffered terrible side effects – such as constantly disappearing and reappearing! Later, others went completely mad. (No wonder!)

THE EVIDENCE

So how do we know about the experiment if it was all so top secret? It wasn't until twelve years after the incident that the Navy were contacted by a man called Carlos Allende. He said he had witnessed the whole thing while he was a deckhand on board a nearby ship. Allende claimed that he had seen the USS *Eldridge* surrounded by a greenish fog (sound a bit 'Bermuda Triangle'?). He had felt a terrific jolt of energy, then the ship disappeared.

A man called Morris Jessup, who had written a well-known book about UFOs, then got involved. Allende had written notes all over a copy of Jessup's book and had sent it to the Navy. The UFO book described Jessup's idea that there was a connection between electromagnetism and flying saucers. Allende read this and thought that electromagnetism could have been used in the Philadelphia Experiment too.

People who believe Allende's extraordinary story think that the Navy, shocked by the results of their weird experiment, stopped all research immediately. They then produced a cover story for the missing men on board, saying they were lost at sea.

What do you think? Do you believe Allende's story? Let's bear in mind that Allende also said that Albert Einstein himself had discussed subjects such as invisibility and faster-than-the speed-of-light travel with him. Likely – or not?

MY MISSION

A particularly tough one on this occasion. Why? Because there really isn't anything for me to investigate. Here's the reality:

- 🌐 After years of naval service the USS *Eldridge* was eventually sold as scrap in 1999. So – no ship
- 🌐 The naval shipyard in Philadelphia was closed in 1995. It was renamed the Philadelphia Naval Business Center, and is now home to various private companies and shops. So – no shipyard

- As the Navy flatly denies that anything happened, we can't talk to them about it
- Carlos Allende, the only witness, died in 1994. He did, however, give a last interview in the 1980s about his involvement in the experiment. He said some interesting things. He described how he had leaned over some railings and actually reached into the force field surrounding the ship. It apparently looked like an ultra-violet glowing haze and felt very strange – 'It kicked,' said Allende. Einstein then saw Allende touching the force field and came over to ask him how it had felt. Einstein then spent the next two weeks with Allende teaching him about the 'physics of invisibility'. Allende remained convinced the USS *Eldridge* was radiated with an energy beam that day in an experiment performed by Einstein. Could any of this be true?

MISSION COMPLETED

When it comes down to it, there are only two positions to take on the Philadelphia Experiment. You either believe it, or you don't. Let's look at the arguments for and against:

1. It Happened – But How?

Now for the tricky science bit. To be convinced of this story, you need to know how it could have happened. It's all down to Einstein's work. But – as I'm no Einstein myself – I'll try to keep it as simple as possible.

Einstein spent many years of his life working on an idea

called a single unified theory – sometimes called the *Theory of Everything*. It seems that he was basically trying to unify the laws of physics, bringing gravity, electromagnetism, and subatomic phenomena together into one set of laws. If you think that sounds difficult, you'd be right! Even Einstein had to admit defeat in the end, and no other scientist since has managed to finish his work.

As we're not brainiac physicists, the most important thing we need to know is that if Albert *had* cracked this theory, the results would have been astounding. It could have made incredible things possible, like travelling through time and finding new sources of energy.

So was the explosives job just a cover for Einstein? Was he trying to test out his unified field theory? Some think that if Einstein had managed to make a connection between gravity and electromagnetism, he might have been able to literally bend light. If light had been bent *around* the ship and not across her, could she possibly have been made invisible?

Others think that Einstein used his unified field theory to make the ship 'teleport'– when all the particles that make up an object are transported to another place. Is this how the ship managed to appear in a completely different location? The whole idea of 'beaming' things elsewhere sounds a bit *Star Trek* – but could science fiction actually be science *fact*?

2. It Never Happened

Many others believe that the Philadelphia Experiment is just a massive hoax – a made-up story. They say it simply never happened and that Carlos Allende didn't see anything that day. They argue that, if it is true, why hasn't the experiment been repeated in the years since? If the ship experiment had worked all those years ago, by now we'd all be making things invisible! There are some other good points on their side too:

- There is no evidence that Einstein was involved in research on invisibility or teleportation
- The Office of Naval Research has stated that the use of force fields to make a ship and her crew invisible does 'not conform to known physical laws'
- There is only one witness that we know of (Allende) – so just one person's word
- Despite all the work done by physicists since Einstein's time, there is still no evidence that it is possible to unify gravity with the other forces – or make a ship disappear

YOU DECIDE

The Philadelphia Experiment is one of those 'hush-hush' mysteries that it's exciting to believe in. But was it all a hoax? Turn to the back and make your choice!

WANT TO KNOW MORE?

If you want to find out more about some of these intriguing mysteries, try these books and websites:

Herbie Brennan's Forbidden Truths: Atlantis and other Lost Civilizations – Herbie Brennan (Faber & Faber)

Can Science Solve? The Mystery of the Bermuda Triangle – Chris Oxlade (Heinemann)

Unsolved! Mysteries of the Bermuda Triangle – Kathryn Walker (Crabtree)

The Mary Celeste: An Unsolved Mystery from History – Jane Yolen and Heidi Elisabet Yolen Stemple (Aladdin)

Unexplained: An Encyclopedia of Curious Phenomena, Strange Superstitions, and Ancient Mysteries – Judy Allen (Kingfisher)

www.nationalgeographic.com – Great for all kinds of information about the world, you can search the site for their views on the mysteries in this book. Also there are some interesting National Geographic TV investigations e.g. *Finding Atlantis* at http://channel.nationalgeographic.com

www.unmuseum.org – An investigation into all things unexplained and paranormal

www.sciencekids.co.nz – Great for science facts, you can also search the site for facts relating to the mysteries in this book

DECISION TIME

So, we've looked at the evidence (which sometimes got a bit too close for comfort, if you ask me). Now it's time for you to sort the facts from the fiction and solve some of the world's greatest mysteries once and for all . . .

Mystery 1: The Lost City of Atlantis

Notes:

_____

_____

_____

Possible explanations:

☐   *1. The Minoans and the Atlanteans Were One and the Same*

☐   *2. Atlantis Is Buried under Mud Flats in Spain*

☐   *3. Atlantis Was Once Part of Cyprus*

☐   *4. It's Just a Story*

☐   *5. Aliens on Atlantis*

☐   *6. Other* _____

Mystery 2: The Mary Celeste

Notes:

_____

_____

_____

_____

_____

_____

Possible explanations:

☐ _1. Sea Monster Attack_

☐ _2. Plundering Pirates_

☐ _3. Foul Play_

☐ _4. Mutiny_

☐ _5. A Curse_

☐ _6. A Sea Quake or Spout?_

☐ _7. A Potential Explosion?_

☐ _8. Alien Abduction!_

☐ _9. Other_ _____

Mystery 3: Mythical Mermaids

Notes:

_____

_____

_____

_____

Possible explanations:

☐ *1. Mermaids Are Sea Cows*

☐ *2. Mermaids Are Real*

☐ *3. Mermaids Are Made Up*

☐ *4. It's Just a Story*

☐ *Other* _____

Mystery 4: The Bermuda Triangle

Notes:

_____

_____

_____

_____

Possible explanations:

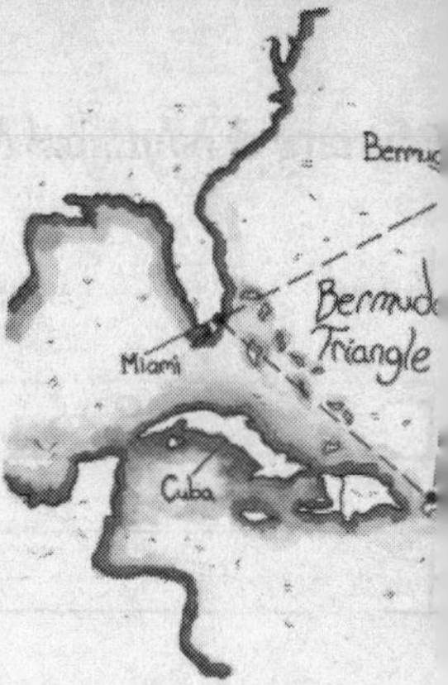

☐ *1. Electronic Fog*

☐ *2. Aliens!*

☐ *3. A Time Portal*

☐ *4. Wild Weather*

☐ *5. A Flatulent Ocean?*

☐ *6. Death by Atlantis?*

☐ *7. Accidents Will Happen*

☐ *8. The Environment*

☐ *9. Other* _____

Mystery 5: The Philadelphia Experiment

Notes:

_____

_____

_____

_____

_____

Possible explanations:

☐ *1. It Happened – But How?*

☐ *2. It Never Happened*

☐ *3. Other* _____

If you enjoyed this book, why not try
the other titles in the series?

GREAT MYSTERIES OF THE WORLD

ALIEN ENCOUNTERS
ANCIENT TREASURES
CREEPY CREATURES

Read every out-of-this-world adventure!

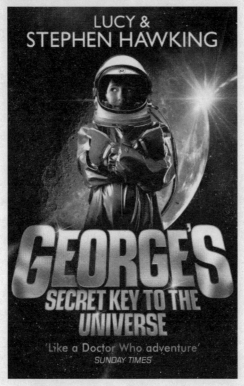

Take a ride through space and discover the mysteries of science and the universe with George and a super-intelligent computer called Cosmos.

But someone else would like to get their hands on Cosmos – someone whose power-hungry plans will lead George to a black hole and sure-fire deep space danger.

LUCY &
STEPHEN HAWKING

GEORGE'S
COSMIC TREASURE
HUNT

What would you do if an alien
got in touch?

George's best friend Annie needs help.
She has discovered something really weird
on her dad's super-computer.

Is it a message from an alien? Could there be
life out there? And if you could talk to aliens,
what would you say?

LUCY &
STEPHEN HAWKING

GEORGE
AND THE BIG BANG

Going back to the beginning
of time . . .

Join George as he battles a sinister rebel-scientist,
who's hell bent on sabotaging the most exciting –
and dangerous – experiment of the century.

A deadly bomb is ticking.
The whole world is watching.
Can George stop the second big bang?

**Meet Itch – an accidental, accident-prone hero.
Science is his weapon. Elements are his gadgets.**

'You'll be itching to read more.' *Anthony Horowitz*

www.itch-books.co.uk

Richard Hammond invites you to journey with him to the planet's most puzzling places . . .

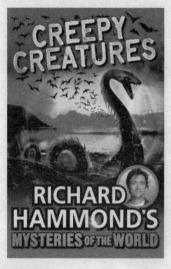

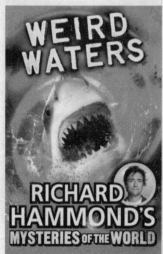

Can you solve the mystery?